I0881055

UNWELCOME SHORES

1 THE UNITED STATES, A HOME AND A REFUGE FOR BLACK PEOPLE?

Zaiway Paye was born in Nimba County in northeastern Liberia in August 1958. In middle school, she first learned about the origins of the country's motto, "The love of liberty brought us here," and why Liberians celebrate Thanksgiving in November. "The American settlers brought us that," she said, referring to Black settlers who left to escape anti-Black racism and slavery in the United States in the nineteenth century.[1] They, with the support of White American plantation owners and abolitionists, founded a settlement that would eventually become Liberia.[2]

After Ms. Paye graduated from high school, she first worked as a cashier in a casino and then as an administrative assistant in a fishing company. In her early twenties, she married a fellow ethnic Krahn man, and together they had four children. Life was not always easy, but for the most part everyone was happy. That all ended when a civil war erupted in Liberia in 1989, and Ms. Paye and her family were targeted because they are Krahn people.[3] After her husband was killed, she fled across the border to Côte d'Ivoire, where she stayed for about fourteen months until she moved to the Buduburam refugee camp in Ghana. There, after several years, she sat for interviews with United Nations High Commissioner for Refugees (UNHCR) officials and staff from an American resettlement agency (also referred to as a voluntary agency, or VOLAG), as well as U.S. immigration officials. Ms. Paye described this "screening" as "very, very, very tough . . . because . . . you have to explain why you left your country, what you went through during the war . . . what caused you to be at risk," all while being able to give "them evidence that would make them believe that truly, 'yes,' you were really at risk to go back." Put differently, Ms. Paye had to demonstrate that she met the definitions of a "refugee" outlined in the 1951 Convention Relating to the Status of Refugees (hereafter referred to as "1951 Convention"), meaning she had a "well-founded fear of being persecuted for reasons of race, religion, nationality, membership of a particular social group or political opinion" and was unable to return to Liberia due to this fear.[4]

She had little hope that these foreigners would provide an avenue out of her dreary life as a single parent with multiple children to care for in an overcrowded refugee camp. When one day her children started shouting, "Mama, your name is up for the program," she was incredulous. But her children were right. Her sister, who was living in the United States, had sponsored her, and the application for Ms. Paye and some of her children to be resettled as refugees in Staten Island was approved.[5] However, due to the nature of the particular U.S. Refugee Admissions Program (USRAP) priority that she was part of, her adult daughters were not allowed to come with her. Instead, Ms. Paye brought her youngest son, one nephew, two nieces, and one of her granddaughters, all of whom she had assumed caregiver responsibility for during the war. Her start in Staten Island, New York, was difficult as she had to make sure she could financially provide for herself and the five children in her care within three months of her arrival. Simultaneously, she knew that her daughters in the refugee camp and other family members in Liberia were expecting remittances. Thus, Ms. Paye started working as a home health aide, a job held by many other Liberian refugees. In her job, she is constantly subjected to anti-Black racism and xenophobia by clients and supervisors alike. In addition to the abuse in the workplace and financial stressors, she has continuously worried about her children growing up in a neighborhood that has had its share of violence and crime. But leaving has not been easy since she likes living in a neighborhood that is home to so many Liberians, but also because finding an affordable place in a different neighborhood in racially segregated Staten Island is virtually impossible. This is only complicated by the fact that Staten Island is the only New York City borough with a non-Hispanic White and Republican majority.[6] Hence, she concluded that "race . . . means a lot. . . . Sometimes you feel inferior . . . because this White person may think . . . they are higher than me." Racist and xenophobic encounters have served as a reminder that at times she is "treated differently . . . because you are not in your country . . . but a refugee . . . running from persecution." More than a decade after Ms. Paye arrived in Staten Island, she felt unsettled and hoped and prayed that she "could calm down a little bit . . . will make a way out nowhere . . . would have a better life, more than this." Objectively speaking, her life is better than the one she had in the Buduburam refugee camp, but she still struggles to provide for her loved ones on both sides of the Atlantic as well as find a sense of belonging in a place that has made it difficult for Black people to do so.

How Zaiway Paye and others like her, who were forced to flee from their homes in Liberia, are among the few fortunate ones who found refuge in the United States, and then subsequently having to deal with stigmas and anti-Black racism is part of the story I tell in this book. The Liberian case is not a singular one; African immigrants are part of the fastest-growing segment of the U.S. foreign-born population. Indeed, Africans make up more than 40 percent of all Black immigrants in the United States today (Tamir 2022).[7] Remarkably, more Africans have arrived in the United States since 1990 than during the transatlantic slave trade (Roberts 2005), many of them as refugees, since other avenues of immigration have not been available to them. Their migration motives are frequently tied to having to escape conflicts that have their roots in American and European exploitation of and involvement in their native countries (see also Beaman and Clergé 2024). The case of Liberia bears just that out; the civil war that brought widespread displacement has its origins in a society and stratification system that is directly linked to the enslavement of Africans in the previous centuries. Despite this, being admitted as a refugee to the United States has not been easy due to a number of overt and covert hurdles Black African refugees have to overcome.

To understand why this is the case and to comprehend Ms. Paye's and her compatriots' lives, their displacement, and resettlement, one must consider the significant role race has played. The salience of race in these different contexts varies. The impetus for Liberia's establishment as a quasi-American colony to protect the institution of slavery in the United States was unambiguously race based. Since becoming an independent country in 1847, Liberia has restricted citizenship to Black people. Consequently, being Black has been a central aspect of the nation of Liberia and what it means to be Liberian. In contrast, refugee resettlement and associated integration measurements by the U.S. government have been framed as race neutral. However, closer examination does not bear this out. Black refugees and asylum seekers have had to overcome additional burdens, with a lower resettlement quota allocated to them and a higher threshold to prove persecution compared to most other refugees. Once in the United States, Liberian refugees, like other Black people, face specific barriers due to systemic and individual anti-Black racism, especially in the racially divided context of places such as Staten Island. Liberian refugees are thus an ideal case study to show how anti-Black racism is deeply ingrained in U.S. refugee and immigration policies, as well as U.S. society.

SELECTIVE REFUGEE ADMISSION: THE SIGNIFICANCE OF RACE AND ANTI-BLACK RACISM

Immigration policies reflect what nation-states want to be. In other words, a close analysis of immigration and emigration policies can reveal a lot of what is not verbalized but practiced by mainstream society and shown in its laws and mores. Looking back to the inception of the United States as a nation, we see that it was never a country where people from all different racial, ethnic, and religious backgrounds were welcome or had the same rights, and most of these disparities continue today. Throughout American history, immigration policies have distinguished between "desirable"/"good" immigrants and "undesirable"/"bad" immigrants in ways usually tied to race, ethnicity, and/or religion, and this has translated to immigration bans and quotas that reflect these preferences (DenUyl 2022; Sáenz and Douglas 2015). After all, immigration and citizenship policies are "about the writing of nations onto bodies . . . writing [that] is defined at a global level by race and racial logics" (Patel 2017, 67; see also Aleinikoff and Rumbaut 1998). This also explains how xenophobia and racism have shaped ideas about who is an American, who can become one, and who cannot because they are deemed unassimilable, undesirable, and/or a threat to the nation (Abdi 2011; Fox and Guglielmo 2012; Ngai 2014). Scholarship has documented how these exclusionary measurements such as the 1882 Chinese Exclusion Act, 1906 Naturalization Act, 1907 Gentlemen's Agreement, and 1924 National Origins Act affected (would-be) immigrants from Asia and Southern, Central, and Eastern Europe. The almost exclusive indirect ban on immigrants from Africa as part of the 1924 National Origins Act has received little attention. Another less-acknowledged fact is that when the U.S. government "created quotas based on the current U.S. inhabitants descended from the foreign region in question, and African Americans were not counted for the purposes of awarding quotas to foreign nations, African countries could not receive a quota allotment despite the large numbers of African descendants already in the United States" (Kolawole 2016, 393–394). While at this time there were only a handful of independent African countries, including Liberia, it is still relevant, as this demonstrates that Africans were not even considered as possible immigrants.

Immigration laws are only one side of how nations shape what they are or want to be (Alba and Nee 2003; Ngai 2014). Laws and actions related to expulsion, proposed and enacted, represent the other side. U.S. history has a plethora of such measurements, too. For example, during the Depression in the 1930s and in 1954 during "Operation Wetback," Mexican immigrants were targeted for removal from the United States. However, a significant percentage among them were actually U.S. citizens of Mexican ancestry, reflecting a dominant view that non-White Mexican Americans were "racially unassimilable" (Fox and Guglielmo 2012, 363). Likewise, people of Japanese descent were forced into incarceration camps during World War II; two-thirds of them were U.S. citizens, leaving no doubt that the U.S. government and large parts of U.S. mainstream society did not consider them "American," but a threat. In addition to these more widely known examples of exclusionary policies, Black people have been targeted over and over as well, and in particular, their Americanness and belonging have been questioned (Carbado 2005; Smith 2015).[8] This includes well-known disenfranchisement laws that have targeted Black people for centuries (Alexander 2010; Bashi 1998) and policies that aimed at their permanent removal from the United States.

In the early nineteenth century, the Society for the Colonization of Free People of Color of America, generally known as the American Colonization Society (ACS), was founded with the goal to address the "problem" that free Black people in the United States presented to the institution of slavery. The proposed solution led to the "repatriation" of free Black people and other Black people who were manumitted only under the condition that they would depart to what would become Liberia. This move cemented the notion that the United States was a society built and designed for White people (Bonilla-Silva and Mayorga 2011; Omi and Winant 1994) and not for Black people, who have been characterized as "denizens" (Bradburn 2009) or "anticitizens" (Esbenshade 2011). A century later, at a time when slavery had been abolished but Black people continued to lack the same rights as other U.S. citizens, the push to make the United States a nation free of Black people was revived when in 1939 Senator Theodore Bilbo of Mississippi, a staunch anti-Black racist, introduced the Greater Liberia Act. Under this proposal, more than 12 million native-born Black Americans would have been deported to Liberia and neighboring areas controlled by France and Britain, which would, in turn for the territory, be forgiven their debts from World War I (Fitzgerald 1997).[9] These examples show that immigration and expulsion policies and structural (anti-Black) racism are greatly intertwined (Treitler 2015); in fact, as Motomura (2019, 543) concludes, "A core feature . . . of immigration and citizenship law [is] to exclude and discriminate by race." Simultaneously, it was the American emigration policy, or rather the expulsion policy of Black people in the United States, that created Liberia and the Americo Liberian settler elite until they were overthrown by Indigenous Liberians in 1980, which ultimately brought on the civil war and displaced half of the Liberian population. Thus, it could be argued that the United States had an obligation to come to Liberian refugees' aid, but it did not.[10] While there may be multiple explanations, I would argue a significant factor is the "anti-Blackness [that] has virtually shaped all aspects of societal life in the United States, including immigration" (Russell and Rivarola 2023, 63).

By drawing on data collected from a longitudinal ethnographic study, I show how race and anti-Black racism have shaped the experiences of Liberian and other Black refugees. I am following here the call of scholars (Sáenz and Douglas 2015; Treitler 2015) who have urged migration researchers to center the role of race in their studies. Similarly, Achiume (2021, 43) points out that "international legal scholarship on refugees has a race problem in that it has not paid sufficient analytical attention to the significance of race . . . a sort of 'racial aphasia.'" Attention to race in refugee policies provides insights into how different refugee groups are (not) selected for resettlement and treated when living in the United States, as well as dominant views about domestic minority groups since immigration law "allows the United States to do at its borders what it cannot do within them" (Johnson 2007, 89). In fact, "racially exclusionary immigration laws . . . reinforce domestic subordination of the same racial minority groups who are excluded. By barring admission of the outsider group that is subordinated domestically, society rationalizes the disparate treatment of the domestic racial minority group in question and reinforces that group's inferiority. Exclusion in the immigration laws must be viewed as an integral part of a larger mosaic of racial discrimination in American society" (Johnson 2007, 153). The experiences of Liberian refugees in this study bear exactly this out: from Liberia's existence because of American slavery, to limiting Black refugees from coming to the United States, to the stigmatization of Black refugees in a similar vein to native-born Black Americans. The parallels between how native-born Black Americans and Black refugees have been treated are striking, and perhaps most vividly exemplified by images of U.S. Border Patrol agents on horses corralling and whipping Black Haitian asylum seekers with their reins at the southern border in 2021, not unlike how plantation overseers brutalized enslaved Black people more than 150 years ago. But this is far from the only analogy. Both groups have been denied full access to American citizenship, either by not being admitted as refugees (or immigrants) or through the continued treatment of Black people as second-class citizens, evidenced by everyday practices and policies. Black refugees have also consistently been portrayed as an economic and welfare burden (Baranik De Alarcón et al. 2020; Dawsey 2018), another similarity with native-born Black Americans (Lamont et al. 2016). An additional commonality is the criminalization of Black people; Black refugees and asylum seekers have been portrayed as cheating the system (Esbenshade 2011), and native-born Black Americans as well as Black refugees and immigrants have been caught in the dragnets of racist policing (Alexander 2010; Palmer 2017). Hence, Neal (2020, para. 4) concludes that "with few exceptions, the lived experience of black immigrants very much mirrors the experience of black American citizens." However, there is more to this, as Black immigrants and refugees "live in the crosshairs of American-bred anti-Black racism and anti-immigrant sentiments" (Palmer 2017, 120).

How Liberian refugees simultaneously navigate barriers associated with being Black and refugees is the subject of this book. On one hand, they went to great lengths to obtain legal refugee (or asylum) status, as this is associated with protection, benefits, and a chance to live in the United States. On the other hand, they have vociferously rejected the informal refugee label, as this does not transfer any tangible benefits and instead works as a racialized stigma for them, mostly because Black refugees have been portrayed as economic migrants and not as "ideologically American" (Haines 2010; Perreault and Paul 2018). While some may expect that Liberian refugees would employ strategies similar to those of other Black immigrants by emphasizing identities alternative to race (e.g., ethnicity, religion, higher socioeconomic status) that could potentially shield them from anti-Black racism, they have not. First, due to Liberia's history and constitution, Blackness and being Liberian are fundamentally connected. Second, emphasizing a "refugee identity," like other refugees at times have done, would not offer Liberians a protective layer because being Black *and* a refugee is often seen as synonymous with being poor. Instead, they cope with anti-Black racism by relying on what I refer to as a *refugee-specific dual frame of reference*. This concept builds on Ogbu's (1994) and Suárez-Orozco and Suárez-Orozco's (1994) "(positive) dual frame of reference," which describes the comparisons that immigrants make when evaluating their current life in their new home country with the circumstances they left behind; often this means that immigrants reason that their financial gains offset discrimination in the United States. Extending this concept to the specificity of refugee experiences, I conclude that refugees make additional comparisons that include, but are not limited to, positive experiences with White people during the resettlement process, the violence and persecution they fled in their home countries, and the urgency to provide remittances for their (still-displaced) family members.

In the end, this book draws attention to the hostile context of reception for Black refugees and illustrates that integration processes are intimately related to race, time, and place. I demonstrate that by centering race as a framework of analysis, we can comprehend how Liberian and other Black refugees' experiences are shaped by centuries-old anti-Black policies and racism. Racial identity also provides a basis for integration into American life. Experiences with anti-Black racism have, in the end, brought Liberian refugees and native-born Black Americans in their shared and disenfranchised neighborhood together. They arrived at this place of concord after years of getting to know each other and overcoming stereotypes and conflicts, and through unions built by 1.5- and second-generation Liberian refugees.

A close analysis of race and racialization as they relate to immigration is especially relevant as we face a growing number of refugee crises that receive unequal attention, compassion, and aid, coupled with increased patrolling of borders, rising nativism, persistent racial inequality, and continued threats and attacks on Black lives. To that end, I offer policy suggestions for national and local policymakers as well as for practitioners involved in refugee resettlement and asylum adjudication. After all, refugee studies were initially designed to make policy recommendations (Black 2001). This research from the outset has been motivated by my desire to make both an intellectual contribution but also policy suggestions, as Turton (1996, 96) advocated that "researching . . . suffering can only be justified if alleviating that suffering is an explicit objective."

WORKING WITH AND STUDYING LIBERIAN REFUGEES: RESEARCH DESIGN

I am often asked why I study the experiences of Liberian refugees. The answer to this is pretty simple. Prior to embarking on this research that began in my first year of graduate school, I had worked for several years at nonprofit organizations that offered services to refugees and immigrants, including Liberian refugees, in the metro Atlanta area. Initially, I had started out in the youth program and then moved into other areas, including, but not limited to, case management, education programming, and interpretation and translation services. In the early years much of what I did was direct-service provision to recently arrived refugees and, to some extent, immigrants. In addition, I worked with other entities (e.g., public schools, health care providers, and social service organizations) to ensure that refugees and immigrants were receiving maximum support and that it was reflective of their diverse cultural and linguistic backgrounds. Toward the end of my time in Atlanta, I was the executive director of a nonprofit organization that I cofounded and that aimed to move toward an asset-based approach to service provision.[11] Overall, these experiences gave me a thorough understanding of how the U.S. government structures "acculturation services" for refugees (e.g., meeting work requirements to continue to be eligible for benefits) and how these services are administered by VOLAGs and other subcontracted providers.[12] Furthermore, during the regular statewide meetings of VOLAGs and other service providers, I heard firsthand how the state refugee coordinator and their staff and VOLAGs discussed newly arriving refugee groups, what they emphasized (e.g., particular forms of trauma and needs), how they compared groups (e.g., Liberian English was erroneously equated to Jamaican Patois), the types of services provided to different refugee groups, and so forth. Government officials and VOLAG staff also talked about how they envisioned that particular refugee groups would be able to integrate into larger American society. Here, I observed that at times the participants drew on common stereotypes about various racial and national groups. It also became clear that often there was not much scholarly literature that could provide cultural background information to staff members, teachers, volunteers, and so forth, who were going to interact with newly arriving refugees. This was particularly the case for African refugees.

Thus, I applied to graduate school with the intention of studying the experiences of African refugees, but I had not settled on a particular national or ethnic group. Serendipity would have it that in the summer before moving to New York, I came across a job posting by a grassroots organization in Staten Island that offered various programming to Liberians. I vividly recall thinking, "That sounds interesting, but it is just too far to commute there several days a week," and so I never applied. Toward the end of my first year in graduate school, when I started to look for a field site, I came back to this organization and reached out to ask if I could become involved based on the work that I had done in Atlanta. And this is how, in the spring of 2009, I first made contact with the Liberian refugee community in Staten Island and began this longitudinal ethnographic study. This type of research methodology allowed me to observe the "long-term and dynamic nature of resettlement" (McMichael et al. 2015, 238) as well as how refugees experience race and racism (Sáenz and Douglas 2015). Indeed, in the past fifteen years a lot has changed: Some of the Liberian refugee children who were barely in elementary school in the early years of this study are now students in my classes. Liberian refugees who were illiterate learned how to read and write, mastered U.S. civics, and became U.S. citizens. Concurrently, national and local dialogues about race and anti-Black racism have been changed by a number of significant events that include the election of the first Black president in the United States, an uptick in overt and covert White supremacy rhetoric and policies such as the Muslim/African refugee ban in the first Trump administration, and the even more anti-Black travel ban in the second Trump administration, immigration raids, increased deportations violent hate crimes, and the Black Lives Matter movement.[13]

Embarking on a longitudinal study afforded me the opportunity to slowly immerse myself in the Liberian refugee community in Staten Island. Initially, I became a volunteer with the aforementioned grassroots organization and eventually also with the Staten Island office of the International Rescue Committee (IRC), a global humanitarian aid and relief organization. In this role of a volunteer, I was able to observe what was happening in the community and build rapport with various community members as someone who cared about their well-being and was not only driven by collecting data. I did this because from my previous work in Atlanta, I was all too familiar with the "over-researched community" syndrome. When researchers just show up, ask questions, and then disappear, refugees not only feel used but also are left to wonder what happened with the information they provided (Byrne 2013; Sukarieh and Tannock 2013). I did not start interviewing Liberian refugees until almost two years after I had entered the community. At that point, I not only had a better sense of the type of questions that I was interested in but also what Liberian refugees wanted to talk about, which I included in the interview guide that I developed. This interview guide consisted of broad topics related to Liberians' journey from West Africa to New York, their initial settlement in the United States, their life in Staten Island, their experiences and encounters with the refugee resettlement system, their interactions with Americans of different racial backgrounds, and anti-Black racism and discrimination, as well as gender dynamics in Liberia and after resettlement. Although this is a book about refugees, I made a deliberate choice to ask no direct questions related to their experiences during the war in Liberia and their subsequent flight. I did not want to retraumatize Liberian refugees, and I knew from my time in the community and my work in Atlanta that most refugees do not want to relive and recount these horrific experiences. Nevertheless, some Liberian refugees who participated in this study decided to share details about the horrors that they or their family members went through. These accounts were similar to those of the Liberians that I had interacted with in Atlanta, as well as those I met through my work as a country conditions expert for asylum cases (details to follow).

To ensure that the sample was representative of the diversity within the Liberian community as it relates to the mode of entry (e.g., refugee, asylee), age, gender, ethnicity, educational level, and duration in the United States, I recruited a purposive sample, meaning that certain people were selected based on their experience or criteria (Maxwell 2004). I located this sample through initiating contact through various points of entry—that is, diverse members of the community (in terms of ethnicity, gender, age, and occupation). This multiple-entry method ensured that I avoided interviewing Liberians involved in only a very limited number of personal networks, which often happens in traditional snowball sampling (Jones-Correa 1998) and could easily have occurred in such a tightly knit community concentrated in a small geographic area.

In the end, I conducted in-depth interviews with fifty-five Liberians, several of whom I interviewed multiple times over the course of the research project, which continued up to the point of writing this book. All but one had lived in Staten Island for at least six months when I interviewed them for the first time. The Liberian research participants were from a variety of ethnic groups (Americo Liberian, Bassa, Gbandi, Gio, Gola, Grebo, Kissi, Kpelle, Krahn, Kru, Loma, Mandingo, Mende, and Vai) and ranged in age from their late teens to their mid-80s.[14] Slightly more women (twenty-nine) than men (twenty-six) were interviewed, reflecting that more female Liberian refugees were resettled in the United States.[15] The vast majority of Liberian research participants (thirty-seven) had at some point legal refugee status, asylum, or Temporary Protective Status (TPS)/Deferred Enforced Departure (DED).[16] There were fifteen Liberians whose legal status was "immigrant." Most (eleven) of these Liberian immigrants had entered through family reunification (child or spouse of a permanent resident or U.S. citizen), while three had "won" their permanent residency through the Diversity Visa Program (DV),[17] and one person had their status adjusted through the Immigration Reform and Control Act of 1986 (IRCA).[18] Eight of these fifteen Liberians with immigrant status had experiences similar to refugees that prompted their migration to the United States. Put differently, if there had not been a war, these Liberians would not have left their native country. Two individuals, in addition to the thirty-seven forcibly displaced people and fifteen immigrants, were U.S. citizens through descent from Americo Liberian (grand)parents but identified as Liberian.[19] I interviewed one Liberian who had been displaced during the war and ended up working with the UNHCR in one of the refugee camps in West Africa, where his fellow country people had sought refuge. While he has never lived in Staten Island, he now maintains a home in North Carolina, where he lives when he is not on an international assignment related to refugee protection. He was not the only Liberian in this study who had been involved with refugee resettlement; there were four other Liberians who were also at some point employed by different VOLAGs.

Additionally, I interviewed a number of non-Liberians. The first group was three individuals (Kenyan, Senegalese, native-born White American) who had all been employed by a local or international nongovernmental organization (NGO) that worked with Liberian refugees. These interviews provided additional data points about Liberian refugee resettlement from the viewpoint of individuals who were not community members. The second group was ten long-term native-born Black American residents living in Park Hill. I conducted these interviews with two of my students, a native-born Black American resident of Park Hill and a second-generation Black Caribbean American from Brooklyn. This set of interviews focused on perceptions that native-born Black Americans living in Park Hill had about race, anti-Black racism in Staten Island, and Africans (esp. Liberian refugees) in their shared neighborhood.

While the interviews with native-born Black Americans were conducted via Zoom due to the COVID-19 pandemic and the availability of the students, the vast majority of the first interviews with Liberian refugees took place at their respective homes. Other times, and in particular for follow-up interviews, I got together with Liberians at their places of work, in public parks, at restaurants, in church vestibules, on the Staten Island Ferry, and in the community rooms in the

Park Hill apartment complex. In other words, I met with Liberian refugees wherever they felt comfortable.

Interviews lasted between one and two hours and were conducted in English, and transcribed verbatim. When given consent, I recorded the interviews while taking notes at the same time. I used the notes to jot down what the audio recording was not capturing, such as gestures and the surroundings.[20] At the end of the initial interview I asked all interviewees to choose their own pseudonym, which for most Liberians in this study also reflects their ethnicity, especially the last name (see appendixes 1 and 2). However, as I describe in chapter 2, many Liberians, not just Americo Liberians, have "Anglo last names" that can be traced back to the names of enslavers in the United States. Throughout the book, I refer to Liberian refugees either with their full pseudonym or use an honorific (Ms. or Mr.) before their last name. In Liberian culture, in most contexts, people are not just addressed by their first name; an older woman's first name is prefaced with "Ma" or "Auntie," and a person of a similar age is addressed as "Sister." (A similar pattern applies to men.) By using honorifics, I hope to honor this part of Liberian culture.

Interview data are complemented by copious field notes that I took as I immersed myself in the Staten Island Liberian community over the past fifteen years. Specifically, I joined Liberian refugees at public and private events—volunteering with different nonprofit organizations;[21] going to baby showers, christenings, and birthday parties; spending time with women at the local African market and during literacy and U.S. citizenship classes; and attending religious services along with a wide variety of ethnic and national celebrations such as the Liberian Independence Day. This allowed me to gather data that capture various aspects of life in "Little Liberia" and a wide range of experiences. While I went to most of these events in person, during the height of the COVID-19 pandemic I also participated in virtual gatherings.

This research is also informed by actual work experience in the field, first with refugees in Atlanta and second as a country conditions expert for Liberian asylum claims and deportation hearings during the past few years. My on-the-ground work experience in Atlanta certainly helped me when I spoke with staff at VOLAGs, who did not have to explain the basics of resettlement and were able to relate to me as a former colleague. In addition, I was familiar with the expectations set by the Office of Refugee Resettlement (ORR) pertaining to fast (economic) self-sufficiency and how this remains a difficult task for many refugees due to their lack of transferable skills, their trauma, (anti-Black) racism and discrimination, and the financial and emotional demands from their loved ones whom they left behind. The vast majority of Liberians in deportation hearings that I have been part of sought Relief under the Convention Against Torture.[22] I will not provide too much context to ensure their anonymity; many of these Liberians arrived as refugees when they were children and later were found guilty of a deportable crime.[23] Working in the spaces of immigration courts has allowed me to use my academic credentials and knowledge to support Liberians and their lawyers while also gaining an additional insight into U.S. immigration and asylum procedures across the country, as I have taken on cases from various circuits in the United States.

In addition to these ethnographic data I also made use of secondary data. Through my work with the IRC, I had access to two data sets that were collected by the IRC: a survey of 1.5- and second-generation youth of Liberian descent ($N = 110$) and focus groups with forty first-generation Liberian parents living in Staten Island. I initially coded these data for the IRC and their grantor and then received permission to use them for this study. Quantitative data from the ORR, the Refugee Processing Center, the U.S. State Department, the U.S. Department of Justice, and the U.S. Department of Homeland Security gave me additional insights on arrival and resettlement for all refugees and in particular Liberian refugees resettled in Staten Island.[24] Finally, census data, publications by local nonprofit organizations, and local newspaper articles were used for background information.

An Immigrant Studying Refugees: A History of Rapport

I am both an outsider and an insider in Park Hill's Liberian refugee community. Like Liberian refugees, I am a foreigner in the United States—but I am an immigrant from Austria who is most of the time racialized as White in the United States. My immigrant identity is important to me since this is how I see and experience the world, but it also reflects how others treat me. Thus, it was always a topic when I first met with Liberian refugees on an individual basis. It often was a starting point, as they mentioned that we shared experiences since we had not grown up in the United States. Liberians made many comments about how we, as foreigners, had to learn a new culture, and, to some extent, language, while figuring out an immigration system that often presented us with arduous hurdles. For example, I could commiserate with Liberians about feeling powerless against immigration bureaucracy since my immigration paperwork from my initial work visa to my permanent residency card had been processed with me listed as a citizen of a country in the South Pacific. For a long time, no objection could convince bureaucrats that they had made an error. The fact that I am not American by birth—I became a naturalized U.S. citizen during this research project—had a definite impact on how Liberians have received me. For instance, one day when I was interviewing a Liberian woman, her elderly mother came to visit. At first, she had assumed I was American. Upon hearing me speak, her entire demeanor changed; her eyes lit up, she took my hands in hers and said, "We are both immigrants. Welcome!" Others made reference to our common experience of having to deal with U.S. immigration authorities and encouraged me to get my U.S. citizenship as soon as possible "because the price keeps going up." The longer the research went on, the more Liberians observed that I have kept my word and have continued to advocate on behalf of the Liberian community. For example, I used my position at Wagner College, an institution that is within a twenty-minute walking distance from Park Hill, to organize for Wagner College students to become involved as after-school and literacy tutors with different grassroots organizations that support West African refugee and immigrant families in Park Hill. In addition, I applied for grants at Wagner College that went to support an NGO that offers programming to the Liberian community. Most Liberians explained my continued commitment to the community through my immigrant background, contrasting it to Americans, who, as they said, only stuck around as long as it was beneficial for their personal or professional gain. I welcomed this emphasis on my immigrant identity, since it made it easier for me to build trust and connections with Liberian refugees.

However, my experiences as a European immigrant certainly differ from those of African refugees. My status as an Austrian immigrant with significant cultural capital in the United States is unlike that of most of the Liberian refugees I studied.[25] Our racial differences were noted by a few Liberians. Some pointed out that we have different complexions and that "God made us so." Other times, especially in situations where I was new to a particular setting (like at an event), the Liberian person who had invited me would say something like, "Don't worry about her skin. . . . She is a family friend. . . . You can trust her, and she is *not* an American" (see Davis 1997; Rhodes 1994 for a detailed discussion on race-of-interviewer effect and cross-racial research).

Unlike most White people in the United States, I also have extensive experience living and being in Black spaces. I spent time in West Africa, and as such, I have some familiarity with certain cultural norms and expectations. In the United States, I have almost always resided in a predominantly Black neighborhood, first serendipitously as I rented an apartment based on affordability and proximity to my job when I moved to the United States, and then by choice to ensure the safety of my multiracial household. But my exposure goes deeper than that. After moving to the United States, I first lived with Black roommates (native-born American, Ethiopian) and since then with my Jamaican spouse, who is racialized as Black in the United States. Because of this, I have witnessed and encountered anti-Black racism, for example, when we sought housing or medical care, and I have also experienced "rebound racism," which is defined as the indirect effect of racism directed at the Black partner, which also affects the White person in financial and emotional ways (Dalmage 2000). While I have not personally experienced anti-Black racism, being in the above situations in my own personal life has made me much more vigilant and aware of the deep-seated anti-Black racism that exists in the United States. This, in turn, also affected my research process, for example, thinking about how and what kind of questions to ask and when to step back and listen.

A Note About Terminology

There are a few key terms that, depending on the context, can have different meanings or are not always clear. Below, I briefly describe how I use them in the book.

Refugee. Throughout the book the term "refugee" describes Liberians in the United States. I do this—knowing that not all Liberians have had legal refugee status—because an overwhelming majority of Liberians came to the United States due to the war in their native country and the resulting persecution, and as such, their motivations to migrate were much more influenced by push factors than pull factors. Many of these Liberians were granted asylum, which shares important legal rights and provisions with legal refugee status. Furthermore, almost all Liberians have had, in one way or another, contact with the USRAP, which distinctly shapes their integration into U.S. society. While the subsequent chapters highlight how different legal statuses have impacted the lives of Liberians, "refugee" describes forcibly displaced people unless otherwise indicated (either explicitly or through the context). As I explain in chapter 4, I use this term even though Liberians do not want to be called refugees because it best identifies migrants who were displaced by violence and (fear of) persecution. Chapter 4 also provides insight into why it is important to distinguish between "legal refugee status," which grants rights, protections, and often government benefits, and the "informal label," which does not.

Black Refugees, African Refugees. While this is a book based on data collected about Liberian refugees, many of their experiences are not entirely unique. Much of my analysis applies to other refugees, especially African refugees, and at times other Black refugees. "African" in this book denotes Africans who are or would be racialized as Black in the United States and therefore does not include Afrikaners (White South Africans). For the most part, when I write about "Black refugees," this includes other African, Haitian, and sometimes Black Cuban, refugees. While there are certainly Black refugees in other areas of the world, there is not enough data and research available to include them in the analysis.

Liberian Culture. When Liberians speak about their culture, they usually do not distinguish between the different ethnic groups that are Indigenous to Liberia. More often, Liberian refugees note the difference between Americo Liberian and Indigenous Liberian culture, as I record in chapter 2 where relevant. However, most of the time the reference was "Liberian culture" or "in Liberia."

LOOKING AHEAD: OUTLINE OF THE BOOK

The next chapter, "When the War Came, Everyone Scattered," describes why Liberians left their country of birth to come to the United States and how this migration is deeply intertwined with Liberia's origin in American anti-Black racism. Liberia, as a country, was conceived by White people in the United States as a way to "deal with" and sustain American slavery. Concretely, Black people from the United States were sent to what would become Liberia to remove them from the United States, to claim an American stake in the African continent, and to colonize the Indigenous Liberian population. The descendants of Black American settlers set up an oligarchy that subjugated Indigenous Africans, which eventually led to the civil war in Liberia. The fourteen-year war caused more than 50 percent of Liberians to flee their homes and seek temporary refuge elsewhere in Liberia or other countries in West Africa. Drawing on the experiences of these Liberians, I recount their tumultuous flight to refugee camps in neighboring countries and Ghana. A very small number of these displaced Liberians eventually found refuge in the United States. While hoping to be selected for resettlement in the United States, most pictured America, their "motherland," as "heaven on earth," where their troubles would disappear, their children could go to school, and they could live freely and enjoy themselves—where, simply put, their "suffering days would be over."

Chapter 3, "Searching for Home in Staten Island," focuses on Liberian refugees' pursuit of this "heaven on earth" and creation of a new home in Staten Island. Much of their "settling down" was facilitated (or hindered) by VOLAGs and impacted by anti-Black racism. Liberian refugees quickly became aware that Staten Island was far from what they had expected; there were no flashy skyscrapers, impeccable infrastructure, multicultural celebrations, or a warm welcome from their "American brothers and sisters." Instead, Liberians found themselves living in Staten Island's Park Hill neighborhood, where crime, drug trafficking, and murder have historically been high. Slowly, Liberians have transformed the neighborhood into "Little Liberia," although not without conflict with their native-born Black American neighbors.

In chapter 4, "Someone Call Me a 'Damn' Refugee," I analyze the contextual complexities that the term "refugee" has for Black refugees. I do so by highlighting that legal refugee status—which provides much greater international protection and access to benefits and resources compared to other (im)migration statuses—is not only a very political issue, but obtaining it requires an enormous amount of ingenuity and, at times, the preferred racial background. Liberian refugees, like other Black refugees, worked hard to beat the odds to secure this highly desired legal status. In the process, they had to vie for one of the rare refugee resettlement slots set aside for African refugees but also had to overcome commonly held stereotypes of Black people to demonstrate that they were vulnerable, victimized people who were worthy of resettlement to the United States. In contrast to the very elusive legal refugee status, the informal label of refugee, which conveys no financial or legal benefits, is readily applied to Black people. For Liberian refugees and other Black refugees, being called "refugee" is not only a constant reminder of their past suffering but also carries a racialized stigma that marks them as "long-suffering Others" and "welfare abusers." This hinders their integration into American society, as they are continuously questioned about their belonging by others and, as a result, even themselves.

Chapter 5, "Whites Are the Boss," focuses on the relationships Liberian refugees have with native-born White Americans. For the most part, relationships with White people in the United States have been contentious, mainly because of deep-seated anti-Black racism and xenophobia. I discuss how Liberians, as Black and African refugees, are stereotyped and discriminated against in the labor and housing markets, in encounters with the police, and in public spaces. Despite this bigotry and stereotyping, Liberians have not always been outspoken about anti-Black racism and prejudice. I argue that this is because Liberians employ what I refer to as a refugee-specific dual frame of reference. Liberian refugees contrast their negative experiences with native-born White Americans in the United States with the historical racial violence of slavery and the Jim Crow era, past discrimination in Liberia during the Americo Liberians' rule and the brutal civil war, and positive encounters with White people during the resettlement process. The latter is an experience unique to refugees compared to immigrants, who are usually not part of organized resettlement and integration programs largely staffed by native-born White Americans. In addition, the ongoing need to send remittances has forced Liberian refugees to stay in less-than-desirable jobs. Finally, many older first-generation Liberian refugees feel that taking on racial injustices in the United States is not their fight, pointing out that they are merely tolerated, not welcomed, and therefore hope to make economic gains in order to return to Liberia eventually.

In chapter 6, "We Have the Same Skin Color," I discuss the different meanings and consequences of being Black in Liberia and the United States. Blackness is the cornerstone of Liberian citizenship. Descent (Americo Liberian vs. Indigenous African) and ethnicity are significant in Liberia as they have impacted a person's status and, often, fate during the country's civil war, but they are generally less important in the United States, where race is a "master status." Consequently, Liberian refugees have to redefine what it means to be Black in their new home, a process shaped through dialogues and interactions with their native-born Black American neighbors and experiences with anti-Black racism in the United States. This development has been neither smooth nor uniform. For example, after some years of contentious relationships between native-born Black Americans and Liberian refugees due to disputes over scarce resources in the neighborhood and claims to cultural and moral superiority, these two groups have forged alliances. These alliances emerged through shared experience with anti-Black racism and relationships and friendships that 1.5- and second-generation Liberian refugees have built with native-born Black Americans. In the end, these coalitions between different Black people have contributed to the election of Black local politicians.

Revisiting the themes, major trends, and findings of the book, chapter 7, "There Are Liberian Refugees in the Future," highlights once more that race has greatly impacted the experiences of Black refugees and their ability to become part of American society. By drawing on Liberian refugees' narratives as well as my applied work in this area, I offer a number of policy suggestions for local and federal policymakers and (inter)national refugee and immigrant organizations with the aim of addressing and combating systemic anti-Black racism and other forms of discrimination in the immigration system and USRAP.

2 WHEN THE WAR CAME, EVERYONE SCATTERED

On February 6, 1820, the *Elizabeth*—frequently referred to as the Black Mayflower (Ciment 2013)—set sail from New York City with almost ninety Black settlers for what would become Liberia.[1] This undertaking took place under the auspices of three White American agents of the ACS and with financial backing from the U.S. Congress. The mood among the passengers, which included farmers, nurses, cooks, preachers, and laborers, was solemn; they had conflicting views about the adventure ahead of them. They, like the majority of migrants, dealt with mixed emotions: feeling sad that they were leaving most of their relatives and friends behind and worried about the unknown but also having a sense of relief knowing that they were leaving the specter of American anti-Black racism behind. The *Elizabeth* was the first ship of many that brought an estimated nineteen thousand Black settlers from the United States and Caribbean islands across the Atlantic. Among them were David Joe's grandparents. They, along with two hundred other Black people from the United States, half of them, like Mr. Joe's grandparents from Jefferson County in Arkansas, left on the SS *Horsa* to Liberia in March 1895. Most of them embarked because, as Isaac Cheeks, David Joe's uncle, said, "Down there, the people was very prejudiced. Only Caucasians had rights.... They didn't have any rights.... They sometimes used to lynch them, tie weight on them, and throw them into the river."

Once in Liberia, Mr. Cheeks and Mr. Joe's forefathers joined other Black settlers and their descendants who became known as Americo Liberians. This group of people, which today makes up about 5 percent of Liberia's total population, established a nation that mirrored the one they had just left. This was not limited to the political and economic stratification that put Americo Liberians at the top and Indigenous Africans at the bottom, but also to the traditions and culture the settlers brought with them. For example, Mr. Cheeks and Mr. Joe's ancestors, like most of their fellow emigrants, operated a farm growing crops typical in the United States, such as sweet potato, corn, collard greens, cabbage, and sugarcane. Similar to the United States, additional labor was needed to operate these farms. This is where Indigenous Liberians came in. They joined Americo Liberian households, where their status varied between quasi family member and indentured servant, but all were exposed to efforts to "civilize" them. Isaac Cheeks remembered growing up with Indigenous brothers who were from the Bassa ethnic group: "My father took in Indigenous boys and raised them right along with us. That was no problem. . . . We all used to work in the farm together, planting . . . picking coffee. . . . We all worked together; we ate together. . . . I was in a bed with a boy that was almost my age that my father raised. . . . But don't misunderstand me, some Americo Liberians, they didn't do that." While Mr. Cheeks stressed that his family treated their Indigenous family members with respect, he also acknowledged that this was not the case for all Americo Liberians. For their part, Indigenous Liberians resented the settlers and were eager to free themselves from their rule. But it would take more than 133 years to end Americo Liberians' reign with a coup d'état in 1980. Following that, Liberia's elite, Americo Liberians such as Mr. Joe—who can often be identified by their last names, the way they speak, and their clothing style—were targeted in retaliation for their long reign, which had left Indigenous Liberians disenfranchised (Advocates for Human Rights 2006, 90). Hundreds of Americo Liberians were imprisoned, tortured, and/or publicly executed. While several thousand Americo Liberians fled the country at that time, David Joe and his family stayed, hoping that things would calm down. But, tragically, this did not happen and they found themselves trapped in a place spiraling into turmoil and war. Mr. Joe was among the twenty-five hundred people—about five hundred of them U.S. citizens—who were airlifted by U.S. Marines out of the mayhem in Monrovia, Liberia's capital, between August 1990 and January 1991 (see also Devroy and Moore 1990). Like so many other Liberians, he was separated from his family in the process. Thus, once Mr. Joe made it to Brooklyn, New York, where he had an uncle, he found a job and started to save money to first bring his wife and two youngest children to the United States in 1994, three other children in 2001, and another son in 2004. Part of the reason why the reunification took so long was that Mr. Joe's wife and children were not registered as refugees with the UNHCR, and thus, they were not eligible for family reunification under the USRAP. Therefore, the Joe family's journey to the United States is different from the more than thirty thousand Liberians, mostly of Indigenous ancestry, who were resettled as refugees in the United States between the mid-1990s and the mid-2000s and who are the focus of this chapter.

Specifically, this chapter gives an overview of Liberia's colonial history and unusual stratification system (Americo Liberians vs. Indigenous Liberians) and discusses how the dynamics involved in the country's very foundation contributed to the civil war, which spurred different waves of immigration of Liberians to the United States. Initially, it was mostly Americo Liberians, like Mr. Joe, who fled, fearing reprisal for their ethnic group's oligarchy. They arrived in the United States using (financial) resources and connections to the United States they had retained during previous stays (e.g., studying at an American college). While they had a more seamless escape from Liberia to the United States, they did not have refugee status, and thus many found themselves, as detailed in chapter 4, in a more precarious legal situation (Reilly 2016; Pailey 2016). Those Americo Liberians, along with Indigenous Liberians, who lacked these connections had to endure years of war and bear witness to or experience (sexual) assaults, abductions, torture, piles of dead bodies, and executions in Liberia, which are detailed in the next pages. Seeking to escape the horrors of the war, many Liberians sought safety in internally displaced persons (IDPs) and/or in refugee camps in Guinea, Sierra Leone, Côte d'Ivoire, and Ghana. There, they hoped to be among the lucky few who would be selected to be resettled in the United States via the USRAP. As these Liberian refugees waited for years, they dreamed of a life in the United States, which Cynthia Sherif, who grew up in Brewerville, an Americo Liberian settlement just outside Liberia's capital Monrovia, described as "the promised land . . . with no dirt on the streets and just beautiful buildings" where they would have a fresh start, free from the trauma that the war and the loss of home, life, and livelihoods had caused and which more importantly would give them and their children a better future.

"LITTLE AMERICA": THE CREATION OF LIBERIA IN RESPONSE TO AMERICAN ANTI-BLACK RACISM

Liberia and the United States are intrinsically linked because of slavery and anti-Black racism; whereas "the U.S. was founded as a nation based on African slavery" (Foner 2018, 1118), Liberia was founded as a colony by the ACS due to American slavery in 1822. The ACS was established by members of the aristocracy of the U.S. South who were profiting from slavery and Northern Quakers in Washington, D.C., in 1816. They agreed, although for different reasons, that it would be better for the United States, and to some extent Black people in the United States, if (free) Black people were "repatriated" to Africa. "Black" back then, and to most extent today, includes anybody who had any African descent, known as the "one drop rule." In fact, most free Black people were of mixed racial ancestry in the United States (Ciment 2013).

Those who enslaved Black people supported the ACS because they were eager to strengthen the institution of slavery and felt that the presence of free and emancipated Black people threatened this endeavor. Quakers joined the ACS, as many were in favor of abolition but were not in support of the existence of free Black people in the United States. Together and independently, both sides raised funds from the U.S. Congress and state governments, arguing for the "repatriation" of Black people to Africa (Ciment 2013; J. Levitt 2005). Other factors that motivated the ACS in this colonization endeavor were the opportunity to Christianize and "civilize" Indigenous Africans through Western education and affording the United States access to Liberia's natural resources, such as rubber, iron, timber, diamonds, and so forth (J. Levitt 2005; Tyler-McGraw 2007). Still, the main purpose of the colony was to offer a potential "solution" to what many White Americans perceived to be a "problem": free Black people living in the United States at a time when the overwhelming number of Black individuals—87 percent according to the 1820 U.S. Census—were enslaved and thus considered property and treated as inferior to White people (Sanneh 2001).

Black people in the North who were technically "free" vociferously opposed the ACS because it conveyed the idea that "blacks were 'really African' (and therefore not 'American') and should return (or be returned) to Africa" (Lubkemann 2017, 84). In contrast, many emancipated and free Black people in the South (and in the Caribbean islands) perceived migrating to Liberia as their only chance to escape slavery, racial segregation, oppression, and terror. This also explains the spike in the number of Black settlers leaving for Liberia in the aftermath of particular violent events such as the killings of free and enslaved Black people by White militias after the Nat Turner Rebellion (1831), the Fugitive Slave Act (1850), and the restrictions placed on Black individuals during and after the Reconstruction Era (1865–1877) (Lubkemann 2017). Thus, these Black settlers to Liberia can, and perhaps ought to, be understood as refugees fleeing racial terror in the United States. In addition, a few other Black people saw the colony as a potential for economic opportunity where they could own "land to farm, trade to pursue . . . businesses to start" (Ciment 2013, 11–12). A smaller number of Black people felt that the "uplifting of Africans in Africa" would consequently "uplift . . . Africans in [the] diaspora as well" (Tyler-McGraw 2007, 153)—in other words, addressing anti-Black racism and bringing freedom to Black people who remained in the United States. Another group of Black settlers did not really have a choice; their enslavers only granted them (and their families) freedom under the condition that they would leave for Liberia. Hence, some have also referred to this as "a period of forced migration *back to* West Africa from the Americas" (Crawley and Fynn Bruey 2022, 110, emphasis in original text).

Overall, historical records suggest that the majority of the Black settlers who left the United States (and Caribbean islands) between 1820 and 1919 (Gershoni 1985) were pushed to leave in search of freedom, which is reflected in Liberia's national motto of "The Love of Liberty Brought Us Here." This promise of freedom was deceptive for several reasons. First, ACS was ruled by White Americans who entrusted White and later Black colonial agents to "establish near dictatorial authority over the settlers" (Ciment 2013, 45)—fueled by "racial paternalism" (J. Levitt 2005, 33) that saw Black people as inferior and thus unfit to govern (J. Levitt 2005). Second, settlers robbed the Indigenous people in Liberia of their freedom.

"Negate Your Name": Americo Liberian Rule

Many Black settlers experienced a comparable fate to White European colonialists in Africa: They had a difficult time adjusting to their new lives and died in high numbers from diseases (Gershoni 1985; J. Levitt 2005). Another similarity was their disrespect of the Indigenous population, which led to the establishment of a society marked by stratification based on descent, colorism, and culture in

Liberia. Despite the promise that Black people would be in charge, White Americans, through the backing of the ACS, controlled every aspect of what happened in the quasi colony, at least until Liberia's independence in 1847. The next most powerful group was Americo Liberians—Black settlers from the United States and the Caribbean and their descendants. This was not a homogeneous group, and there were many frictions, for example, between free and emancipated Black people who often differed not only in their complexion but also in their formal education, skill level (artisan vs. farmhand), and financial capital. This led to a replication of what was already happening at that point in the United States: a small light-skinned elite in positions of power (Ciment 2013), which Liberian refugees in Staten Island commented on. For example, Memba Wesseh, an ethnic Bassa, originally from Monrovia, described the complexion of Liberian presidents and noted that "if you see the pictures . . . they were White. . . . White people almost . . . Joseph Jenkins Roberts, James Payne, Daniel B. Warner, everybody." Understandably, darker-skinned American and Caribbean settlers and their descendants, including Edward Wilmot Blyden, a father of Pan-Africanism, resented those in power, and felt that, due to their biracial ancestry, light-skinned settlers and Americo Liberians could not be trusted but also were "genetically unstable and unable to govern Liberia" (Tyler-McGraw 2007, 175). Gradually, colorism became less of an issue among Americo Liberians because of increasing intermarriage and their combined focus on uniting against Indigenous ethnic groups and encroaching European powers, who all represented a threat to their rule (Ciment 2013; J. Levitt 2005).

Over time Americo Liberians were also joined by about five-thousand "Congo people," Africans seized from slave ships that tried to cross the Atlantic after the trade of enslaved humans was abolished (Singler 2015). All of these groups and their descendants—who are interchangeably referred to as Americo Liberians or Congos—established a society in Liberia modeled after the Antebellum South in terms of culture and social hierarchy. There are countless similarities between Liberia and the United States, especially around how the settlers in both places treated the Indigenous population and how they established the nations. Like Native Americans in what would become the United States, the sixteen Indigenous ethnic groups (Kpelle, Bassa, Grebo, Gio, Mano, Kru, Loma, Gola, Kissi, Krahn, Gbandi, Dei, Belle, Mandingo, Mende, and Vai) of the Liberian territory neither wanted to give up their land nor be ruled by outsiders, which resulted in conflicts and wars.[2] Despite being the original inhabitants of the land, Indigenous Africans were not acknowledged in Liberia's Declaration of Independence (July 26, 1847)—modeled after the U.S. Declaration of Independence of 1776—rather, it stated that "We, the people of the Republic of Liberia were originally inhabitants of the United States of North America." Indigenous ethnic groups were denied Liberian citizenship and the right to vote until 1964 (S. Ellis 1999);[3] yet another resemblance to the United States, where U.S. citizenship was extended to/imposed upon all Native Americans in 1924. Liberia followed once more the U.S. example when it duplicated citizenship laws that were based on racial exclusion. In the United States, the Naturalization Act of 1790 limited citizenship to free White people. Pailey (2016, 5) argues that "Liberia's constitution of citizenship . . . reflected a settler male ethos, ruling indigenous, non-Christians, women of both Indigenous and settler orientation, and non-blacks." Specifically, the Liberian Constitution limits—to this day—citizenship to only "Negroes or persons of Negro descent."[4] The origins of this race-based citizenship are unequivocally linked to the history of the United States and its racial exclusion of Black people. Essentially the construction of Liberia as the redemption and elevation of the Black/African race (David 2014) is the counterpart to the United States, as it provided a space where Black settlers and their descendants had citizenship, a right that was denied to them in the United States until the ratification of the Fourteenth Amendment of the U.S. Constitution in 1868. Consequently, Blackness became an integral part of Liberian (national) identity and one that Liberia's founding fathers sought to protect against any non-Black control with a race-based limitation of citizenship.[5] And the threat was real, as European nations were eager to bring the entire continent of Africa under their control, which also explains why the Liberian Constitution includes a clause that only allows Liberian citizens to own land (Ludwig 2016a; Pailey 2016). At the same time, this right and other privileges did for a long time not extend to most Indigenous Africans, who, in the eyes of Americo Liberians, were morally and culturally inferior, uncivilized pagans (Gershoni 1985). The Black settlers' views were informed by the "White racial frame," which purports a negative view of Africa and its people and "White culture" as superior (Feagin 2009b). Many Black settlers had lots of disdain for the Indigenous population; some of them described them as "heathen and barbarous people" (J. Levitt 2005, 82), "lazy and duplicitous," and even "lumped . . . together with monkeys" (Ciment 2013, 71), the same degrading language that White people in the United States have used to describe enslaved Africans, the ancestors of these Black settlers. This sentiment was also echoed by Isaac Cheeks as he recounted popular perceptions of the Indigenous population among his fellow Americo Liberians:

> The people that left here, they dress like they were . . . here, but the Indigenous, they tied their lappa . . . put chalk on their face.[6] They would tell them . . . "Go wash the chalk, take bath, put perfume on," things like that. . . . Most of them wanted to eat with their hands, and they would tell them, "No, you eat with spoon, knife, and fork." . . . They had a culture that the Americans were not accustomed to. And they used to cook different because they used to make corn bread, biscuits, short bread, gravy. And most of the Indigenous women didn't know how to do that. But they soon learned. . . . [Americo Liberians] forced them to go to church . . . and become civil.

In other words, many of the Black settlers were implementing the very rules they had just escaped, with an important exception that they did not enslave Indigenous Africans. Another difference was that White Americans in the United States justified slavery based on their imagined racial superiority, while Black settlers rationalized that their cultural superiority (following and adhering to cultural practices in the Antebellum South) put them above Indigenous Africans. As Mr. Cheeks states, Indigenous Liberians could only improve their standing in Liberian society if they were "civilized," meaning adopting Americo Liberians' cultural norms and values; shedding their Indigenous languages, dress, customs, and traditions; and getting baptized. This often happened through the "ward system,"[7] which was legally recognized in 1838 (Liebenow 1969). This cultural practice among Indigenous Africans, which predated the arrival of Americo Liberians, involves sending children to stay with wealthier family members. With the presence of Americo Liberians, more Indigenous children went to live with Americo Liberian families instead of their Indigenous relatives to receive an education and sustenance. There were other ways Indigenous Africans could become part of the Americo Liberian group, such as if they were the children of an Americo Liberian man and his Indigenous mistress,[8] also known as a "country wife," and then came to live with the Americo Liberian wife and husband (Ciment 2013). Furthermore, some Americo Liberians took it upon themselves in their quest to "educate" and Christianize the Indigenous population and went to the hinterland,[9] where they recruited Indigenous children who then stayed with them. Regardless of how the children arrived in an Americo Liberian family, they had to adopt Americo Liberian customs and practices, including Christianity. James Paye, a Gio who was born in Nimba County, described his own experience: "When you . . . live with the settlers . . . you have to negate your name and adopt the name of your foster parents in order to be civilized . . . incorporate you in a so-called Western culture. . . . I was flocked fifteen lashes . . . when I spoke Gio . . . told . . . not to speak that heathen language anymore." Another important aspect to being accepted as "civilized" was having an Americo Liberian name such as Jenkins, Roberts, Cooper, Reeves, or Payne, which ironically, Americo Liberians had been given by their own or their forefathers' enslavers. Wright Talley, a Krahn who prior to the war had worked in the Ministry of Finance, explained the origins of his real-life, typical Americo Liberian last name: "The only way that you as an Indigenous Liberian can . . . fit into Americo Liberian society is you got to carry on . . . their name. . . . They must have godfathers to live with, and so this is how my grandfather got his name. He was living with the [Anglo-American name] family, and so they changed his name to [Anglo-American name]. You are asked to take the [Anglo-American] name because if you don't do that, you cannot get the required education."

While some Americo Liberian families thought of and treated the Indigenous children and teenagers in their household like family members, as Mr. Cheeks had described, others saw them as servants (Dolo 2007; Gershoni 1985) with "little difference to domestic slavery" (Liebenow 1969, 16). Osiemeo Boye, a Bassa who was born in the Bomi Hills but was sent by his sister to live with an Americo Liberian family in Monrovia because "she didn't have money," recounted his unpleasant experiences during his youth: "I live there like a houseboy, carrying garbage, throw garbage away. . . . Everything happen in house . . . they blame me. They didn't see no wrongdoing of their kids. Everything they want me to do it, I did not hesitate; I did everything. Every day I carry garbage on my head to the dumping site." It seems shocking that people, in this case the Black settlers who not long ago broke free from anti-Black racism and also often enslavement, would turn around and oppress others in a similar inhumane way. So why did Black settlers and their descendants choose to mistreat the Indigenous groups in Liberia? Feagin (2009a, para. 3) offers the following explanation: "Racism inevitably reproduces itself in the minds of the oppressed in order to rise." Beverly Coleman, who is of both Americo Liberian and Vai ancestry, echoed, "The people that left from here, they were slaves. . . . They were treated less than a human being. So, when they get to Liberia, they were given the position and power. They began to oppress their own people. Because that's what they were used to . . . for so many years before they set them free. So, if you used to being . . . treated . . . with disrespect, when you meet other people, you're gonna treat them with disrespect." As Ms. Coleman described, the relationship between Black settlers and Indigenous Africans was stratified, with a clear hierarchy that ensured that Americo Liberians dominated the country economically, culturally, and religiously. For example, Americo Liberians appropriated the land, coerced Indigenous Africans to work for them for little to no pay, and subjugated them to taxes. This only got worse as the ACS's influence waned, and thus the financial support from the United States dwindled. Additionally, they, like all colonizers, tried to (forcefully) convert the Indigenous population to their religion, Christianity. This commitment to Christianity was enshrined in Liberia's Declaration of Independence (Ciment 2013) and remains very important in Liberia and for most Liberians at home and in the diaspora today. According to the 2022 Liberian Population and Housing Census, 85 percent of Liberians are Christian. This is in stark contrast to neighboring countries such as Guinea and Sierra Leone, where Islam is the dominant religion.

Culturally speaking, ties initiated in the nineteenth century between Liberia and the United States are still present today. For instance, Liberia's lingua franca is English, although it is a Liberian version of English, which reflects grammar and vocabulary from English spoken by Black settlers as well as local Indigenous languages (Singler 2015). Similarly, the Liberian flag also reveals the historical connection; it differs from the U.S. flag solely in the number of stars and stripes. Furthermore, many Liberian cities and counties are named after U.S. presidents or locations in the United States, two examples being Liberia's capital, Monrovia, after U.S. President James Monroe, an enslaver who supported the ACS, and Maryland County after the U.S. state of Maryland (see map 2.1).

Overall, U.S. involvement with Liberia has continued past Liberia's independence. It includes the long, historic transatlantic movements between both countries, as well as the American economic, political, and military investments. For instance, in 1942 the United States built Roberts International Airport

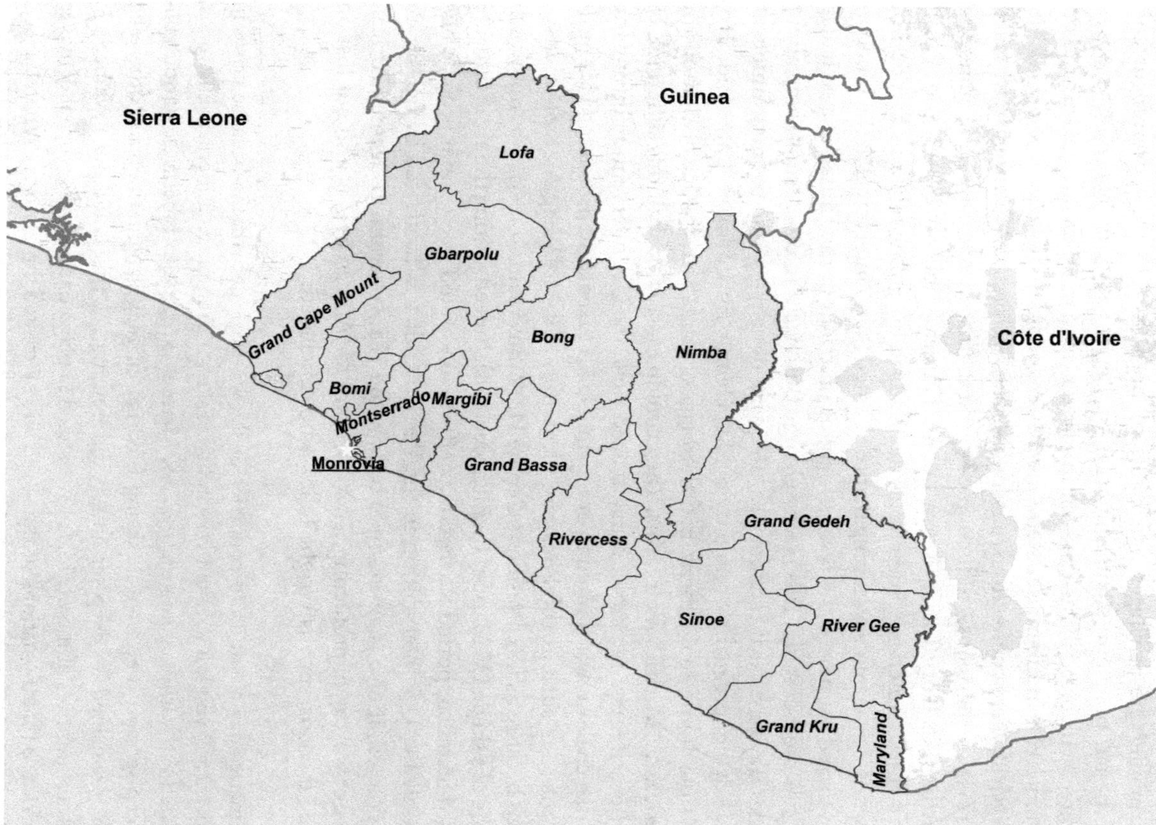

MAP 2.1. Liberia. Map created by Gerold Ludwig.

just outside Monrovia as a base for the U.S. Air Force, where B-47 bombers could refuel. After World War II, the airport more or less remained under American control and was operated by Pan American Airlines until 1985. Firestone, a U.S.-based company, created agreements with the Liberian government from the 1920s on that eventually gave Firestone unprecedented access to rubber production while undermining the privileges and rights of both the Liberian government and the Liberian people in significant ways (J. Levitt 2005). In fact, Firestone was (in)directly involved in the civil war in Liberia (for a more detailed discussion on Firestone's role in Liberia see Reno 1995; Stier 2009).

Given all these connections, it is logical that, as Dorgbah Weemongar, who fled Monrovia in the 1990s, said, people in "West Africa, especially in neighboring countries like Ivory Coast, Sierra Leone, Guinea . . . but in Liberia too . . . call Liberia 'Little America.'" Sometimes this leads to imagining relations that do not even exist, for example assuming that the United States intervened in the Liberian civil war and supported the resettlement of Liberians to the United States. Janjay Waggah's mother said, "This is why George Bush went to do . . . something about Charles Taylor's hardheadedness. . . . He was destroying our country, innocent people dying, pregnant women dying. So, George Bush look at it and said, 'No, this is our home too.' Liberia had the biggest plantation, rubber plantation for America. . . . So, that's their farms. They couldn't just look at all this suffering." In fact, her statement is a rather romanticized view; the U.S. intervention during the Liberian civil war was limited to evacuating U.S. citizens and protecting U.S. business interests such as the Firestone plantation that Ms. Waggah's mother mentioned because as U.S. President George H. W. Bush said, "Liberia was not worth the life of a single US Marine" (S. Ellis 1999, 168). Indeed, during the same time the United States supported Kuwait in its efforts to ward off Iraq's annexation. While certainly the U.S. intervention in the Persian Gulf was motivated by fear about access to oil, it also is an example of how the U.S. government deemed African lives not worthy of protecting. This disregard for African lives is also not lost on some Liberians, such as Wright Talley, who concluded:

> America pay attention to countries of the world . . . not African because crises in Africa are, you know, taken very lightly. Take for example . . . Liberia in the 1990s, when the war was going on, the U.S. Marines . . . came to Liberia . . . stationed in deep sea and they were . . . seeing Liberian citizens slaughtering each other and they remained on deep sea and . . . did nothing. . . . That could not have been in other countries of the world. . . . They need to play a decisive role when it comes to Africa so that the nations of the world will be treated the same. . . . When they . . . throw out dictators, it should be all over . . . not only be in the Middle East . . . Europe . . . Asia . . . but it should also be . . . in Africa.

But there was very limited involvement by the United States in Liberia's civil war.

LIBERIA'S CIVIL WAR

After more than a century of maltreatment and exploitation at the hands of the Americo Liberian elite, Indigenous Liberians' efforts for equal rights and political inclusion, as well as combating widespread poverty, galvanized in the 1970s. Initially, these efforts were organized by the Movement for Justice in Africa, a group based at the University of Liberia, and the Progressive Alliance of Liberia, which was founded by members of the Liberian diaspora (consisting of Americo Liberians and Indigenous Liberians) in the United States (J. Levitt 2005). However, these groups were unable to get the Liberian government, under the leadership of President Tolbert, to commit to reforms that would lead to the inclusion of Indigenous Liberians.

Two events in 1979 ultimately led to the overthrow of the Americo Liberian oligarchy. First, President Tolbert curtailed voting rights by "invoking 150-year-old constitutionally based property ownership rules" (J. Levitt 2005, 195).[10] Second, the Liberian government, under the pretense of addressing rising rural-to-urban migration, raised the price of rice, Liberia's staple food, from twenty-two Liberian dollars to thirty Liberian dollars for a one-hundred-pound bag when the average household income was eighty Liberian dollars per month. In reality, the increase was designed to benefit Tolbert and his network of Americo Liberians who owned the rice farms, and to decrease the government's debt. Indigenous Liberians, and in particular the younger generation, responded to the proposed changes by joining a demonstration initiated by the Progressive Alliance of Liberia. The dispute was met with harsh treatment from Tolbert's government forces, resulting in the death of more than forty protestors (Ciment 2013; J. Levitt 2005). Shortly thereafter, Tolbert sought to regain control by involving the military, reversing the increase in the price of rice, and releasing some of the activists who had been jailed in the aftermath of the protests.

However, Liberia remained politically unstable, a situation which a young master sergeant in the Liberian military, Samuel Doe, a member of the Krahn ethnic group, used to seize control in a coup d'état on April 12, 1980.[11] This was the first time in the country's history that an Indigenous Liberian held power as head of state. Ultimately, the coup "arose from a continuum of interdependent conflict histories woven into the political fabric of Liberia's sociopolitical order" (J. Levitt 2005, 197), where Indigenous Liberians were systematically excluded "from the economic, political, and social arenas" (Advocates for Human Rights 2006, 59). In the aftermath of the takeover, Doe had former President Tolbert and most members of Tolbert's cabinet publicly executed on a beach in Monrovia. But Doe and his supporters' wrath was not limited to Americo Liberian politicians. Ordinary Americo Liberians—regardless of their social standing—were targeted because of the group's past injustices against Indigenous Liberians and because they held most of the political and economic power, prompting, as discussed earlier, hundreds to flee, among them David Joe, who was introduced in the opening vignette.[12]

The majority of Indigenous Liberians were hopeful that Doe would bring prosperity to all citizens. Doe began his administration by creating a government comprising various ethnic groups, including Americo Liberians, but it became a Krahn hegemony before long. From the early days of military rule under Doe to the end of his reign as "elected" president in 1985, Doe and his supporters displayed contempt and enormous hostility toward the opposition.[13] In 1985, Thomas Quiwonkpa, an ethnic Gio from Nimba County and one of Doe's former comrades-in-arms, attempted to oust him but failed and in turn was mutilated and killed by Doe's followers. Doe did not stop there; he and the Armed Forces of Liberia (AFL) retaliated with brutal attacks against the Gio and their allies, the Mano, which included heinous crimes such as drowning babies and women in wells (Advocates for Human Rights 2006). By exploiting "ethnic divisions which had been dormant for well over a century" (J. Levitt 2005, 201), Doe made it difficult for different ethnic groups to build a united front against his increasingly autocratic rule. Doe's reign was so atrocious that Liberians, including Isaac Cheeks, noted that Doe "killed more of his own Indigenous people than the Americo Liberians ever killed" (see also J. Levitt 2005).

As time went on, more and more Liberians suffered and thus became disenchanted with Doe and his totalitarian regime. When Charles Taylor, a Liberian of Americo Liberian and Gola descent who had been educated in the United States, (re)emerged on the scene, many Liberians cheered him on in his pursuit to remove Doe. In this endeavor, Taylor was supported by the National Patriotic Front of Liberia (NPFL), which consisted mostly of Gio and Mano fighters, in his plan to oust Doe starting in December 1989. What Liberians had not expected, however, was that Taylor's potential rise to power, rather than being a hopeful turn of events, would be the beginning of a civil war. As Taylor and his fighters started to make their way from Nimba County and Grand Gedeh County (which border Côte d'Ivoire) toward Monrovia, they brutally attacked Doe's forces and the civilian Krahn population (since Doe was a Krahn) as well as members of the Mandingo ethnic group.[14] The NPFL's tactics included "staging battles in highly populated areas, attacks on unarmed civilians, widespread rape and sexual violence, hostage-taking . . . interruption of food supplies for civilians, looting, and extremely brutal violence" (Advocates for Human Rights 2006, 129). Furthermore, the mostly untrained and "undisciplined" fighters established checkpoints throughout the country as they progressed toward the West. These "checkpoints provided the rebels a means to target, extort, abuse . . . [and] terrorize individuals" and also at times torture and kill them (Advocates for Human Rights 2006, 133). This warranted that any person who tried to move from one point to another had to give up something for safe passage, which included, but was not limited to, money, food, and their bodies (e.g., for sexual favors).

Within several months, the NPFL controlled most of the country. But this was not the end of the fighting as another faction formed in July 1990, the Independent National Patriotic Front of Liberia (INPFL) under the leadership of Prince Johnson, a Gio. This new group, along with the NPFL, staged a battle for Monrovia where they fought the AFL, government forces under Doe's command. After months of brutal fighting, which once again involved the torturing and slaughtering of thousands of civilians—including the infamous St. Peter Lutheran Church massacre by government forces—Johnson and his INPFL troops prevailed, capturing Doe and torturing him to death on September 9, 1990. Despite brokered peace agreements, fighting continued involving the AFL, INPFL, NPFL, and new rebel groups, some of which were also backed by neighboring countries such as Sierra Leone and Guinea. At that point, Taylor controlled most of Liberia—with the exception of Monrovia—and thus also the country's natural resources, including timber, metals, and diamonds, which allowed him to continue the war and his quest to bring the capital city under his control.

On July 19, 1997, war-fatigued Liberians, fearing Taylor's wrath in the event of a loss, elected him president, after a campaign in which he championed the shocking slogan, "He killed my ma, he killed my pa, I will vote for him." Many Liberians and the international community expected peace to return to the country, and thus Liberians came back from their places of exile, including refugee camps in other West African countries. But, to the disappointment of Liberians and the rest of the world, peace did not last. Like his predecessor, Taylor quickly curtailed the freedom of the political opposition and the press, tortured and raped suspected opposition supporters, and conducted extrajudicial executions (Advocates for Human Rights 2006, 183). While Liberians of all ethnicities did not feel safe from Taylor and his various security forces, which included his own paramilitary force, the Liberian National Police, and the AFL (that he now controlled as the Liberian president), Krahns and Mandingos were especially targeted. This forced thousands of Liberians who had just returned to their homes to flee once again. Danny Gayflor, a Liberian UNHCR employee who grew up in Lofa County, reflected on this series of events: "When Charles Taylor won the election, people thought everything was over; many people started returning. And then after some time, the other warring parties were not . . . in favor . . . that Charles Taylor won, they say it wasn't fair . . . so they also went back to the bush to continue fighting. So, those that returned also had to flee again." Trepidation over Taylor's authoritarian regime, along with his involvement in Sierra Leone's armed conflict, eventually led to an insurgency of the conflict, driven by two militia groups: Liberians United for Reconciliation and Democracy (LURD) and Movement for Democracy in Liberia (MODEL). Both armed groups were supported by Guinea and Côte d'Ivoire, respectively, which explains why the war eventually affected these neighboring nations as well (J. Levitt 2005).

After more than fourteen years of countless atrocities, including random executions, sexual assaults, abductions, hacking off of limbs, and sacrifices of pregnant women, fetuses, and babies (Stepakoff 2007) committed by all sides of the conflict, including a high number of child soldiers (some as young as six years) and targeted torture of aforementioned ethnic groups, as well as others, Liberians were exhausted.[15] In July 2003, in a desperate cry for help to finally end the war, Liberian women in Monrovia piled up the mutilated bodies of murdered Liberians in front of the U.S. embassy, as they felt that this was the only way to flood international newspapers with pictures and get the United States' attention and get them to intervene as Liberia's former "colonial power" (Moran 2012; Sengupta 2003). The next month, the United States sent 150 Marines, who supported ECOMIL, the Economic Community of West African States (ECOWAS) mission in Liberia to support their peacekeeping after the Accra Comprehensive Peace Agreement had been signed the same month. Here again, it was Liberian women who were instrumental in getting this peace agreement (Gbowee and Mithers 2011; Moran 2012) that ended with Charles Taylor finding temporary exile in Nigeria before he was tried and convicted of war crimes and crimes against humanity for aiding and abetting rebel fighters in Sierra Leone's civil war.[16]

"Hide in the Bush": Fleeing Violence

As already alluded to, throughout the war, the battle zones between the different factions constantly changed, thus forcing civilians to flee more than once and to "hide in the bush, so they didn't get killed," as Younger Dugbo, who fled with her aunt and several siblings and cousins to Côte d'Ivoire, recalled. The loose organization of armed groups—all trying to gain control of Liberia—made it very difficult to distinguish between ally and foe. Dorgbah Weemongar remembered April 6, 1996, one of the multiple times when extensive fighting took place in Monrovia, where he was at that time: "You couldn't tell who is who because those that were fighting the war, they were not in uniform. So, you see a lot of people . . . carrying . . . assailant weapons and . . . guns . . . et cetera." In fact, some of the fighters, particularly children and teenagers—high on drugs—only wore pants and T-shirts; others were shirtless.

Whereas Mr. Weemongar was fortunate to escape these attacks unharmed, this was not the case for thousands of Liberians. Many of the Liberians who found refuge in Staten Island endured and witnessed immense cruelties similar to those of the harrowing accounts that other Liberians throughout the United States gave to the Liberian Truth and Reconciliation Commission. For example, one Liberian man detailed what AFL soldiers under Doe's command had done to his family: "My father's body was terribly mutilated. My mother's stomach was ripped open. She was eight months pregnant. I was so frightened I couldn't even touch them. My sister had been shot right in the middle of her head. I was in a terrible state. I couldn't even look at them closer because I was just in shock. I mean even to see my father was hard. I could just recognize him by his watch which was still on his hand" (Advocates for Human Rights 2006, 146). Another account shows that all sides of the war were capable of atrocities. Here a Liberian woman describes how Taylor's security forces tortured her family in the fall of 1998 because they accused them of supporting the INPFL:

> Without a search warrant, they went from room to room searching for the alleged hidden arms. In the meantime, the entire household which included my father, step-mother, my siblings and myself were tied with nylon twine on chairs and beaten with gun butts and any object they could lay their hands on. I was severely beaten with a gun butt in my abdomen. I sustained serious abdominal injury that led to me undergoing abdominal surgery in Ghana. The same soldier that beat me in my abdomen also pierced my feet with sharp rusty iron. The scars of this barbaric treatment are on my feet to this date. The blows to my abdomen caused me to faint. My first cousin who was also tied tried to reach me and help me stand. Seeing his effort, one of the armed men who referred to himself as Turtle shot my cousin in his forehead killing him instantly. They never found the arms and ammunition that were allegedly hidden in the house. Yet, they took away my father for interrogation. He was detained for a few days and released. When he returned home I observed that he had lost one of his front teeth as a result of being beaten while in detention (Advocates for Human Rights 2006, 189–190).

Violence, such as described here, propelled Liberians of all ages, genders, and ethnic groups to flee and hide because "during the heat of the war," as Garpu Garbleh, who left Liberia after the April 6, 1996, battle in Monrovia, said, "Anything that moved was targeted, and if . . . anyone catch you, you're dead." At least two-hundred fifty thousand Liberians—then the equivalent of about 10 percent of the population—were not able to escape and were killed during the fourteen-year-long conflict. Others only survived because they continuously moved around in search of refuge. During the entire time of the conflict, more than 50 percent of the Liberian population were forced to flee; one-third sought refuge in Guinea, Sierra Leone, Côte d'Ivoire, Ghana, and Nigeria, and two-thirds were internally displaced (UNHCR 2006).

Liberians' flight routes were very diverse, as the experiences of Varney Konneh and Nowa Namo show. Varney Konneh, a Mandingo, who also claims Gbandi ethnicity since his family lived among them for two generations but perhaps also because he is Christian, grew up in the Kolahun District in Lofa County, which was the site of very heavy fighting in 2000. He described how he had to leave his home in search of safety and refuge:

> I moved to rebel territories. I was there for one and half year and that was one of the most terrible times I ever had in my life because . . . I didn't have any shoes, nothing. I have only one trousers and one shirt for one and half year. . . . I didn't have briefs to wear [*laughs*], no underclothes. . . . I was always moving from place to place. When there's something going on this side we move to another place. . . . In the IDP camp we were receiving some handouts some of the time. Sometimes also you wouldn't get it because the fighting would make the U.N. workers not come around. . . . You have to spend some time in the bushes. . . . Anyone who

> have the opportunity during the war in Liberia to leave will leave. But, I didn't have the opportunity because I was not even close to the seaport.... If I had the opportunity I would have gotten out. It was really difficult.... I think I was even worse than those who left the country [*laughs*] ... because I was under rebel command, you know, mental torture was there. You don't have food, the reason why I only have one trousers and one shirt because the rebels took everything from me.

As Mr. Konneh said, IDP camps were not safe places as they were frequently attacked by various rebel groups (J. Levitt 2005). Hence, those who could tried to find ways to leave Liberia for a neighboring country. But this was "not an easy journey because I had children. There was no transportation at the time, so we had to walk not knowing where we were going.... We walked for days, for weeks," recounted Nowa Namo, a Kpelle from Grand Gedeh County. Initially, she and her family found refuge in Côte d'Ivoire. Ms. Namo and her family stayed there for almost seven years. But "when the war came to the Ivory Coast, everyone scattered and I went to Guinea," she said. Here, Ms. Namo is referring to the fall of 2002 when Côte d'Ivoire descended into civil war after a failed coup attempt. This happened quite often to Liberians who found temporary refuge in one of the neighboring countries, only to be forced to migrate again because war erupted there as well (Agier 2011; Porter et al. 2008). Frequently, this meant that families split up to increase their chances of survival, as in the case of Ms. Namo, as she shared, "When the war started ... in Ivory Coast ... my mom was so afraid, she said, 'But then let me go back to Liberia.' She said, 'When I'm going back, I'm going to carry the little girl with me because I don't want to be just running from place to place,' so she carried her. So, she went with her grandma." Ms. Namo and her mother decided it would be easier for Ms. Namo if she only had two children to look after. Now, more than two decades later, Nowa Namo's youngest daughter is still living with her grandmother in Liberia, whereas her other children are in the United States.

Other Liberians, like Cynthia Sherif, lost one or more family members and/or did not know about their relatives' whereabouts for years. Indeed, this was the case for most Liberian refugees (Stepakoff et al. 2006). Ms. Sherif's father was executed at the beginning of the conflict because he was an Americo Liberian, which prompted his wife and children to flee "into the bushes for a couple of years," as she recalled. When they all fled, Ms. Sherif had been visiting a relative in another town and thus found herself on her own, searching for refuge while not knowing anything about the state of her family, except that her family's house had been bombed. "The last information that I got, they were all in the house. So, three years, I didn't know if my family was alive or dead.... It was really, really hard.... They didn't know how to get in touch with me because they couldn't take anything because they had to run for their lives.... I have a cousin who the rebels took and kept ... for years, and finally she resurfaced." Many Liberians found themselves in refugee settlements and camps in other countries in West Africa, awaiting news about their loved ones. They were forced to remain there and anticipate what their options for the future were, while holding out hope that the war in Liberia would finally end.

"IT WAS TOUGH": LIFE IN REFUGEE CAMPS

Refugee settlements and camps "are framed as a temporary stop on the path to one of the UNHCR's durable solutions" (Trapp 2015, 31). But due to the conditions leading to many refugee situations around the world, including that of Liberians, being protracted, it means that twenty-five thousand refugees from the same nationality are forced to live in exile for five years or longer "with little or no prospect of a durable solution to their predicament" (Zetter 2011, 1). Additionally, all refugee camps start out with much smaller populations only to increase rapidly over time, often resulting in squalid living conditions. For example, the Buduburam refugee camp in Ghana initially hosted five thousand Liberians and at the height of the war as many as forty-five thousand (Agblorti and Grant 2019; Omata 2012b). In the beginning, Liberian refugees came to Ghana by air or vessels and ships that left Monrovia under the coordination of ECOWAS. Over the years they were joined by those who had found refuge in Côte d'Ivoire and/or Guinea but were displaced again (Dick 2002a). No matter in which West African country Liberian refugees stayed during and after the war, they were presented with the three durable solutions that the UNHCR pursues for refugees: (1) (voluntary) repatriation, (2) local integration in the first country of asylum, and (3) resettlement in a third country. Since 1985, (voluntary) repatriation has become the preferred choice for the UNHCR and host and donor countries. In reality, it has been more like involuntary returns since this is what donor nations and the UNHCR have been pushing since the mid-1990s (Chimni 2004). It is not coincidental that this policy shift occurred right as the number of displaced Africans increased compared to that in other regions of the world.

Many Liberian refugees were reluctant to return to Liberia. Nevertheless, organized voluntary repatriation occurred at two different times: After Charles Taylor was elected president in 1997, the international community (and some Liberians) assumed the war was over and Liberian refugees could return; indeed, the UNHCR promoted Liberians returning to their country of birth, and simultaneously the Ghanaian government was pushing to close the refugee camp (Dick 2002a). But as described earlier, the fighting in Liberia began again, and thus many people had to flee once more. Starting in 2004, the UNCHR resumed yet again voluntary repatriation of Liberian refugees (Omata 2012a).[17]

Without a doubt, many Liberian returnees were happy to be reunited with their surviving family members and to be back in their native country. Nevertheless, many Liberian refugees in Ghana were hesitant to return and refused to be repatriated, desperately hoping to be part of another solution (Byrne 2013; Essuman-Johnson 2011; Holzer 2015). They feared having to live among those who caused so much harm while endeavoring to rebuild their lives amid the overall precarious economic situation in Liberia (Dick 2002a; Omata 2012a). In addition, the UNHCR repatriation packages did not include sufficient funding for Liberian refugees to start anew in their native country (Holzer 2015). Asha Onyango, a native Kenyan who worked with the UNHCR in the refugee camp in Buduburam, recalled how Liberian refugees turned to prayers, which intensified once the United States started to drastically reduce the number of applications accepted for resettlement in 2006:

> The churches took advantage of this. They . . . told people, "We're having prayer sessions for you to go to America." . . . Even the U.S. had come with the U.N. to tell people that the situation now in their country has stabilized. . . . They were stopping or were reducing the resettlement from the camp. But they did not believe this. So, they have prayer sessions to open the way for resettlement. . . . They have this perception that they could be resettled to America. Many of them up till now don't . . . want to go back to Liberia. They're still in the refugee settlement, especially in Ghana . . . and some of them are still persisting.

In 2024, there were still several thousand Liberians remaining in Ghana, despite discontinued humanitarian aid and protection,[18] the demolition of the Buduburam refugee camp (Adombila 2024), and joint efforts by the UNHCR and Ghana to close the refugee camp in favor of repatriation to Liberia or local integration. However, this group, like most other Liberians, has rejected these durable solutions. In fact, only very few Liberians became part of Ghana's society because they generally preferred resettlement; the Ghanaian government only haphazardly supported the effort and they overall felt not welcomed by the local Ghanaian population (Agblorti and Grant 2019; Byrne 2013) and also did not have access to the general Ghanaian labor market (Hampshire et al. 2008).[19] In addition, Ghana's stagnant economy and high unemployment rate and most Liberians' inability to speak Twi, the lingua franca in the southern part of Ghana, have presented additional obstacles (Ecke et al. 2016).

Contrary to popular belief that "all refugees want to go home," resettlement in a third country, and the United States in particular, was by far the favored option among Liberian refugees (Essuman-Johnson 2011, 107; see also Holzer 2015; Porter et al. 2008). This preference among Liberians is striking given that relocation to third countries is an option for only about 1 percent of the global refugee population (Dwyer 2010). The hope of emigration was omnipresent in the camps. Those who received remittances on a regular basis from relatives and/or friends in the United States especially saw this move as their ultimate goal (Dick 2002a; Trapp 2015). Liberian refugees were swayed by photos, which frequently accompanied the money. These pictures created unrealistic images of the United States, as Ms. Onyango described:

> Most of these people in the camp had family members who had already been resettled. . . . They were having a better life. . . . I saw some of the photographs that were sent. . . . They showed happy people, well dressed like . . . standing in front of good malls or good shops, which is something they don't have in their country or even in Ghana. . . . So, it's a thought of moving from a developing country to . . . the land of opportunities. So, to most of these people it was a hope of your life changing. Because . . . when you stay in a camp, it's like you're in limbo for a while. . . . It's like you're stuck. So, for them, resettlement gives them an option . . . to get out of this situation.

But Liberian refugees did not just want to be resettled to any country in the Global North; there was a clear affinity for the United States, which is directly linked to the historical ties Liberia has had with the United States (see also Crawley and Fynn Bruey 2022; Trapp 2015). Danny Gayflor, the Liberian UNHCR staff member, explained, "Because the country was established primarily by free slaves from America . . . they consider America to be their motherland. . . . They don't even consider any European country. . . . Many of them consider America to be the only place they can easily live for the fact that they have many friends, many relatives there. You don't have to go to . . . a strange place where you don't know anybody as compared to going somewhere where you have relatives and friends." All the Liberians I spoke with, regardless of whether they are of Indigenous or Americo Liberian ancestry, emphasized this connection between the United States and Liberia. This is important to point out, since the majority of refugees in the camps in West Africa and those who were ultimately selected to go to the United States via the USRAP are of Indigenous ancestry. (As stated before, Americo Liberians also fled, but they mostly came directly and on their own—often on temporary visas, sometimes with green cards, and on rare occasions with U.S. citizenship—to the United States (see chapter 4; Reilly 2016).

Before being selected for settlement in the United States or elsewhere, Liberian refugees endured lots of hardship in the camps. And, although all lived through the trauma of flight and displacement, each person's daily existence in the camps was quite unique. Specifically, the geographic location where Liberian refugees found refuge, (lack of) access to remittances, socioeconomic status, household/family composition, age, and gender, among other factors, impacted how they lived. Even most basic things, such as getting water for drinking, cooking, and washing, were challenging. Sunday John, who was a teenager when she lived in refugee camps in Côte d'Ivoire and Ghana, illustrated this when she said, "A refugee life is not . . . a good one. . . . Being on the camp . . . was hard. . . . As time went by, they kept increasing the prices of . . . water. We go to some place to get water . . . and we put chlorine in the water to kind of filter it to be able to wash or cook. . . . We used to wake up early in the morning because . . . you had to rush . . . and be in line. . . . It was tough." These subsequent examples demonstrate the wide variety of what Liberian refugees experienced during their time in refugee settlements and camps.

In contrast to Ghana, Guinea, and Sierra Leone, where the UNHCR operated refugee camps, there were no official camps in Côte d'Ivoire (see map 2.2). Instead, the Ivorian government had authorized Liberian refugees to live in villages and small towns in a *Zone d'Accueil des Refugies* (Refugee Reception Zone). Garmuyou Dyemene, who had finished high school in Liberia, recalled the three years he spent with his family there: "It wasn't a camp; it was a town. It was a nice town they call Danané in Ivory Coast.... Most of us that lived there were in homes because we were sponsored by our parents from this side.... It was not like a refugee camp." Although not quite like in Côte d'Ivoire, conditions in the Buduburam refugee camp in Ghana improved over time for those Liberians who received remittances. With the support from overseas some Liberian refugees were able to build concrete houses, although on Ghanaian land (see also Agblorti and Grant 2019), leading several, including Osiemeo Boye, to feel that "people living like they already in America.[20] A man there, he have a satellite dish over the house. He's a refugee in the refugee camp; he has a flat screen TV in a room... got telephone, everything. Even the man who live in that country who's a citizen don't have what you have." The significance of remittances was not lost on Liberians, including the younger generation. Wannie Jacobs was only three years old when she fled with her three brothers and mother to Danané and then relocated to the Buduburam refugee camp, where she stayed until she was eleven and was resettled to Staten Island. Although still a child at that time, she remembered how her relatives in the United States sent food, clothes, medicine, other provisions, and money: "They struggled... because... if you don't have a family back here in America sending you money... to feed you... your family... won't know when your next meal is coming.... But for my mom and us... my grandmother was our support system.... My grandmother was sending us food and money and she... make sure... we were safe." As Ms. Jacobs indicated, those who were not recipients of remittances had a much more difficult time; this was especially the case as time went on and the initial assistance from the Ghanaian government and local Ghanaians dried up (Omata 2012b).

Liberian refugees, particularly women, also engaged in a variety of economic entrepreneurial activities inside and outside the camp to supplement their (food) rations (Porter et al. 2008). Those who received monetary support from relatives and/or friends abroad were once again in a privileged situation, as this allowed them to set up small businesses.[21] The less fortunate had to sometimes pursue activities in and around the refugee camps that were not legal. For example, some sold parts of their food rations, and others were involved in robberies, peddled drugs, and/or "rumbled... the red-light streets,"[22] as Asha Onyango said (see also Dick 2002b; Porter et al. 2008).

In a few cases, the combination of remittances, income generated through the different business opportunities, and/or employment with Ghanaians, allowed

MAP 2.2. Major refugee camps and settlements in West Africa. Map created by Gerold Ludwig.

Liberian refugees, in particular those who had (more) formal education, as Danny Gayflor described, to live outside the camp: "There was a limited population of literate ones. . . . They found some ways of leaving the camps to improve their lives, yeah maybe finding jobs in the city center instead of sitting in the refugee camp. Because the more literate you are, the easier it is for you to manage. . . . They moved and rented some houses." Sometimes, the ability to find and afford housing beyond the camp can lead to "informal local integration" in the first country of asylum, such as Ghana (Campbell et al. 2006, 103). However, many of these Liberian refugees, just like those in the refugee camps, still dreamed of a life in the United States.

"PLENTY OF EVERYTHING": IMAGINING AND PREPARING FOR LIFE IN THE UNITED STATES

Life in the refugee settlements and camps was hard. Years, sometimes more than a decade, living in limbo with no outlook to a solution wore on Liberian refugees greatly. Most fantasized about a life in the United States; for those who had been accepted into the USRAP, there was actually a chance of this dream becoming reality. But it took an additional eighteen to twenty-four months until they could leave West Africa as they had to go through different "vetting" stages, which included background checks by multiple U.S. agencies, such as the U.S. Department of Homeland Security's U.S. Citizenship and Immigration Services (USCIS), U.S. State Department, Federal Bureau of Investigation, Central Intelligence Agency, and others, and a medical screening to identify diseases of public health significance (Capps and Fix 2015; Ludwig and Reed 2016).

Universally, Liberians in the refugee settlements and camps had high expectations for their future lives in the United States (see also Covington-Ward 2017). Many of these hopes were shaped by the media and television, where "everything you saw was good. There was nothing bad in America. . . . People in flashy cars . . . high-rise buildings . . . plenty of food and plenty of everything," as Varney Yarkpolo, who initially found refuge during the war in Guinea and then flew to the United States to seek asylum, remarked. In addition, according to Garpu Garbleh, another asylee, relatives and friends living in the United States depicted it in their stories as "a small heaven . . . streets paved with gold." Thus, not surprisingly, Liberians anticipated an "easy life" that would be, in the words of Saah Kandakai, who became separated from his young family during the war, "like bread and butter, all is good, all is honey. . . . There are trees around and maybe you could just see money and pick it." For Liberian refugees, not much could be more difficult than experiencing and witnessing atrocities, surviving war, and enduring the hardships of flight and refugee camps. Being selected for the USRAP meant being "given a green light . . . that was to follow them all the way to the United States . . . where things were gonna work out for them," as Varney Yarkpolo, who worked as a caseworker for a VOLAG, described. Simply put, there was "a belief that . . . once you come to America, you're no longer suffering," as he said.

With these images of an easy and sorrow-free life on their minds, Liberian refugees above the age of fifteen entered the predeparture Cultural Orientation Education Program (Cultural Orientation) sponsored by the U.S. government and delivered by VOLAG and International Organization for Migration (IOM) staff, who sought to prepare them for their new lives in the United States. This orientation heavily emphasized work life in the United States, no doubt because in recent decades refugees have been supported by government funds for only a short period before they have to become economically self-sufficient (see chapters 3 and 4). Part of being economically self-sufficient in the United States is also having a good credit score. This is something that refugees learn when they are still abroad and have to sign promissory notes stipulating that they will start to repay the travel loans they received from the IOM for their transportation costs to the United States. Refugees begin payments within three to six months of their arrival in the United States and are expected to pay them off within three to five years. This is not a small feat, given that travel expenses for large families usually are above $10,000.

In addition to becoming familiar with economic requirements, Liberians learned about time management, housing, paying bills, and other aspects of U.S. culture. For example, the trainers instilled in the refugees "that they've got to stop beating on your children. . . . Men . . . have to stop abusing women. . . . Don't drink alcohol in public spaces," as Memba Wesseh, who was involved in resettlement efforts when he lived with his family in the Danané refugee settlement, recalled. Estella Konde, who had fled with her aunt also to Côte d'Ivoire, was surprised to hear that you "have to call someone . . . before you go . . . to let them know that you are coming. Because you can't just get up and go because everyone is at work here." One cultural aspect that received little to no attention is anti-Black racism and other forms of discrimination; instead the focus was on "America . . . a country of opportunity. And that once you subscribe to the rules and laws, you will be given the chance to excel," as Varney Yarkpolo pointed out. However, this intentional oversight of all forms of discrimination during the Cultural Orientation has impacted Liberians and other refugees, in particular Black refugees. Indeed, as some of the following chapters show, Black refugees have paid a high price for not being prepared for the specter of anti-Black racism in the United States.

While the Cultural Orientation highlighted economic opportunities, staff were keen on making sure that Liberian refugees lowered their expectations about their future in the United States. Sunday John remember what she had been told: "At the orientation . . . they kind of showed . . . the two sides. I mean like what life actually was gonna be like here. . . . Because I always thought that in America . . . the money is just on the floor and you just walk on it like that. So, when we went for the orientation, the guy showed us that sometimes it's tough. . . . And they showed us some places, some people were sleeping in the train, and they also bring the better side of it. And say people living so large, luxury life, and then they'll show another part of it where you see maybe homeless and stuff like that." During the preparation for their lives in the United States, IOM staff emphasized to single parents, of whom there were quite a few given the high mortality rate during the war, that their adjustment would be more difficult than for a household with two parents. Janjay Waggah, who left for Staten Island from Côte d'Ivoire with her six children and five nieces in 1998, remembered that warning that the IOM staff gave during the workshop: "Don't think that you're going to America . . . all your trouble is over. . . . It's the beginning of this struggle. . . . America is not good with one person alone. One parent cannot make it. It's hard . . . because you're gonna meet up with bills. . . . You're gonna pay for the place, you gonna pay before you eat, you gonna pay for everything . . . all alone. . . . So, I want for you to have that to back of your mind." Many Liberians found the information presented at the Cultural Orientation helpful since it conveyed to them that "reality is . . . different from the expectations," as Zubah Kpadeh, another refugee who had spent his childhood in the Danané refugee settlement, said. However, others, especially those with more formal education, including Memba Wesseh, felt that the Cultural Orientation, at least certain aspects of it, was not that important because they already were familiar with American cultural values given Liberia's historical relationship with the United States. "In my country . . . it's almost like here, so people know . . . what is what. . . . So, the only thing that is different is that we speak a different dialect. . . . So this is why we have accent. . . . We had the same school system. . . . Everything is after America. . . . They call Liberia 'America's stepchild.'" But despite Liberians' familiarity with some U.S. cultural values and the best intentions of those who conceived of and facilitated the Cultural Orientation in the refugee camps, the orientation did not prepare Liberian refugees sufficiently. In truth, many refugees had several obstacles to deal with while preparing for resettlement to the United States, such as limited literacy, the severe trauma and stress of living through war and IDP and/or refugee camps, and the short time span in which they had to learn about America's expectations of them. Also, some of the trainers were not that familiar with the United States. Garpu Garbleh, a former resettlement caseworker, explained what he perceived the main problems were: "This is . . . where the refugee program . . . performed very poorly. . . . Orientation was meant to prepare them to live in America. Unfortunately, some of the teachers never been to America. So, I once asked them, 'How will you effectively teach Cultural Orientation of America when you have never been to the U.S.?' You know it's a joke. You must experience it before you can actually teach it. They talk about credit card; you have never used a credit card before, and you're telling refugees about credit card. . . . They had Ghanaians teaching Cultural Orientation [*chuckles*]." What is evident, however, is that the Cultural Orientation tried to dampen Liberian refugees' expectations of "an easy life" in the United States by emphasizing work expectations but not so much any other problems that could make life hard for them, such as anti-Black racism and other forms of discrimination. Still, for so many of those seeking a new life in the United States, it is possible that the notion of what constitutes an "easy life" is relative. In other words, after escaping war and surviving years of dreadful living in a refugee settlement, the prospect of a moderately peaceful life, a roof over one's head, and access to education could very well be considered "easy."

FROM NEW YORK CITY TO LIBERIA AND BACK: A UNIQUE MIGRATION

One could argue that the migration of Liberian refugees to the United States closed the circle that was started with the emigration of Black settlers—under the auspices of the ACS—from American shores to Liberia in the early nineteenth century. Although that would oversimplify what really happened. These Black settlers fled enslavement, anti-Black racism, and systematic disenfranchisement in the United States in the hope of finding liberty on the West African coast. Once arrived in what would eventually become Liberia, they limited claims to liberty, prosperity, and representation to their own kind (Americo Liberians), effectively excluding Liberia's Indigenous population. Over the next century, Americo Liberians built a society that imitated the United States in many ways: the constitution, cultural and religious practices, their dealings with the Indigenous population, and so forth, although with one main difference: Blackness being central to Liberian (national) identity. But a shared racial identity did not translate to equal rights for all in Liberia because society was stratified along descent, ethnicity, and culture. This is why, after more than a century of subjugation, Indigenous Liberians rose up and supported a rebellion, which ended Americo Liberian rule and started years of bloody mayhem that would end the lives of more than 250,000 people and force more than half of Liberia's population from their homes. The first group to be targeted and thus to flee were Americo Liberians; many ended up seeking—what they had assumed to be temporary—refuge in their forefathers' birthplace, the United States. But that was just the beginning. During the civil war, rebels and government troops subjected the entire Liberian population to brutal atrocities that frequently intensified for some ethnic groups. More than a million mostly Indigenous Liberians fled their homes and sought shelter in neighboring countries and Ghana. In these refugee settlements and camps, Liberians waited for the war to stop so they could return or be among the coveted few who were selected for refugee resettlement in the United States. Those hoping for resettlement imagined a life without suffering and with opportunities for themselves and their children. Though, as the next chapter details, their struggles were far from over once they arrived in Staten Island.

3 SEARCHING FOR HOME IN STATEN ISLAND

Beatrice Akoi was born in 1993 in Côte d'Ivoire, where her Liberian parents initially had sought refuge from the war in their native country before migrating to the Buduburam refugee camp in Ghana. Ms. Akoi does not remember much about her time in Côte d'Ivoire but rather recalled her childhood in the Buduburam refugee camp, where she and her family, along with many other Liberians, hoped and dreamed about being resettled in the United States—a place that they imagined as heaven and where, as her aunt, Yassah Flomo, said, "Every other problem [would] be over." Understandingly, when Ms. Akoi found out that she was leaving for the United States, where—based on videos that she had seen—she expected everyone to be "wealthy and stuff, no homeless people," she was the most excited she had "ever been in life." Except this was about to change quickly. In March 2010, Ms. Akoi arrived with her siblings and parents at JFK airport in New York. While waiting to be picked up by her older sister, who was sponsoring the family to come to the United States, and the caseworker from Lutheran Social Services (LSS), a VOLAG, she noticed an old bulldozer. In disbelief, she kept staring at it until her mother noticed and asked her what she was looking at, to which a stunned Ms. Akoi could only respond, "That old stuff right there. Why is it, they have old things in America?"

But this was just the first indication that America was quite different from what she had imagined. The next morning, Beatrice Akoi, still traumatized from the old machinery she had seen at the airport, remembered waking up in the morning and seeing a cockroach. "I'm . . . 'Oh my God we brought a roach in the people's country,'" she said, laughing, only to be corrected by her sister, who told her that roaches are rather common in New York City too.

With the help of resettlement caseworkers, Ms. Akoi and her family aimed to get adjusted to living in the Park Hill Apartments in Staten Island's North Shore, where ceilings frequently crumble and a variety of insects and rodents can be seen. After two months in the United States, the family decided to move to Philadelphia, where they had more family. However, Ms. Akoi did not like it there and returned to Park Hill, where she lives with Yassah Flomo, who had originally been resettled in North Carolina. Both women were drawn to Park Hill because they perceived North Carolina and Philadelphia as "too boring" and places where getting around for work and school depends on having a car, which they could not afford. In contrast, living in Park Hill gave them access to New York City's public transportation system and placed them in very, very close proximity to other Liberians. While they enjoyed these things, at the same time, Ms. Flomo and Ms. Akoi complained about the drugs, smoking, and violence they observed in Park Hill. In addition, Beatrice Akoi noted that living among native-born Black Americans was not always easy because she felt that they were bullying Liberian refugees at times. Yet, Ms. Akoi also acknowledged that being a refugee gave her access to some programs, most of which she learned about from the staff at VOLAGs. For example, they helped her and other refugees with furniture for their apartments and enrolled them in government benefits and youth programs run by VOLAGs.

This vignette shows that the vast majority of Liberian refugees had high hopes for their future in the United States. Although happy to have left the war and refugee settlements and camps in West Africa behind, their efforts to find and create a new home in the United States, and especially in Staten Island's Park Hill neighborhood, have been challenging. Initially, Liberian refugees received assistance from VOLAGs and the U.S. government. While some of this support was to facilitate their cultural and emotional adjustment to the United States, the bulk of this aid was geared toward becoming economically self-sufficient. Taking into consideration that most Liberian refugees had experienced trauma and many lacked literacy skills and formal education and had to adjust to a new sociocultural environment shaped by anti-Black racism, this was not an easy task to accomplish. The need to become economically self-sufficient within such a short time often propels refugees into a perpetual state of stress (Sowa 2009).

But these were not the only obstacles Liberians encountered in Staten Island as they strove to adjust and create a home for themselves and their families. Like many other refugees (Besteman 2016; Tang 2015; Sackett and Lareau 2023), Liberians were resettled in neighborhoods that have cheap housing but limited infrastructure and have been plagued by crime, drugs, and violence since the 1980s. This holds true for Park Hill in Staten Island but also other cities where Liberian refugees were resettled, such as Philadelphia and Brooklyn Park, Minnesota (Haddow 2015; Reilly 2014). This lack of safety has made it difficult for Liberians to embrace places like Park Hill as their "home away from home." Though over time Park Hill has become safer, and today the neighborhood is no longer known as "Killa Hill" but as "Little Liberia," negative perceptions have remained. The conflation of Black neighborhoods and crime is, as scholars have concluded, much more about the persistent stereotypes about Black people that are only intensified by continued residential segregation and institutional disinvestment (J. R. Logan 2013; Wilson 2012).

It is in this environment where Liberians practice their culture, speak their native languages, and buy and eat "African food" but also seek respite from widespread anti-Black racism, which is prominent in the very racially segregated borough of Staten Island.

"JUST LIKE HEAVEN": RESETTLING LIBERIAN REFUGEES

The U.S. government and VOLAGs are heavily involved in resettling refugees. This goes from literally selecting the state, city, and apartment/house where refugees will live to furnishing the homes—following government guidelines—to matching them with job opportunities. All of this is driven by ensuring that refugees become economically self-sufficient within a short time after arrival. VOLAGs do this for around seventy thousand refugees every year.[1] Here, I discuss how this played out for the Liberian refugee community in Staten Island, which is part of the close to thirty-five thousand Liberians who were resettled between the 1990s and 2024.

The majority of these Liberian refugees, who arrived between 1990 and 2008, were resettled in New York State,[2] followed by Minnesota and Pennsylvania (Worldwide Refugee Admissions Processing System [WRAPS] data; Mott 2009). Within New York State, Staten Island was the main resettlement area. These resettled Liberian refugees have been joined over the years, just like in other states, by other Liberian refugees and immigrants. However, Staten Island, due to its density, has the highest per capita concentration of Liberians outside of Liberia (Reilly 2014). Liberian refugees who were resettled in Staten Island were all Priority 3 (P3) cases,[3] implying that a family member had sponsored them.[4] This meant that VOLAGs worked with Liberian families, such as Beatrice Akoi's sister, to help them prepare for the arrival of their refugee relatives. The selection of the Park Hill neighborhood in Staten Island was not arbitrary. VOLAGs selected this neighborhood due to the availability of larger-size apartments and, as I explain later in more detail, because they believed there would be racial and cultural affinity among the incoming Black refugees and long-term native-born Black American residents.

Once Liberian refugees, including Ms. Akoi and her family, boarded planes in West Africa, their VOLAG and family members were notified so they could meet them at the airport. Often Liberian refugees arrived very excited to be reunited with relatives whom they had not seen in years, at times even decades, and with diverging views of what the future would hold for them. Some Liberians, like Wannie Jacobs, who came to Staten Island as a teenager, expected—based on what she had heard from adults—America "to be just like heaven . . . where you could do anything . . . eat whatever you want to eat, be whoever you wanna be. . . . Nobody . . . was struggling to make ends meet" (see also Covington-Ward 2017b; Sackett and Lareau 2023). Other Liberians were a bit more careful in their assessment of the future and abandoned images "about manna falling from heaven," as Danny Gayflor, the Liberian UNHCR staff member who worked with Liberian refugees in West Africa, said, and braced themselves that they would have to work hard when they got to the United States and that "things were not gonna be very easy."

Regardless of their expectations, the lives of Liberian refugees, especially during their early months in the United States, were controlled and monitored by the bureaucratic system of refugee resettlement (Nawyn 2010; Ong 2003; Sackett and Lareau 2023). This started with a visit to one of the VOLAGs' offices. Since the majority of cases in Staten Island were handled by LSS, that implied that refugees either met their caseworker at the main office in Manhattan or at the branch that LSS operated two days a week from 1998 to 2007 on the second floor of a church in Staten Island's North Shore. Both the church and the Liberian caseworkers have continued to be an integral part of the Liberian community, most certainly because the caseworkers themselves are Liberian and the church's congregation is predominantly West African.

In the first as well as subsequent meetings with their caseworkers, Liberians, like other refugees, received assistance in adjusting to life in the United States. Some of this support was provided through programs such as employment services and English language or literacy instruction by VOLAGs. Many refugees also attended a domestic Cultural Orientation aimed at reinforcing what they had been told about life in the United States in their overseas Cultural Orientation and "to ensure expectations of refugees . . . [were] not too high" (Dwyer 2010, 24). In fact, most refugees, like Nowa Namo, who arrived in the United States in the summer of 2003, did adjust their expectations of what their lives would be like in the United States. She remembered what she had been told by a caseworker and her subsequent reaction: "He said . . . you work hard. . . . He said, 'But . . . you'll start from down and . . . you be climbing up little by little.' . . . I said, 'OK, what is the place that you have to start before you climb up?' [*laughs*]. . . . He said, 'They got a minimum wage job. . . . Sometime you go clean people house, clean the street . . . mop people's floor, dust people's windows.'"

In addition to programs that sought to facilitate refugees' adjustment, Liberians, like other refugees, received monetary assistance. For some this meant three months of Refugee Cash Assistance (RCA), and if they met the eligibility requirements, Medicaid, Medicare, Supplemental Nutrition Assistance Program (SNAP, colloquially referred to as food stamps), Supplemental Security Income, and other government aid. All these benefits are given with the explicit goal to get refugees "job ready," as Varney Yarkpolo, a former caseworker, explained: "For the first three months, you're . . . well taken care of. We process your documents. We put you on welfare. . . . And the program pays your rent, food, and other items for three months. And we believe that within these three months you should be job ready. . . . The job developer has to make sure that they work . . . within three months. . . . So, you have to get them prepared so that they can be independent."

To conclude, the caseworkers at the VOLAGs were busy dampening the Liberian refugees' expectations while at the same time assisting them to find work—not an easy task given most refugees' low human capital and traumatic experiences.

"They Expect You to Pay the Bills": Economic Self-Sufficiency

Many Liberian refugees in Staten Island did not receive RCA but rather were enrolled in the Matching Grant Program, which is explicitly for low-skill menial jobs that often are in ethnic niches and which "support existing gender and racial/ethnic hierarchies in the labor market" (Nawyn 2010, 150). Refugees participating in this program receive a combination of cash assistance and employment services for three to six months, again with the goal that they will be economically self-sufficient within that time period. Funding for this employment and training program comes from the ORR, an office within the U.S. Department of Health and Human Services, and local communities and employers who contribute cash (at least 20 percent) and in-kind goods and services. But since a large number of the Liberian refugees were illiterate and did not have many transferable skills or work experience, it was difficult to secure job training and employment opportunities for them. Fortunately, as Varney Yarkpolo pointed out, LSS found companies that were willing to give refugees a chance. Subsequently, the vast majority of Liberian refugees in Staten Island who participated in the Matching Grant Program were enrolled in job training programs for a limited number of jobs. Many of these job placements were at fast-food restaurants, while a few were with security companies. However, most Liberians, in particular women, were placed with different home health aide agencies in Staten Island, which is similar to other Liberian communities across the United States (Corrie and Radosevic 2013), reflecting both a general trend of African immigrants' high rate of employment in the health care field (Covington-Ward 2017a; Showers 2023) but also a perpetuation of gendered stereotypes of (Black) women as "natural caregivers."

Liberian refugees acquired jobs not only through the employment services provided by VOLAGs but also through referrals from family members and friends. For example, Nowa Namo, an illiterate woman, secured a job as a home health aide via a connection that her son, who had sponsored her to the United States, had with a Ghanaian immigrant. Relatives and friends were not the only sources of contacts for potential jobs. Some Liberians benefited from the fact that Enid Browning, a fellow Liberian woman who has been living in Staten Island since 1979, worked at one of the home care agencies in the same borough. She recalled how it all started: "They got the information by word of mouth. It is the oldest way to tell a story, to give news. . . . It only took probably one Liberian to know that a Liberian was working in that office to have it go around to every other Liberian coming in needing a job. . . . And because they knew I was there . . . they came, and I helped them." Ms. Browning assisted Liberian refugees in finding placement in homes across Staten Island, but more importantly, she helped with the necessary paperwork. The agency where Ms. Browning worked, like most others, required home health aides to have a high school diploma, which many of the Liberian refugees did not have. And so, Ms. Browning circumvented the official hiring process by completing the forms herself and thus, made sure that despite not meeting the minimum educational standards, Liberian refugees were hired by the agency's supervisor because she reasoned, "They knew how to clean. . . . They were nurturing caregivers . . . and for that, you don't need a diploma."

The government's mandate to become quickly economically self-sufficient (Haines 2010) did not allow Liberian refugees to enroll in school but rather forced them to take on menial jobs, ignoring their and other refugees' pleas for better positions for which they may have qualifications (Covington-Ward 2017b; Nawyn 2010). Varney Yarkpolo described this requirement: "Most people . . . wanna go to school. . . . But we find it difficult to just say, 'Go to school' because whoever brought you to this country have responsibility, and they expect you to pay the bills." For Liberians who wanted to further their education or had held professional jobs in Liberia, like Dorgbah Weemongar, a Bassa man who had lived in Monrovia before the war forced him to leave, accepting these jobs was very degrading, as he shared with me: "Let me be frank. . . . I was frustrated [*laughs*]. I felt what I was doing . . . was just downgrading my status. . . . Before I came here, I used to work at the Ministry of Health in Liberia, health statistics. . . . I came here, and I went to do home health aide training to go work at old folks' home. I was extremely discouraged. . . . I told my sister, 'You know what . . . just buy me a ticket; I am going back.'" It is worth noting that being pushed to accept jobs that are below one's educational level and/or forgo educational opportunities can "contribute negatively to refugee mental health, as well as keep refugees in poverty" in the long run (Hess et al. 2019, 769). But the USRAP focuses more on short-term goals and thus regards having a paying job and not being dependent on welfare as one of the first steps, and perhaps the most important one, to becoming a "productive" part of American society (Nawyn 2011). Employment data—because they are readily available, tangible, quantifiable, and appear "objective" (Colic-Peisker 2009, 178)—are often used to measure refugees' integration (Haines 2010; Tang 2015). In practical terms this leads to VOLAGs focusing most of their services on employment at the expense of other important areas, such as educating refugees about American culture, discrimination, racism, and so forth. However, it is not just the federal government and VOLAGs who use gainful employment as an indicator of successful integration. Liberian refugees—in Staten Island and in other cities in the United States (Covington-Ward 2017a; Reilly 2014)—like other refugee groups (Warriner 2007; Hess et al. 2019), view this as an indicator of success. Concretely, Liberians regard their entrance into the workforce as a step in becoming, at least partially, members of American society. Being "productive" members of society allowed refugees to reclaim some agency and responsibility for their lives, which they frequently were forced to surrender during the war, in IDP/refugee camps, and during the resettlement process.

Having a job mattered not only for the individual Liberian refugee and VOLAG caseworkers who could record having met the major goal of the USRAP mandate, but also for Liberians' relatives and friends on the other side of the Atlantic. Those left behind, either in Liberia or in refugee camps in West Africa, depend on remittances that Liberians in the United States provide (Dick 2002a; Omata 2012a). This obligation to help family members abroad prompted many Liberian refugees not only to put their personal needs and feelings second to those they have been supporting overseas but also not to dwell on the anti-Black racism that they have encountered in their jobs (see chapter 5). For example, Saah Kandakai, who despite having an undergraduate degree in engineering from the University of Liberia, could, for a long time, only find employment as a caregiver in a group home for individuals with mental and physical disabilities. Rather than complain, he simply concluded that "while you are here and you [are] . . . like great help down there. . . . So, you make sure . . . you have any job with disposable income," allowing him to take care of his extended family in Liberia. Similarly, Cynthia Sherif, who is employed in the same field as Mr. Kandakai, continues to support many of her family members in Liberia. She said that she receives calls not only from close family members asking for money but also distant relatives and even long-lost acquaintances with whom she grew up. Declining the request is not a simple task, as Ms. Sherif stressed: "It's hard to tell them 'I don't have it' because they have no other means of getting money. . . . When you hear that somebody didn't eat in days and they have little children . . . ten dollars goes far there . . . and they are so grateful that you did something."

But this devotion toward relatives in Africa has made it even more difficult for Liberian families to create a thriving home in the United States; their small salaries cannot maintain multiple households unless great sacrifices are made. While older Liberians who were born and raised in Africa are more willing to do so, 1.5- and second-generation Liberians, like Samuel Black, have sometimes resented their parents who forced them to forgo things:

> My mother has people in Africa. She have family members over there while all of her family that she gave birth to is over here. . . . She cares about back home. But we, we don't have nobody back there. So, we don't really care that much. My mom lives with my sister like ten years now. She's been trying to build up some type of foundation back home. . . . So, my mom didn't get her own place to raise us by herself. . . . I used to go to school wearing my older brother's pants. It was like living a bad life then. As a kid, you are not enjoying it. . . . I wish my mom could have saved some money in the United States to build up her life over here, make us strong. . . . Make herself a better person and then try and do something back at home. But not try to do, like she is trying to do a lot for people back at home at the same time basically we was suffering over here.

Overall, Liberian refugees try really hard to find and keep jobs; many have succeeded, but it comes at a price and is far from what they dreamed their life would be when they were refugees in West Africa. Many Liberian refugees are stuck in menial, dead-end jobs that leave little time to focus on getting acculturated to life in the United States. Similarly, Liberian refugees were busy supporting other Liberians, including those who did not have refugee status. On one hand, because Liberian refugees had jobs and housing, they could provide affidavits of support to the Diversity Immigrant Visa (DV) Program "winners" in Liberia.[5] One of these beneficiaries was Varney Konneh, a former IDP who obtained a permanent residence permit through this program. He explained the vital role that Liberian refugees played for DV winners like him: "Most of those who won the DV... have to get a sponsor... because you have to have a place to come.... They have friends or relatives on refugee status... who send affidavit of support." Liberian refugees' assistance to these immigrants did not stop with the affidavits of support; they also shared the knowledge and network they had acquired through being part of the USRAP. In this way, they were like Bashi's (2007) "hubs"—veteran migrants—serving as migration experts for the "spokes" (the newcomers). This did not mean that refugees no longer needed support; in fact, they frequently, even more than a decade after living in the United States, have turned to their former caseworkers with their questions and concerns.

"He's Like a Godfather to Us": Interactions with Caseworkers

Besides finding employment for refugees, VOLAG caseworkers also assisted Liberian refugees in Staten Island with enrolling their children in school, setting up medical appointments, filing for adjustment of status and U.S. citizenship applications,[6] and providing access to other resources, and as such, strove to make them feel welcomed in their new home. Officially, these services were only available to those with legal refugee or asylee status. However, Varney Yarkpolo, the former caseworker, reassured me that he and his colleagues also assisted Liberians without these statuses, even though they did not receive reimbursement from the government for the provided services.

Still, accessing these services and caseworkers' help was not the same for all Liberians. Lack of information about the programs, illiteracy, and the cost of transportation kept some Liberians from obtaining them. This was especially true for the elderly. For example, Kormassa Kollie, who during the course of this study learned how to read and write and, consequently, was able to pass the U.S. citizenship requirements, never goes outside of Park Hill without her son. This dependency leaves her and others in a precarious situation since all service providers are located outside of Park Hill. Fortunately for Ms. Kollie and others like her, many of the caseworkers conducted home visits where they provided assistance with applications for government benefits or other things of that nature. This personal connection and attention and their shared Liberian heritage explain why most Liberians in Staten Island, including Osiemeo Boye, continue to speak highly of their caseworkers: "He helped more than one thousand people to come here... because when he came, he started working with the resettlement agency and then he helped. He's, beside God, he's like everybody's godfather here. . . . God forbid, when they say [name of the caseworker] is sick, everybody would want to know what they can do for him because . . . he opened his heart to everybody." This close relationship that many of the Liberian refugees developed with their former caseworkers can readily be observed in Park Hill. The former caseworkers attend many of the community events and are always acknowledged publicly. Even today, some Liberian refugees continue to seek out their former caseworkers—although they now have different jobs—with a wide variety of concerns, such as finding a job, filing an application to become a U.S. citizen, and settling marriage disputes.

In addition to the practical services the VOLAGs provide for refugees, including Liberians, they are also charged with assisting refugees with adjustment to cultural and social patterns of the new society and surroundings through the domestic Cultural Orientation. This training is mandated by the federal government for all refugees and seeks to improve upon what refugees had already learned in the overseas Cultural Orientation prior to their resettlement. Given the historic, political, and cultural connections between the United States and Liberia, VOLAGs assumed that there would not be much need for such training but rather that Liberian refugees' acculturation would be (much) easier compared with other refugee groups. This is also something that I recall from the meetings that I attended as a refugee service provider in Atlanta in the early 2000s. There, the state refugee coordinator and their staff presented similar arguments as Varney Yarkpolo, the former caseworker in New York, who recalled about the VOLAG leadership, "They felt that when Liberians come here, everything will be smooth sailing. They weren't expecting to have any problems. . . . In Liberia, we . . . speak English . . . so integrating into the society, it was something that they felt it would have been very easy. . . . They met a lot of barrier and resistance in terms of their cultural background." The reality is, the process of acculturation has been difficult for Liberian refugees in Staten Island but also in other cities (Covington-Ward 2017a; Reilly 2014; Weine et al. 2011). While English is the official language in Liberia, most Liberians speak Liberian English among themselves, which for outsiders can be difficult to understand. And even when Liberians speak standardized English,[7] Americans often do not comprehend them because of their Liberian accents, which I saw quite often when my college students tutored Liberian refugees in literacy and U.S. citizenship exam prep classes over the years. This of course has been devastating to Liberians who assumed that they would return to a familiar environment since they regard "the U.S. as our mother country," only to find out that "Americans know nothing about Liberia," as David Joe, who came to the United States in 1989, put it.

While Americans' lack of knowledge about Liberia is disappointing, so was the realization that the borough of Staten Island does not at all resemble the common images of New York City as the epicenter of skyscrapers and celebrations of multiculturalism and immigrant heritage; it was quite the opposite.

"RACISM IS HIGH IN STATEN ISLAND": NEW YORK'S CONSERVATIVE BOROUGH

To many New Yorkers, Staten Island is known as the "forgotten borough," and it represents an anomaly in the city (C. Brown 1994; Viteritti 1992); it is not linked to any other borough by the subway system, and the only forms of public transportation connecting it to the rest of New York City are buses from Brooklyn, the Staten Island Ferry at the tip of lower Manhattan, and since 2021 the St. George Ferry from Midtown via Battery Park.

Staten Island differs from the other boroughs in its demographic makeup. Not only does it have a much smaller population (498,212 in 2024 compared to 8,478,072 for the entire city), but until recently, Staten Island was overwhelmingly non-Hispanic White. In fact, non-Hispanic White people are still the numerical majority, which is not the case for the other boroughs. In 1980, a remarkable 85 percent of Staten Island's residents were non-Hispanic White, and only 7 percent were non-Hispanic Black. In 2024, according to the American Community Survey, these numbers were 55 percent and 12 percent, respectively. This stands in stark contrast to New York City as a whole, where 31 percent were non-Hispanic White and 23 percent non-Hispanic Black. Some of this increase in racial and ethnic diversity stems from the rapid growth of the immigrant population. So, one may say, parts of Staten Island have the flavor and characteristics of "new immigrant destinations" (Massey 2010). In 1980, when 24 percent of New York City residents were foreign-born, the figure was only 10 percent in Staten Island. Most immigrants in Staten Island then were Italians who had come decades earlier compared to newly arrived Asians, Latin Americans, and Caribbeans who had begun to dominate the immigrant population in the city as a whole.

By 2024, 25 percent of Staten Island residents were foreign-born. The immigrant presence is especially pronounced in the North Shore, the northern part of Staten Island. This section of Staten Island has a much larger non-Hispanic Black population than elsewhere in the borough; a fifth of the population of the North Shore Community District 1 was non-Hispanic Black in 2024. It is in this part of Staten Island that Liberians have become a new part of the ethnoracial mix.

Staten Island has also acquired a reputation—sustained by many newspaper articles (J. Berger and Urbina 2003; Sjursen 2017), blogs (Cohen 2009), books (Taibbi 2017), and observations and conversations I had with native Staten Islanders of all racial backgrounds—as a borough where anti-Black racism has been rampant.[8] Perhaps this is best exemplified by Eric Garner's murder and the subsequent handling of the case. In July 2014, Eric Garner, a native-born Black American man, was killed by an illegal chokehold by Daniel Pantaleo, a White native Staten Island police officer with previous misconduct charges, in Tompkinsville, a neighborhood in Staten Island's North Shore. Despite national criticisms of how then–Richmond County district attorney Dan Donovan handled the case, he was elected as U.S. representative for New York's Eleventh Congressional District in

2015 and reelected in 2016, but in 2018 he lost to Max Rose, a Democrat.[9] Two years later, Rose lost to Republican Nicole Malliotakis in the two subsequent elections. In her first campaign in 2020, Malliotakis chastised Rose for his participation in a Black Lives Matter protest.

Hence, not unexpectedly, many Liberians, including Garsuah Janjay, an older Liberian Bassa man, feel that "racism is high on Staten Island . . . and is very visible." They, but also some local politicians such as Michael McMahon, often contrasted it with the other New York boroughs, where they said racism was less of an issue (see also Reilly 2014).[10] Liberians frequently cite residential segregation, demarcated by the Staten Island Expressway, also referred to as "Staten Island's Mason-Dixon Line" (J. Berger and Urbina 2003), which separates the more racially diverse North Shore from Mid-Island and South Shore, which are both mostly non-Hispanic White. While there is certainly residential racial segregation in other New York boroughs, for the most part people intermingle there because many use public transportation, which is much more limited in Staten Island. Thus, it is not uncommon for Liberians to have never been to Staten Island's South Shore. For many Liberians, the Staten Island Expressway represents a boundary that can, or better, should not be traversed. This was echoed by Sam Collins, who grew up in Park Hill and subsequently has lived in New Jersey and Georgia. He compared the segregation he experienced while growing up in Staten Island to other places in the United States: "Nobody is inviting you over dinner. . . . When school is over, we went one way; they went the other way. And so, it was a clear sense of segregation. . . . Atlanta, in contrast . . . yes, it's segregated in some part but your subdivision have people of different racial groups."

Like so often in the United States, due to systemic anti-Black racism, a "Mason-Dixon Line" not only separates different racial groups, but by default this also means socioeconomic groups. This is not different in Staten Island. According to the American Community Survey, the median household income in 2021 was $109,500 for the South Shore, $77,170 in the North Shore, and significantly lower for the Park Hill neighborhood ($39,222). These differences were also reflected in the poverty rates, which were in 2021, 6 percent for the South Shore, 16 percent for the North Shore, and 54 percent for Park Hill (see map 3.1).

These racial and socioeconomic differences are also mirrored in the (local) politics. Whereas the North Shore has consistently voted for Democratic candidates on the local, state, and national levels, Mid-Island and the South Shore have almost always supported Republican candidates. Given that the North Shore has fewer residents/voters than the other two areas, it is not unexpected that the island as a whole has reliably been Republican.[11] This tendency to vote for Republican politicians, who are much more likely than Democrats to favor strict immigration and refugee policies and are overall less supportive of rights for ethnoracial minorities and welfare benefits (H. E. Brown 2013), has certainly impacted the local reception and consequently Liberians' ability to become part of Staten Island. This is important to note since this local context is very different from

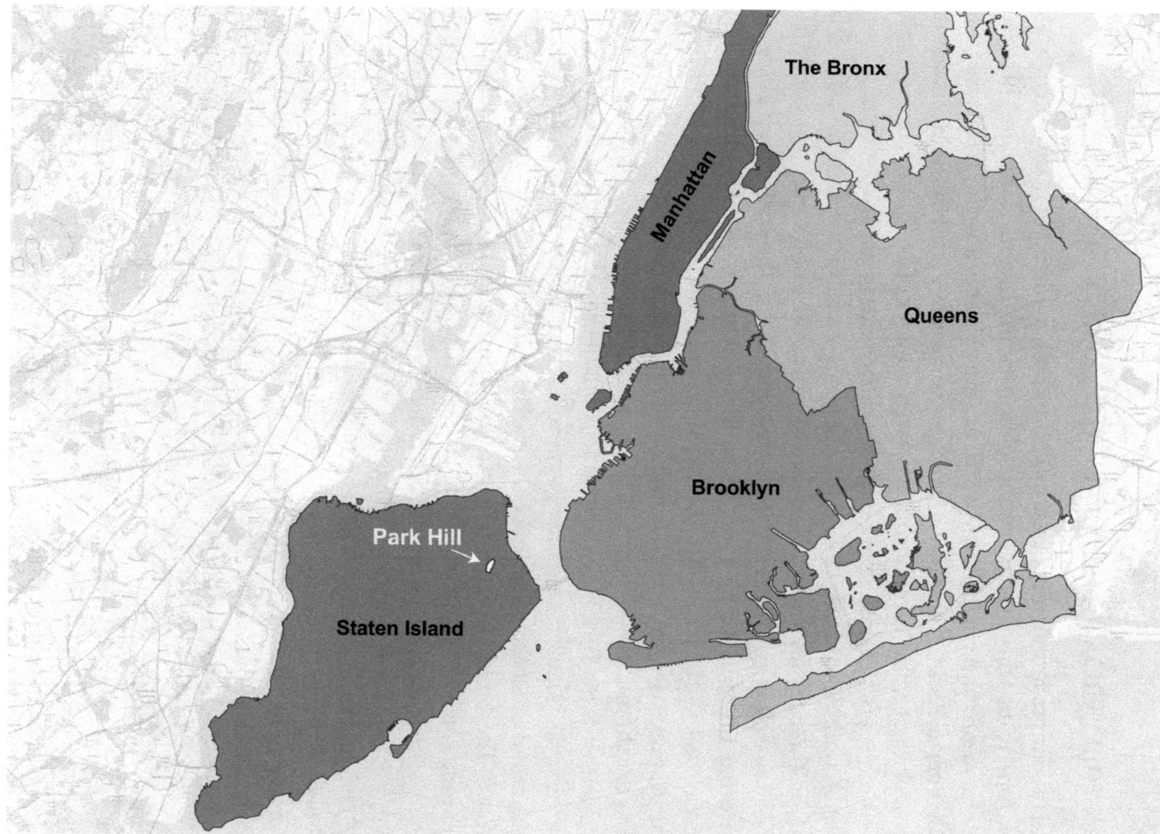

MAP 3.1. New York City with Park Hill neighborhood. Map created by Gerold Ludwig.

larger New York City, which is often seen as a bastion of the Democratic party, and as such, anti-immigrant feelings factor in less in the lives of immigrants who tend to live in other boroughs and therefore is not discussed in the literature. Hostility toward Liberians is not limited to those in the larger Staten Island community but also occurs in Park Hill.

PARK HILL: FROM "KILLA HILL" TO "LITTLE LIBERIA"

Park Hill is a predominantly Black neighborhood, made up of many native-born Black Americans who were joined by West Africans (mainly Liberians, but also Sierra Leoneans and Ghanaians), as well as some Caribbeans and Hispanics (primarily Puerto Ricans). Because a large percentage of Park Hill residents are of Liberian heritage, this neighborhood is often thought of as "Little Liberia." Little Liberia is not a typical immigrant enclave, which tends to have a lot of ethnic businesses. A walk down Park Hill's main shopping area, Targee Street, makes this obvious: There are fewer than a handful of African-themed stores that offer African food as well as sold West African DVDs and CDs in the earlier days. There are a few other stores in the neighborhood; these include sad-looking bodegas that advertise that they accept WIC (Women, Infants, and Children program) and SNAP, laundromats, phone stores, and beauty parlors. While Targee Street can be seen as the shopping area, Park Hill Avenue is the heart of the community. More specifically, it is the Park Hill Apartments, built in the 1960s, and 55 Bowen Street from the 1970s. All of these buildings are collectively referred to by both Park Hill residents and other Staten Islanders as "Park Hill," "the Park Hill projects," or "the projects." The buildings of the apartment complex physically resemble those owned and run by the New York City Housing Authority, but in fact they are not; they are a mix of privately owned and federally subsidized low-income housing (see figure 3.1). The six-story buildings in the fifteen-acre complex making up the Park Hill Apartments were originally built for middle-class residents and over time became home to low-income individuals.

Among these initial residents were also some Liberians, including Enid Browning, who came to the United States as a young bride in the late 1970s. Ms. Browning remembered how the neighborhood was transformed:

> The change was . . . drastic. . . . In 1979 it was safe; I could leave my keys in the door overnight, and my keys were still there in the morning. I didn't get burglarized or killed or anything. . . . Mid or late '80s, things began to change, when . . . drug dealers . . . [and] welfare recipients moved in and . . . didn't seem to care about their environment or the atmosphere at all. And many of them didn't want to work. . . . They accepted a particular system and then did other things on the side. So, there was lot of burglary and other things happening, people . . . on the street corners selling . . . [and] taking drugs. So, the whole atmosphere of Park Hill . . . changed drastically. It would make you wanna leave and move out of there.

FIGURE 3.1. Center of Park Hill neighborhood, Staten Island, New York. Photo by Gee Bee Productions.

The crime that Ms. Browning referenced was also the reason why Park Hill acquired its reputation as "Killa Hill" and "Crack Hill." The deterioration of the apartments and the neighborhood was detailed by Gerald Barclay,[12] a Liberian filmmaker who grew up in Park Hill, in the 2009 documentary "Killa Hill: The Park Hill Documentary" and a 2025 docu-series "Killa Hill." The productions' title reflect the neighborhood's moniker made famous through the music by the Wu-Tang Clan, a group of rappers, some of whom had grown up in Park Hill. They immortalized the neighborhood and the prevalence of crime and drugs in their songs, including "Gravel Pit" on *The W* album, when they rapped, "From Park Hill, the house on haunted hill / Every time you walk by your back get a chill."

Hence, predictably, the issue of crime, including drugs, guns, and violence, is the most frequent complaint cited by Liberians when asked what they dislike about living in Park Hill. For example, survey data showed that more than one-third of youth in Staten Island's North Shore felt unsafe, in particular because of gang violence (68 percent) and the presence of guns in the community (51 percent). The arrest of several members of a drug ring that operated in Park Hill and other areas of the North Shore confirms that the youth's fear is in response to very real happenings in the neighborhood (U.S. Attorney's Office, Eastern District of New York 2011; Tracy 2022). Gun violence also remains of great concern to adult Liberians and native-born Black Americans living in the neighborhood. Nearly all Liberian refugees I spoke with either mentioned having seen or heard a shooting in Staten Island's North Shore. In addition, like Ms. Browning, they have frequently witnessed drugs being peddled either on the street or in the hallways of the apartment buildings, causing some to be caught in the crossfire of rival gangs. Juah Nimley, who came to Park Hill as a teenager just before the outbreak of the war in Liberia, remembered how many times she had barely escaped becoming a target of stray bullets. Here she recalled an encounter from the 1990s:

> There was a party. . . . We didn't tell Mom early enough. . . . We weren't allowed to go. So, we had to make a plan to leave the house while she was asleep. . . . When my mom was snoring, we got our clothes . . . got dressed, took our shoes . . . [and were] coming down the stairs. When we got in the lobby of the building, the gunman is standing at the end of the building shooting at this other guy running toward us. The gunman is standing on the other side by the elevator and shooting direct at this guy. . . . It was like we're trying to put our shoes on and didn't even realize what was going on. When I lifted my head up, what I heard was pa, pa, pa; this guy is running and the shoes, the pocketbook wherever it went, we were back in the house.

For Liberian refugees, gang violence and shootings were the last things they expected to encounter once they left the refugee camps in West Africa. But the reality is that for many, it felt as though they had just escaped one war to find themselves in another war zone yet again. Listen to Desai Kpoe Monbello's experience when she was selling her vegetables and palm oil on the streets of Park Hill a couple of years ago: "One time . . . in the early part of July we were selling over there, on that spot right behind the . . . green car [pointing to the other side of the street]. As soon as I put my things there, we heard the gun right here. We started hiding ourselves, then we saw the boy coming. . . . As soon as he saw the police car coming he run away. . . . The shooting made me come from Liberia and come here; people started shooting outside here, especially in the summertime." While fortunately, crime rates have dropped since the mid-1990s in Park Hill, as in other New York City neighborhoods, murder, rapes, robbery, and burglaries continue to happen even today.[13] Liberians, along with much of the general public, have different ideas about who was responsible for the committed felonies and what caused the decrease in crime. Some Liberians suggest that the city's "tough on crime" policy made the neighborhood safer. More explicitly, Mr. Boakai gave credit to former New York City Mayor Giuliani and his pursuit of the "Broken Windows" theory (Kelling and Wilson 1982). Mr. Boakai, who settled in the early 1990s in Staten Island, went as far as saying, "If Giuliani . . . had another four years . . . Park Hill would have been a paradise garden." News coverage (Bernstein 1994) from the mid-1990s about an increase in police raids targeting drug trafficking and prostitution in Park Hill seems to corroborate Mr. Boakai's view. At the same time, these very same raids led to disproportionately high arrests of Black people in New York. But there is another explanation that far more Liberians support. They believe that their own arrival contributed to the decrease in violence and crime in Park Hill. Many social scientists would agree. A correlation between a decline in criminal activities and an increase in immigrant population has been confirmed by scholars, such as Robert Sampson (2008). The perception that Liberian refugees improved Park Hill was explicitly expressed by one of the former resettlement workers, Garpu Garbleh: "Park Hill, from the beginning of the resettlement program, was not a very healthy environment in terms of crime, but when the Liberian refugees came in, they somehow diluted that. . . . There were more Liberians coming in and . . . those bad ones leaving . . . so . . . the crime rate dropped." At the same time, he also acknowledged that some Liberian refugees—"the young ones that came and that were misdirected"—joined the drug trade and participated in violent acts, which have continued in the neighborhood, although on a much smaller scale. In the same breath, Mr. Garbleh pointed out that the problem was not the Liberians who had come to the United States in the 1970s and 1980s—with precarious visa statuses and, thus, too afraid to take the chance to make quick money through illegal means—but refugees who arrived with secure legal status. Although it should be noted that those with legal refugee status and also permanent residents can be and are deported if they are found guilty of an aggravated felony, drug crime, or other crimes (see chapter 6).

Violence is not the only problem that has plagued Park Hill residents. Signs of decay, such as water leaks, broken windows, and chipped ceilings, are everywhere. Although some of the buildings underwent renovation in 2011 and 2012, it was getting worse again in 2019 (Liotta 2019) and has continued since then (Alves 2021; Shahi 2025). Rodent sightings are also common. During an interview with Loko Pella, who initially came to the United States in 1989 to take care of her sick sister, in her home in Park Hill, one of the children she was watching squirmed after having discovered a cockroach on the floor. Ms. Pella calmly responded by saying that the Liberian children in Staten Island are afraid of these insects; she was not concerned about the cockroaches but feared the rodents. She said, "What we don't like here is, we deal with the rats . . . something we didn't even see in Liberia in our homes. . . . We didn't have roaches; we didn't have rats. Not like here." Apprehensively, I lifted my feet from the floor and asked whether the rats came into the apartment as well, to which she replied, "Yes. Here, a lot of rats. Trying to get rid of it, we can't even get rid of it."

In addition to having to deal with crime and pests, Park Hill residents endure other hardships in the buildings. For example, while some winters the apartments were, as Samuel Black described, "ridiculously hot, like 100 and something degrees, like project heat," in 2016, 2023, and 2025, residents did not have gas for cooking and hot water or heat for weeks. The apartment buildings' environs are also not appealing; papers, leaves, and garbage are a common sight. But despite these problems, Liberians have established a bustling and vibrant community in Park Hill, one that, as noted earlier, is often referred to as "Little Liberia."

"They Feel at Home": Creating an Ethnic Neighborhood

Today between six thousand and eight thousand Liberians and Liberian Americans call Staten Island, in particular the area around Park Hill, home. While there are other neighborhoods throughout the United States such as Brooklyn Park, Minnesota, and Southwest Philadelphia that have similar numbers of Liberian residents, the concentration of so many Liberians in such a small geographic area makes it the only neighborhood in the United States that can "so readily [be] identified as Liberian" (Reilly 2014, 139). This is also because other settlement areas of Liberians in the United States are more ethnically diverse and include more Africans from other nations (Osirim 2010; Reilly 2014). Why Liberians initially settled in the community is not known, but there was a small community as early as the 1970s and 1980s, which mushroomed as a result of refugee resettlement efforts in the 1990s and early 2000s. Former resettlement caseworkers recalled a special outreach program to inform Liberians in Park Hill about the possibility of sponsoring relatives to come to the United States as refugees. This information spread mostly through word of mouth, as Garpu Garbleh, one of the caseworkers, remembered: "Information is power. So, most people in Park Hill . . . didn't just sit on it. . . . They got the information that there's a refugee program, and they went after it. There were others living in different boroughs, but they thought that it was not true until people started resettling in Park Hill like crazy." Subsequently, Liberians in other boroughs also contacted VOLAGs to help them get their relatives to the United States. VOLAGs advised them that they should move to Park Hill because of affordable and available apartments, some with multiple bedrooms that could accommodate their arriving family members.[14] In addition, Park Hill, in the eyes of senior New York VOLAG staff, had the added benefit that Liberian refugees would be living among native-born Black Americans with whom VOLAG staff assumed Liberians shared a racial and cultural affinity.[15] Garpu Garbleh, who worked as a caseworker for one of the VOLAGs, recounted how his supervisors made this decision: "The expectations of Lutheran [Social Services] was that the African Americans would be very receptive to their African brothers, which was to the contrary. You know, that's how my White bosses were thinking. . . . And I had to report to them that they were not as receptive as they were thinking." Thus, resettling African refugees into native-born Black American neighborhoods is not by accident but the manifestation of the "racialized geography of settlement. . . . African refugees [are] living in peri-urban spaces of Black segregation and poverty, while non-African refugees live in majority White suburbs" (Watson 2024, 858). In fact, resettling Liberian refugees in a resource-poor, high-crime, and neglected neighborhood led to many conflicts between the newly arrived Liberian refugees and long-term residents that marked their relationship, as detailed in chapter 6, for many years.

Despite the friction with native-born Black Americans and ongoing anti-Black racism in the borough, other Liberians moved on their own to the Park

Hill neighborhood. These Liberians include refugees who had been resettled in different states and immigrants, asylum seekers, and asylees who lived elsewhere. Many Liberian refugees, who have migrated to Staten Island from other U.S. cities, had initially been scattered around the country in accordance with the Migration and Refugee Assistance Act of 1962. Initially, scatter policies were promoted by the federal government to avoid a "second Miami," referring to the concentration of Cuban refugees there. The goal was to minimize the impact of a refugee population on local populations and local resources/governments through dispersal (Desbarats 1985), as well as to promote incorporation by preventing the creation of large ethnic enclaves and thus propelling immersion into the larger "mainstream American" community. However, scatter policies have not been able to prevent the creation of geographic refugee clusters through secondary migration. "Secondary migration" is the term used in the USRAP and by VOLAGs to describe refugees who move from one U.S. state where they were originally resettled to another one within the first year of being in the United States. Liberians, like other refugee groups (Besteman 2016; Sackett and Lareau 2023), continued to move in search of a "lower cost of living and cheaper housing" (Weine et al. 2011, 34), to be near relatives and friends, and to find better jobs and benefit prospects. Most secondary migrations are initiated and facilitated through networks that these refugees have in the desired destination; this holds true for Liberians who moved to but also, on occasion, away from Staten Island.

The decision to relocate is also a clear sign of agency among refugees. It demonstrates that they reject the settlement location that others, namely the VOLAGs, made on their behalf and that refugees are able to activate their own personal networks to locate job opportunities that prompt their relocation (see also Besteman 2016; Mott 2009). Refugees make these decisions regardless, or more often unaware of the fact that many resources allocated to the VOLAGs by the U.S. government for the initial resettlement period are not transferable to another VOLAG (Weine et al. 2011). To put this another way, Liberians who were originally resettled in Pennsylvania or any other state and moved to Staten Island shortly thereafter lost their right to some of the initial resettlement services, although not to government benefits (such as Medicare, Social Security, and food stamps). Despite these deterrents, the longing and need for affordable housing, better job opportunities, public transportation, and higher government benefits, as well as the desire to be near family, proved to be strong motivations, prompting Liberians, like Flomo Yakpazua, who initially had settled with his wife's family in Minnesota, to move to Staten Island. He reasoned that one "can live in Staten Island for . . . five, ten, almost fifteen years without owning a vehicle" and "get to work, see friends," whereas in other states this was not possible.

Regardless of when or how (resettlement, secondary migration, etc.) they came, together Liberians have built a community in Park Hill over the years, and today their presence is immediately felt due to its density. There are Liberian flags on many of the apartment windows and in parked cars. Liberian, other West African,

FIGURE 3.2. West African outdoor market in Park Hill. Photo by Gee Bee Productions.

and also American music can be heard through the open windows in the summer or year-round in the hallways of the apartment buildings. Flyers on doors to residential buildings frequently announce Liberian-themed events, and especially on weekends, the building hallways and streets come alive with women dressed in African garments and chatter in Liberian English. It is hard to miss when you have entered "Little Liberia," as Winnifred Fassah, an illiterate single mother who was resettled along with four children in the early 2000s, pointed out: "They call Park Hill 'Little Liberia' because everything you see in Liberia . . . you see it on Park Hill. . . . Just how you see the people . . . sit down, gossip . . . and . . . talking loud. It's the same, the way of life, so everything if you go . . . and look at the movement of the people . . . the dishes that they eat. . . . Just what you see, that's just what happen in Liberia. . . . So, what you see on Park Hill, the friendliness . . . that's just how it works in Liberia." Over the years, I observed that when Liberians in Park Hill meet someone they do not know but believe to be a fellow Liberian, after correctly identifying them as such, they often then greet each other with a smile and a Liberian snap handshake.[16]

Many community activities take place in common area rooms in the basements of apartment buildings, on the sidewalks, and in Liberian churches nearby. One of the most visible centers of the lively Liberian community is the outdoor market held daily outside during the warmer months (see figure 3.2). Originally, the market was set up on one of the sidewalks in the neighborhood. However, many native-born Black Americans in Park Hill complained about it, and subsequently, the market women were forced to move within the neighborhood several times. In the fall of 2012, through collaboration among the Liberian leadership, a prominent native-born Black American leader, and the building management, a permanent space for the market was secured. This new location brought some other changes. Additional women started to sell, and the variety of items being sold subsequently grew. When the market was still transient, as many as twenty West African women sold vegetables and food, including African peppers, palm oil, cassava leaves, potato greens, and smoked fish. The market women buy many of the vegetables in New Jersey and bring them to the neighborhood. In addition to food items, women peddle a variety of African fabric and clothing and other items. More recently, the market women also started selling barrels that Liberians fill with groceries, clothing, and other necessities to ship to Liberia.

One could say that Liberian women have adapted their West African lifestyles to Staten Island's landscape and the demands of the Liberian diaspora. This market provides women, who hail from Liberia, Sierra Leone, and Ghana, with a type of employment in which many were already engaged in West Africa. "Sometimes you will see it, they cook outside. . . . It's like Africa, selling the vegetable on the street," Diasa Minong, a Senegalese community activist, observed. Women often supplement what they receive from the government in welfare benefits and/or Social Security payments with earnings from selling at the market. For those who buy products, as well as those who sell them, the market is crucial in combating loneliness that many older Liberians experience in the community. The market allows Liberians, especially those of the older generation, who are often semiliterate or illiterate, to socialize, and it gives women an opportunity to leave their apartments (Koyama 2015; Ludwig and Reed 2016). Everliner Ethridge, who, as the wife of one of the former Staten Island Liberian Community Association (SILCA) board members, was actively engaged with the community, remarked, "The old mas were very grateful that they had a place, especially after leaving a war-torn country. . . . And I think they are happy. . . . They were able to come together and establish themselves into a little group to . . . make market because that is what they used to do back home in Africa. Indigenous people bring their stuff together and make a little business. . . . And so . . . I would say, they feel at home because in order for you to do that, you have to be comfortable." Kormassa Kollie, who was a market woman in Lofa County before the war and sold for years at the market in Staten Island, echoed this sentiment. When Ms. Kollie first came to the United States, she stayed with her son in another North Shore neighborhood. While she was glad to be reunited with her son, she was unhappy with the living arrangement. She remembered that she was by herself in the home since her son, daughter-in-law, and grandchildren would "leave at daybreak." And so, Ms. Kollie asked her son to secure her an apartment in Park Hill so she could "go sell . . . at the market" and keep company with other Liberian women of her own age.

In addition to serving as a place where Liberian market women can escape the isolation of their apartments, practice cultural traditions, and earn money, the market provides services for other Liberians and West Africans who live in Park Hill and elsewhere in Staten Island. There, they can buy fresh vegetables and other food typically unavailable in their neighborhood grocery stores and connect with a bit of "home," as Annie Quide, a Grebo woman who had been displaced multiple times in West Africa before being resettled, described: "Park Hill is comfortable and for my community . . . like I'm at home. I'm back in Africa. Because in the summertime, the old women on the streets, they're selling their stuff and you don't have to go a long distance to get some African food, is right there so it's . . . a convenience and you meet people in the street, they know you . . . say 'hi' to you with a smile on their face, you smile back at them. . . . Everybody looking out for everybody and that's one of the joyful things about it." The market has another important function; it helps Liberians to retain and pass on aspects of their culture to the next generation who were born in or, like Wannie Jacobs, spent most of their lives in the United States. But this happens in a very gendered way since it is almost exclusively women, dressed in traditional West African lappas and headscarves, who are "making market." To be fair, there are sometimes one or two older men who sell fish from their car trunks on a nearby street corner, but men are less visible in this space. Hence, Liberian women, like in most other cultures, are, as Eva McGovern, who worked with refugee youth at one of the VOLAGs, observed, "the caretakers of the community" and as such "keepers of culture and tradition." Wannie Jacobs elaborated on how the Liberian women and the market were important to her, especially when she was a child and teenager: "It gives you a sense of home. For us . . . teenagers or children who grew up in America who don't know much about the homeland, it kind of gives us some type of security because this is where . . . I learned most of my culture . . . like during the summer. You will have . . . the old women selling . . . African food outside and they will be roasting . . . chicken. . . . This is . . . 'Little Liberia' . . . feeling of being at home. So, it's kind of . . . like home away from home. . . . I will always come back to Staten Island because this is where I could say I grew up, and this is where a lot of my ethnicity comes from."

As a result of many of the activities I have described, Park Hill has slowly been moving away from the image of "Killa Hill" to "Little Liberia." This kind of process is not unique to Park Hill. Often, residents of neighborhoods with dreary conditions and negative images try to redefine the identity of their neighborhood and engage in activities that construct a positive image. Liberians have done this by establishing an ethnic enclave in Park Hill. Ethnic communities are important for immigrants but particularly for refugees, as Valtonen (1999, 483–484) noted, because they have "a restorative effect on culture disruption caused by displacement, regardless of the level of intragroup contact." Such communities also offer opportunities for (re-)creating social networks. These social networks are especially important for Liberian women who say that they are grateful for the large number of Liberians in Park Hill whom they can ask for help. Zaiway Paye, who was introduced in chapter 1, elaborated: "Sometimes you don't have anything to cook, you run to your friend, 'I want this. Let me check your freezer.' You know . . . we are like family . . . especially on this Park Hill. There are more Liberians that we knew way back. . . . Sometimes when I'm going somewhere I just call one, 'Please can I leave my daughter with you because I need to go somewhere,' and I would be happy because I have a babysitter here."[17] Thus, Park Hill also provides some opportunities to find work inside the community. Many of the older women watch Liberian American children for a minimal fee. While some may see the exploitation in the miserly pay, for most Liberian refugees it is a way to build a community, giving the older female generation something meaningful to do, allowing the middle generation to earn money, and exposing the children, who were mostly born in the United States, to Liberian culture. Perhaps most importantly, all of these activities have created a "home away from home" for Liberians but also mark the neighborhood as "Liberian" and/or "African," which did not always sit well with many native-born Black Americans living in Park Hill. The following occurrences typify this. In the spring of 2016, the Business Center for New Americans wanted to mount a sign—identifying the market, which they had created in coordination with the West African market women—near the entrance to the African outdoor market. But the sign was barely hung when one member of the native-born Black American leadership in Park Hill and ripped it down, accompanied by a derogatory comment and exclamation, "This is not an African neighborhood."[18] Another example involved an annual Liberian cultural festival, organized by a local grassroots organization, that lasted until the COVID-19 pandemic ended it. The highlights of the festival were the traditional Liberian dances that were performed by 1.5- and second-generation Liberian American girls. The youth studied these dances under the guidance of Liberian women and a male Liberian drum instructor. The organization started this initiative after learning that most of the Liberian youth felt ashamed of their heritage and knew very few positives about Liberia. But learning and performing these dances changed much of this. Their pride and joy were unmistakable as they danced in traditional Liberian outfits for the community. Several native-born Black American neighbors resented this public display of West African traditions. They expressed that the Liberian American girls should also learn and perform tap, along with other "American" dances. For these native-born Black Americans, this open performance and celebration of Liberian culture marked Park Hill as "African" territory, something that they did not always appreciate. While some could possibly interpret it that way, they could only do so if they overlooked that the girls also eagerly danced to Beyoncé and other American artists.

More recent developments also show that the different cultural groups can and do coexist. In May 2019, despite pouring rain, the Park Hill community (both native-born and foreign-born) came out to celebrate the naming of the area as the "Wu-Tang Clan District" in honor of the rap group from the neighborhood (see figure 3.3). Just a few years later, in April 2022, the presence and impact of Liberians in the neighborhood were acknowledged when the corner of Sobel Court and Park Hill Avenue was named "Little Liberia Way" (see figure 3.4). Disagreements

FIGURE 3.3. Wu-Tang Clan District. Photo by author.

FIGURE 3.4. Little Liberia Way in Park Hill. Photo by author.

between Liberian refugees and native-born Black Americans still continue to exist, but as the years have gone by and a new generation has come of age, more coalitions have been formed.

CONTINUED STRUGGLES FOR LIBERIAN REFUGEES

Prior to their arrival in Staten Island, Liberian refugees were full of hope for what their new lives in the United States would be. Instead of shiny skyscrapers, trees stacked with money waiting to be picked, and mint infrastructure, they found themselves in a neighborhood that has been plagued with crumbling buildings, safety concerns, violence, drug trafficking, gang activities, and generally was the opposite of common flashy New York City images. This, combined with the urgent need to become economically self-sufficient, caused many Liberians to be disappointed and frustrated. But over time, especially with the assistance of VOLAG caseworkers, Liberian refugees have prevailed. They have found employment—often not their dream jobs, but ones that have enabled them to sustain their families in Staten Island while also sending remittances to relatives in West Africa. In addition, Liberian refugees have started to make claims to Park Hill as their new home. In short, in the face of many problems and obstacles, Liberians have created a "Little Liberia" that offers comfort and a connection to their heritage culture and makes them feel at "home." The Africanization of the neighborhood is evident in an outdoor market during the warmer months, Liberian festivals, people wearing African garments on the street, and Liberian parties held in the apartment buildings. This concentration of Liberians in a small geographic area also helped Liberians recreate their lives in the United States. Certainly, living in Staten Island changed Liberians. They reunited with family members from whom they were separated in the war but also created new families. But Liberians are not the only ones who have changed in the past twenty years or so. Their presence in Staten Island has contributed to the alteration of the borough's ethnoracial makeup. However, as the following chapters illustrate, the borough continues to be a place where anti-Black racism is omnipresent.

4 SOMEONE CALL ME A "DAMN" REFUGEE

In 1992 Mr. Boakai Boakai, then forty-nine years old, arrived in Staten Island with an immigrant visa that his brother, a U.S. citizen who served in the U.S. Army, had sponsored. Even though Mr. Boakai had worked for years at the U.S. embassy in Monrovia, he never planned to emigrate to the United States, but the war in his native country forced him to do so. When he first came to Staten Island, he was not able to bring his family with him. They were scattered throughout Liberia and other countries in West Africa because of the war. Some of his family members were registered refugees with the UNHCR in the Buduburam refugee camp in Ghana.

Once in Staten Island, he got a job and learned from VOLAG caseworkers who were conducting information sessions in New York about the possibility for his displaced family members to be resettled as refugees in the United States. Subsequently, Mr. Boakai completed the necessary application to sponsor his relatives to come to the United States. As part of the process, his family members in the Ghanaian refugee camp had to be interviewed by U.S. immigration authorities and prove that they were both *bona fide* refugees and actually Mr. Boakai's kin. This entailed demonstrating that they had been persecuted due to one or more of the five grounds listed in the 1951 Convention Relating to the Status of Refugees (1951 Convention) and establishing that they were indeed close relatives of Mr. Boakai. They were able to "pass" the interview because they credibly conveyed just that by using the appropriate terminology paired with a display of agony that others expect of refugees. Since resettlement does not immediately happen after the interview, Mr. Boakai's relatives had to wait, deciding to pass the time in Liberia, where fighting had subsided in some areas.[1] However, when their time came to board a plane to the United States, they migrated once again to Buduburam since eligibility for resettlement in the United States was contingent on their living in the refugee camp and having no viable option of safe return to Liberia.[2]

When Mr. Boakai's relatives finally arrived in the United States, they qualified for assistance through the USRAP. They and Mr. Boakai were very appreciative of the services and (financial) resources they received due to their legal refugee status, as it made their transition to U.S. society easier and decreased the monetary burden on Mr. Boakai. At the same time, they started to actively try to distance themselves from the informal refugee label that others loosely applied to them due to their Liberian and African heritage. This label does not hold any benefits but instead serves not only as a reminder of what they had witnessed and experienced during the war but also of their status as poor and "homeless" outsiders.

This vignette is an example of how legal refugee status is an elusive status that is very difficult to obtain. It requires a coordinated effort and agency on the part of refugees. They not only have to search for and find refuge in the right place (in most cases by crossing an international border), but they also have to be able to express their experiences in a way that deems them credible and resonates with UNHCR and U.S. immigration officials' views and guidelines of what and who refugees are and how they act. This means refugees must downplay their agency to render themselves in need of protection by emphasizing that they are at the mercy of the external forces that displaced them in the first place (see also Malkki 1996). While most refugees experience these challenges, they are, as I document in this chapter, particularly pronounced for African refugees. The main reason for this is the systemic anti-Black racism in both global and U.S. refugee and immigration policies. This includes, but is not limited to, the lack of humanity that many Black refugees and asylum seekers are afforded, as their suffering is taken less seriously, given that war, violence, and authoritarian regimes in the African context have often been normalized. Their experiences do not fit the narrative of "exceptional violence," which elicits outrage, shock, horror, and often a humanitarian response (Springer 2012; Swanson and Torres 2016), such as the Hungarian, Cuban, Syrian, or Ukrainian refugee crises. Furthermore, I demonstrate how refugee policies and anti-Black racism are intertwined and the implications this has for African refugees. For example, the USRAP has for most of its existence allocated the lowest quota to the African continent compared to other regions, but it has also limited avenues and programs through which African refugees can apply for and receive legal refugee status, all while maintaining a higher threshold that African refugees must surpass to prove the degree of their persecution compared to other refugee groups. To be clear, as noted in chapter 1, this applies to Black African refugees, not White South Africans (Afrikaner) who were designated as "refugees" by the second Trump administration. In contrast to the legal refugee status that is out of reach for many African refugees, the informal label "refugee," which confers not advantage but stigma, is readily applied to Africans but also to native-born Black Americans (Masquelier 2006; Sommers et al. 2006), rendering them perennial outsiders and indigents who are, for large parts of the population and media in the Global North, synonymous with being an economic burden (Gale 2004). Put differently, legal refugee status is highly coveted but almost unattainable for Black refugees, be it Africans or Haitians. The informal refugee label instead is generously applied to Black people and thus is experienced as a burden on themselves. For them, this label, unlike the legal refugee status, does not yield any tangible benefits and thus is only experienced as a burden and therefore rejected. Distancing oneself from this informal refugee label takes a similar effort as advocating for oneself to be granted legal refugee status. Hence, this chapter makes an important contribution to our understanding of the experiences of displaced people by making explicit the roles that race and anti-Black racism have played in the USRAP and in the way refugees are treated once they are in the United States. To contextualize the experiences of Liberian refugees, this chapter starts with a historical and theoretical overview of the (legal) concept of "refugee" and its relation to the USRAP.

"EVERYWHERE BUT AFRICA": A BIASED RESETTLEMENT PROGRAM

The term "refugee" is frequently used in the (social) media, but most often in these contexts it is an informal label and not the legal status. Indeed, as I detail in this section, the legal status in U.S. immigration law is a rather recent distinction but has since its codification been fraught with bias and tainted with (anti-Black) racism that has left many who are in search of refuge looking for different avenues to secure some kind of (temporary) protection.

Today, U.S. legislation clearly distinguishes between refugees (who leave their home countries because of persecution or fear of persecution (with the exception of the recent designation of Afrikaners for whom this does not apply) and immigrants (who come to the United States to be reunited with family members or for economic reasons), but this has neither always been the case nor been applied the same to all people who have been forcibly displaced.

Until the mid-twentieth century, "refugees were essentially considered a subcategory of migrants" (Long 2013, 4). The 1951 Convention changed this, defining a "refugee" as

> someone who, owing to a well-founded fear of being persecuted for reasons of race, religion, nationality, membership of a particular social group or political opinion, is outside the country of his nationality and is unable or, owing to such fear, is unwilling to avail himself of the protection of that country; or who, not having a nationality and being outside the country of his former habitual residence as a result of such events, is unable or, owing to such fear, is unwilling to return to it.

While the 1951 Convention appeared to be far-reaching, it was mostly restricted to events occurring in Europe before January 1, 1951, thus marking a clear racial distinction of who could be a refugee.[3] This geographical, and thereby racial, and time limitation was lifted with the adoption of the 1967 Protocol Relating to the Status of Refugees (hereafter referred to as "1967 Protocol") (Chimni 1998; Malkki 1995).[4]

None of these definitions really mattered, however, for refugee admission to the United States, which was driven by Cold War politics until the 1990s. It began with the Displaced Persons Act of 1948, which provided a legal avenue for more than four hundred thousand European refugees to enter the United States. This legislation was necessary since the 1924 National Origins Act had brought almost all immigration from Eastern, Central, and Southern Europe to the United States to a halt. The Displaced Persons Act of 1948 presented the first in a series of acts that regulated the resettlement of refugees to the United States. In the 1950s several impromptu legislations, such as the Refugee Relief Act of 1953, the Refugee-Escapee Act of 1957, and the Hungarian Refugee Act of 1958, were passed in response to other refugee crises brought on by Eastern and Central Europeans trying to escape Communist regimes. Fidel Castro's ascent to power in Cuba launched another wave of refugees waiting to be granted access to the United States. Again, numerous programs were created to resettle and assist Cuban exiles; some of these, with modifications, are still in use today. All of these refugee groups received a warm welcome because they "were universally positioned as groups that maintained certain racial traits that would allow them to assimilate quickly into 'good' Americans" (Current 2008, 45). Specifically, there were U.S. government–sponsored campaigns that aimed at creating support for these refugees by highlighting their cultural and political affinity with Americans and that these Cubans were "'definitely-not-black'" as well as downplaying the real extent of the financial support provided to these refugee groups (Casavantes Bradford 2019, 70). In this light, it is not surprising that there were no protective measures for Africans who sought to escape Communist regimes in Angola, Benin, and the Republic of the Congo. They, after all, were Black. Hence, this is an indication that anti-Black "racism [is] embedded in . . . refugee policy" in the United States (Esbenshade 2011, 180; see also Lennox 1993).

While African refugees' plight has historically often been ignored (El-Enany 2016), it was harder to do that for Southeast Asians who were displaced during and after the destruction of their countries in proxy wars. A significant number of these refugees had supported the U.S. military, and as such they, like Eastern and Central Europeans and White Cubans, were seen as ideological allies who presented an opportunity to bolster U.S. ideology by "discredit[ing] authoritarian regimes, to glorify core American values (e.g., freedom) and economic practices (capitalism)" (Haines and Rosenblum 2010, 392).[5] Given this rationale, and based on the assumption that the Southeast Asian refugee crisis was temporary, the U.S. government, under President Ford, passed the Indochina Migration and Refugee Assistance Act of 1975, which allowed hundreds of thousands of refugees to enter the country and provided some assistance to them (Haines 2010).

A few years later, recognizing that the influx of refugees from Southeast Asia, Cuba, and now also the Soviet Union would continue, the U.S. government enacted the Refugee Act of 1980 (Aleinikoff 1996; Haines 2010). With this new legislation, the United States finally adopted the international definition of "refugee" set forth by the 1951 Convention and the 1967 Protocol. Until then, "refugees," according to U.S. immigration law, were exclusively defined as those fleeing certain

Communist countries or the Middle East (Refugee-Escapee Act of 1957). Thus, it is evident that the distinction made between "refugee" and "immigrant" by the U.S. government has "not reflect[ed] empirical reality but policy intentions" (Long 2013, 7; see also Zolberg et al. 1989) as well as racial preferences, namely excluding Black refugees (Charles 2006; Esbenshade 2011). The Refugee Act of 1980 tried to correct this overt bias.

Although, a racial bias toward refugees from Eastern and Central Europe, Asia, and the Middle East is still evident, as annual quotas and admission numbers show; over the years consistently fewer African refugees have been resettled to the United States compared to those from other geographic regions (Esbenshade 2011; Krogstad and Radford 2017).[6] This is even more confounding considering that the vast majority of protracted refugee situations have been in Africa (Hyndman and Giles 2011; UNHCR 2020). Furthermore, there have been "surge" operations or other relief efforts for refugees or other displaced people in all geographical regions except for Africa. Surge operations occur when resettlement countries such as the United States allocate additional quotas for a particular national group, and their resettlement is "fast-tracked"; this included Vietnamese in 1975, Kosovo Albanians in 1999, Iraqis in 2007, Syrians in 2016, Afghans in 2021, and Ukrainians in 2022.[7] While all of these national groups were allocated additional quotas, there are important differences among them. Some were granted legal refugee status with all the benefits, whereas others have been parolees (Afghans and Ukrainians), a temporary status with fewer benefits. In addition, for certain groups (e.g., Ukrainians) fees were waived, and applications were processed at a much faster pace than for other groups (e.g., Afghans) (Bolter and Chishti 2022). However, the U.S. government espoused toward all of them a policy that was "favorable" or "receptive," similar to that toward Southeast Asian and White Cuban refugees decades ago (Portes and Rumbaut 1996). This has not always been echoed by the larger American society; instead, the societal context of reception for these groups, with the exception of White Cubans, has mostly been "prejudiced." For Black refugees (e.g., Haitians and Cuban Marielitos), according to Portes and Rumbaut's (1996) typology, the "context of reception" was always negative—"hostile" from the U.S. government and "prejudiced" from the larger society.[8] That this is due to anti-Black racism can be seen through the experiences of Cuban Marielitos. They were, just like the earlier wave of White Cubans, fleeing an authoritarian Communist regime, but because they were predominantly Black and portrayed as individuals with criminal convictions, their arrival and integration was marked by hostility and prejudice from the U.S. government, the larger U.S. society, and the White Cuban refugee population already living in the United States (Gosin 2019; Portes and Rumbaut 1996). Hence, for some refugees it is advantageous to identify or be identified by others as White when they have (legal) White racial identities or the proximity to Whiteness, such as in the earlier discussed case of the first wave of Cuban refugees but more recently also for Syrians (Ajrouch and Jamal 2007; Gualtieri 2001). Syrian refugees, like White Cubans before, have at times portrayed themselves and have been "conceptualize[d] . . . as ideologically American" (Perreault and Paul 2018, 91), wearing "western clothes . . . [and having] professional careers such as engineering, medicine and education . . . [who] want to come to America to serve as architects and doctors" (Perreault and Paul 2018, 93), balancing other accounts that portray Muslim refugees and immigrants as a threat.[9] On the contrary, Black refugees have never been characterized as "ideologically American" nor had access to any of these surge operations, meaning the United States did not conceive that they were in need of expedited or additional refuge. Rather their plight has been framed by mainstream media and dominant society as economic misery and a threat to the native (White Anglo-Saxon) population (Lenette and Cleland 2016; Perreault and Paul 2018) due to their perception as being culturally backward (Achebe and Lyons 1998; Boaz 2011) and criminal (Chisholm 1982).

Several Liberians, including Zubah Kpadeh, who came as a sixteen-year-old with his grandfather to Staten Island, noticed this bias in how the United States has responded to humanitarian crises around the world and how this at times translates to creating resettlement opportunities for refugees. He and other Liberians felt that the "United States . . . choose to assist some . . . countries and . . . not to assist other country in terms of war. . . . They go . . . everywhere . . . but Africa." For Liberians, this is even more painful, as the United States did not intervene during the civil war in Liberia despite the historical relationship between the two countries. Thus, it is fair to state that refugee admission is both a highly political and racial issue, which played out during the first Trump administration when, within days of his taking office, the USRAP was suspended and then significantly reduced the quota of resettled refugees per fiscal year.[10] Even more blatantly, this was the case during the second Trump administration when White South Africans were designated as "refugees" as their resettlement was fast-tracked within three months whereas other refugees have spent years waiting.

Governments are not only important in deciding who gets admitted as a refugee, but they are also instrumental in "creating" refugees through policies and (in)action that cause refugees to flee (Lacroix 2004; Zolberg et al. 1989). And as such, refugees and other forcibly displaced people differ from immigrants in an important way when it comes to the significance of push (and pull) factors. For example, from the standpoint of individual migration motives, the first concern of a refugee/asylum seeker/IDP is to flee an intolerable or life-threatening situation. Indeed, for this group of people, the concept of destination choice is less relevant than the overwhelming "push" (FitzGerald and Arar 2018; Zolberg et al. 1989). This was also reflected by how Vanessa Jallah, who was resettled as a child with her mother and siblings, stressed the element of force when she said, "A person that fled her land, her country. . . . You're running away, so you are a refugee. . . . During the war, a lot of us had to flee over the border. . . . That's how we are considered refugee because we had to flee over the border . . . for safety." In contrast, immigrants usually choose their destination according to employment opportunities, wage levels, and/or where they already have contacts. The immediate threat that causes most refugees and other forcibly displaced people to leave their homes in a hurry, often without any of their legal documents, also does not allow for planning strategically for migration. Subsequently, most refugees and asylees are, compared to immigrants, less prepared to embark on a new life in a new society. The U.S. government recognizes this and provides various forms of government assistance to refugees and asylees that are not available to immigrants.[11] Hence, gaining legal refugee status or asylum can—as I detail later in the chapter—be very beneficial.

Despite the juridical distinction of a "refugee" as a "figure of humanitarian rescue" (Long 2013, 7) rather than an "economic migrant," most migration flows are actually mixed. Put differently, economic migrants and refugees "have multiple reasons for mobility" (Castles 2003, 17), which often overlap and therefore lead to shared social networks and migration routes; and per se, "these categories are not divided by bright boundaries but blurry ones" (Reed et al. 2016, 605). As a result, many social scientists argue that refugee status is a legal distinction made by the federal government to determine admission categories and eligibility for government services (Gold 1992; Heeren 2015) and to provide an opportunity to define who is "worthy" of being rescued. This is vividly demonstrated by the case of the admission of Afrikaners under the refugee category.

For this reason, as already stated, the differentiation between those who receive legal refugee status or not hinges foremost on the policies the U.S. government pursues at a time, as well as on the public and the (social) media's perception of particular ethnoracial/national groups and, to a lesser extent, on individual people's agency in pursuing legal refugee status. For example, (White) Cubans have been historically seen as defectors of Communism—and thus *bona fide* refugees—regardless of whether this was their motive to leave, while others, namely Africans and other Black asylum seekers, such as Haitians, are almost universally viewed first and foremost as economic migrants who migrate because of hunger and poverty (Charles 2006; Hanson-Easey and Augoustinos 2010).[12] This matters because governments, including the United States, are not immune to popular views but rather take these into consideration when making (immigration) policies. Thus, if there is broad support and extensive favorable reporting, governments respond and increase refugee resettlement for certain groups (Alboim 2016; Vásquez 2021). But the opposite can occur, as evidenced by the refugee and immigration policies enacted by Trump. The decision about who is declared "a refugee is therefore not a matter of personal choice but of governmental decision based on a combination of legal guidelines and political expediency" (Portes and Rumbaut 1996, 23) and "say[s] more about the . . . States themselves (and their 'moral community') than . . . the migrants" (Reilly 2016, 99). Therefore, displaced people who are excluded and/or not looked upon favorably must go to excessive lengths to make a case as to why they should receive legal refugee status. This plays out especially in the case of African refugees who, as a geographical group, as noted before, have historically been allocated proportionally fewer slots to be resettled in the United States and generally also lack powerful advocates (e.g., lobbies, politicians) or a constant (positive and negative) presence in the media that some other refugees have been afforded (Hawkins 2008; Patterson 2019).[13] The absence of news coverage of the plight of Liberians during the war and as refugees is even more perplexing given the unique history between the two countries, which had led Liberians to expect that the United States would intervene in the civil war in their native country and also grant them protection. The United States did not do that; instead, it sent troops, aid, and attention to other conflicts (e.g., former Yugoslavia, Iraq), thus validating Zubah Kpadeh's observation, "They go . . . everywhere . . . but Africa."

What Makes Someone a Liberian Refugee?

Since the routes to arrive as a legal refugee in the United States are limited, in particular for Africans, some Liberians pursued other avenues to escape the violence in their native country in search of refuge. Among them were (upper) middle class Liberians who traveled on visitor or student visas to the United States. Given this mode of travel and entrance, not everyone in the Liberian community agreed that they should be classified as refugees. For example, Janjay Waggah, who arrived in the United States via the USRAP, felt that because "they came here like immigrants . . . only those who came on the refugee program are refugees." However, her son-in-law disagreed and noted that "a lot of people came on . . . student visa, visiting visa, and just end up staying. . . . I consider them refugees because they all came here against their will because of the status of their country at the time." While there was some disagreement about who could be counted as a "Liberian refugee," as the next examples bear out, this also shows the complexity of exit from Liberia and entrance to the United States. Generally, it was understood in the Liberian community that they were in the United States because of the war, even if their legal status did not always reflect that. Some Liberians were forced to make some really difficult decisions that ultimately determined their legal status as refugees or immigrants in the United States, as the ordeal that Ms. Maymay Bensing, who fled to Sierra Leone with her son during the war, shows:

> My mother filed . . . for refugee status. . . . My sister was on the list, but I could not find my sister. . . . But not my son. . . . So, the choice was to just come like as young girl who don't have a kid. . . . But I thought it was too selfish. Coming that way means . . . my son and my sister will not have the opportunity to come to America. . . . So, I told my mom I wasn't coming if I couldn't come with my kid. Because she left us and came and I know how we struggle. I wasn't about to leave my son alone . . . to come to America. And I had to find my sister. . . . So, I'm not a refugee because I didn't come . . . on a refugee status . . . but I could have. . . . It's the war that made me go Sierra Leone.

Similarly, other Liberians who arrived on visitor visas, escaping the (potential) harm in Liberia, were conflicted about whether they were "refugees" or not. This is embodied by Sam Collins, who came to the United States in the early 1980s, following his parents, who had left Liberia because they were, as Americo Liberians, targets following Doe's coup d'état. He reasoned, "I didn't come as a refugee. I came after the coup, I guess, and probably I would have been called a refugee at the time . . . but . . . the war was raging and you were picked up by helicopters . . . or you got on a bus or were forced to exit. . . . That's what I see as refugee. We got on a Pan Am flight. So, it wasn't as bad as that. At the time, I guess I wouldn't [be] categorized as a refugee, but when Taylor became president everybody that came . . . they were all refugees."

Although he is keenly aware that he never had legal refugee status, he knows that he shares some experiences with Liberians who had legal refugee status. However, given the circumstances of their arrival in the United States, such a status was never an option for him and his brother. So instead of having this legal protection and access to benefits, the two teenagers became undocumented after their visas expired. Fortuitously, they were able to obtain legal status through IRCA.

Other Liberians who were in the United States on temporary visas received a reprieve starting on March 27, 1991, when Liberian nationals became eligible for TPS.[14] The U.S. government had estimated that up to fourteen thousand Liberians in the United States were eligible to apply for TPS, but only between thirty-six hundred and four thousand did, for a combination of reasons (Nyamwange 2014; Reilly 2016).[15] This status remained in effect until September 30, 2007, when it was replaced by DED, a status set to expire on June 30, 2026.

These temporary "nonstatuses" (Heeren 2015) of DED and TPS are decreed by the U.S. president to nationals of countries that are deemed unsafe to return to because of ongoing armed conflicts, environmental disasters, or other extraordinary and temporary conditions and protect them from deportation and allow them to legally work and live in the United States. In essence, individuals with TPS/DED status are recognized as "*de facto* refugees" (Frelick and Kohnen 1995, 341, emphasis in original text), but they lack most of the rights and services that those with legal refugee and asylum status are entitled to. For example, they are not eligible for most government benefits (Bergeron 2014; Simmelink 2011), cannot sponsor their family members to join them in the United States, and need to apply for authorization if they want to travel outside the United States. Most importantly, in contrast to refugee status and asylum, because TPS and DED are designated as temporary, they do not provide a pathway to permanent residency and U.S. citizenship. Rather, they were conceived to make it almost impossible for individuals to adjust their status "even if they acquire some other route for doing so, such as marrying a legal permanent resident or U.S. citizen" (Heeren 2015, 1141).[16] This puts holders of these "nonstatuses" in a "state of perpetual uncertainty" (Heeren 2015, 1119), providing only "liminal legality" (Menjívar 2006) despite the fact that the reasons why they were displaced in the first place are often the same as those with legal refugee status.

This is only exacerbated by the fact that TPS and DED have continuously been renewed for short periods of time, and sometimes just days before the expiration date. As a consequence, for decades Liberians on TPS/DED have lived in fear that they would be forced to return to Liberia or become undocumented. In addition, as James Paye, a former social service provider, described, they have been distressed by the degree of uncertainty in their lives: "They're . . . demoralized. They feel powerless. . . . They live in a constant fear of deportation . . . are stuck . . . can't move forward." Such a precarious immigration status, or "nonstatus," affects not just the individuals themselves but also close family members like children, siblings, and parents who may have legal refugee status, asylum, or be U.S. citizens (Enriquez 2015; Menjívar and Abrego 2009).

Fortunately, this time of fear ended for just over twenty-two hundred Liberians who applied for and qualified to become legal permanent residents under the Liberian Refugee Immigration Fairness Act, which was passed in December 2019.[17] Whereas this reprieve was welcomed by Liberians and their allies, it should be noted that this was the first time that such a path to legal permanent residency was offered to any African de facto refugees, while other groups have experienced this type of relief before. For example, the Nicaraguan Adjustment and Central American Relief Act of 1997 legalized the status of many Nicaraguans, Salvadorians, Guatemalans, Cubans, Yugoslavs, Albanians, and nationals of the former Soviet bloc countries who were de facto refugees (the majority had pending asylum applications). There is also the unprecedented case of the Chinese Student Protection Act of 1992, when in response to the Tiananmen Square protests of 1989 the United States granted permanent legal residence to close to fifty-five thousand Chinese nationals who were in the United States, despite the fact that they were not de facto refugees since only a few hundred had spoken out publicly in support of the protests.[18] Hence, these examples show the favoritism that the U.S. immigration system has had toward certain national groups, reflecting dominant political and racial priorities. Other forcibly displaced people have only been granted temporary protection. In fact Africans have been overrepresented among nationals designated as TPS.[19] It is, therefore, clear that while U.S. immigration law uses and assigns distinct legal categories, not every displaced person has the same chance to be recognized as a refugee; instead this is contingent on a person's geographic origins, often a proxy for race, and how well a displaced person is able to relay "their story" to an adjudicator, which I describe in the next section.

"THEN THE WAR CAME AND I HAD TO FLEE": SEEKING SAFETY AND REFUGE

Most often legal refugee status is not something that is simply bestowed on individuals. Rather, individuals must actively pursue it. This is a very complex and strenuous process but also one that cannot always be planned, as the immediate goal of safety takes precedence over long-term (re)settlement plans. In addition to various state policies that impact who has a realistic chance of getting legal refugee status, a lot also depends on where individuals are located (e.g., inside their country of citizenship or outside) when they are seeking refuge; this has especially been the case for African refugees. The physical location, as I detail, determines whether a person can become a refugee, an IDP, or an asylee (see also Reilly 2016). Another important factor is an individual's ability to prove to others (e.g., UNHCR and U.S. immigration authorities) that they are in need of protection. However, such "storytelling" does not happen in a vacuum but against a backdrop of anti-Black racist state policies and gatekeepers' (e.g., immigration officers) stereotypes about geographic origin, race, gender, and other factors.

On Becoming Refugees or Not

The conflict in Liberia took place in many regions of the country, and as such, citizens fled to the nearest safe place. For some this was another Liberian county, while others, as Varney Konneh, whose travails were detailed in chapter 2, explained, "walk for days and weeks to cross counties to cross into other countries," such as Côte d'Ivoire, Guinea, or Sierra Leone, which he was unable to do. During certain time periods, Liberians living in and close to Monrovia "were running to the ship" in Freeport of Monrovia, where Nigerian and Ghanaian vessels were docked to evacuate their own citizens (Crawley and Fynn Bruey 2022). Several thousand Liberians also seized the opportunity to leave Liberia this way.

Although all of these people were forced from their homes, their legal, and thus protective, status was not the same. Those who left Liberia had a chance to be declared refugees, who are "persons outside their country of origin for reasons of feared persecution, conflict, generalized violence, or other circumstances that have seriously disturbed public order and who, as a result, require international protection" (UNHCR 2013, 3).[20] Having this legal status of "refugee" provides special protection based on the 1951 Convention and the 1967 Protocol. Refugees then become subject to the laws of the state (e.g., Guinea, Sierra Leone, Côte d'Ivoire) in which they are seeking refuge and should be guaranteed protection under international refugee law. In turn, they are not supposed to be repatriated if their lives or liberty are at risk (non-refoulement principle in international law). Often host governments jointly with international organizations such as the UNHCR provide aid to refugee populations. This aid can include basic necessities, such as food, and shelter, as well as assistance to apply to one of the resettlement programs.

Almost all Liberians who crossed into neighboring countries, or Ghana, and registered with the UNHCR upon arrival were granted prima facie refugee status.[21] This status is conferred to individuals by the UNHCR—and not by the government of the country of first asylum (e.g., Côte d'Ivoire, Ghana)—during a mass exodus where prevailing conditions have substantially the same effect upon a large population and when it is not possible to carry out individual screenings. It means people fleeing do not have to prove that they are individually persecuted because of grounds outlined in the 1951 Convention, but rather each civilian from this country is deemed a refugee, prima facie—in other words, in the absence of evidence to the contrary (Albert 2010). In Africa, refugee status is often granted on a prima facie basis, which reflects the expanded definition of "refugee" that the Organisation of African Unity (OAU) adopted in 1969.[22] Liberians continued to have this prima facie refugee status until the UNHCR, in collaboration with the countries of first asylum, evoked the cessation clause on June 30, 2012, which effectively ended their international protection, including against refoulement (Dobbs and Edwards 2012; UNHCR 2005).

While losing international protection was hard for Liberians who were still living in Ghana,[23] those Liberians who were internally displaced, meaning they never crossed an international border, wished they even had that for a short period. IDPs, like Varney Konneh, are often more vulnerable than refugees because they remain under the legal system of their own government, often one that they are trying desperately to escape (Kälin 2000; Gupte and Mehta 2007). Situations during a war, just like in Liberia, are so dangerous that international relief organizations do not enter conflict zones, and consequently, IDPs receive less aid than refugees. Furthermore, "unlike [for] refugees, there is no legally binding instrument upholding the specific rights of internally displaced persons" (Ferris 2014, 6).

Hence, many Liberians were advised by family members living in refugee camps or in the United States to make their way to Côte d'Ivoire or another country to avail themselves of international protection but also to perhaps become eligible for resettlement in a third country. A former refugee resettlement caseworker, Baka Wehjay, explained, "If you're a refugee, you cannot be in your own country, and so based on that, most of the refugees were living outside of Liberia in order for them to get that status to come. So, even if their spouses were still in Liberia, their relatives in the United States would tell them to go to the neighboring country because they fear that . . . the U.S. immigration official would say, 'Well, we cannot give you the refugee status because your life is not in danger.'"

While this was true for displaced Liberians, the United States has recognized the danger for other populations. Specifically, the United States has—sometimes in collaboration with the UNCHR—granted refugee status through "in-country processing" (described in more detail further below) to IDPs and people living in their own homes in their native countries. Throughout history, the United States has never done any "in-country" processing for Africans, despite the fact that Africa has consistently had more IDPs than any other geographical area (Internal Displacement Monitoring Center 2023), and IDPs have remained extremely vulnerable (Zetter 2011).[24] Hence, this is why Mr. Boakai's relatives, who were introduced at the beginning of this chapter, had to be present in the refugee camp in Ghana to have a chance of being resettled to the United States. To conclude, for individuals it is not enough to flee life-threatening conditions and/or oppressive situations—they need to be strategic in where they seek refuge; this is particularly true for Africans, as they have limited avenues to resettlement.

"You Have to Go There and Tell Your Story": Applying for Refugee Status in Africa

Making it to a refugee settlement or camp often is just the beginning for forcibly displaced people in search of a more permanent solution. While the majority hope to return home one day, especially at the beginning of their displacement, they, like Liberians, also learn that there is the possibility of resettlement, and a good number of them put every effort toward getting themselves and their family members a chance to be eligible for resettlement. The first step is to be given the opportunity to be interviewed by staff from the UNHCR and USRAP. This legal and administrative procedure is referred to as Refugee Status Determination (RSD). During RSD, displaced people have to find the right balance between asserting themselves and being passive enough victims deemed worthy to be selected for resettlement. This is far from an objective process, as is demonstrated by the following accounts and analysis.

For refugees, including Liberians, in camps, the desire for resettlement has been driven by an "increased ease of communication with the diaspora, expanded knowledge of entitlements, and the high visibility of resettlement processing" (Jansen 2008, 569). In other words, Liberians living abroad, like Mr. Boakai, shared this information with their family members and friends in West Africa. Despite the perceived "large visibility," resettlement to a third country (e.g., the United States, Canada, Australia) is only an option for a negligible number of refugees and even less so for African refugees. But the odds are not the same for every refugee.

Several factors determine whether one is selected. To begin, being African generally reduces one's chances for a number of reasons. This is due in part to the aforementioned low quotas that the USRAP, since its inception, has allocated to African refugees, a practice also common among other popular resettlement countries, such as Canada (Hyndman 2019). However, this is not reflective of actual need, as "resettlement needs in the Africa region continue to be the highest globally" (UNHCR 2021, 33), but a global refugee resettlement system that has always discriminated against Black refugees.

Although this was not the only obstacle in the way of Liberians' chance to be resettled in the United States. In contrast to the prima facie refugee status they were granted in the first countries of asylum in West Africa, they had to prove in the RSDs that they individually experienced or feared personal persecution based on one of the grounds stipulated in the 1951 Convention (UNHCR 2005). Liberians described RSDs with UNHCR and U.S. immigration staff as having to "go there and tell their story . . . some gruesome story that would make you wanna come to America," said Wannie Jacobs, who spent much of her childhood in refugee camps. But there is more involved than simple storytelling. Increasingly, forcibly displaced people have been viewed with suspicion rather than compassion; they, but in particular Africans, are assumed to be opportunistic/bogus/economic migrants until proven otherwise (Mascini and van Bochove 2009; Sigona 2014).

While many refugees around the world have to contend with this (Swanson and Torres 2016), there is an added layer of scrutiny for African refugees who have been stereotyped as endemic cheats (Jansen 2008; Kibreab 2004) and "lying . . . antagonistic, distant and fantasists" (Jubany 2011, 83). These cultural stereotypes matter because they can, and most certainly have, along with (un)conscious anti-Black racism, influenced how those conducting RSDs assess a displaced person's narrative as well as their character (Ahmad 2002; Sigona 2014).

Furthermore, refugees' statements are not just evaluated for facts but frequently also on their performance of normative gender expectations (Llewellyn 2017; Oxford 2005) as well as racialized views about African refugee women, for example, who "are expected to be more emotional than white women" (Spijkerboer 2000, 65). This means, that (African) women seeking refugee status (or asylum) are expected to have experienced persecution in the private sphere and show distress while recounting their experiences; appearing "indifferent" or failing to cry during the interview is interpreted as a sign that the persecution or (sexual) assault did not occur, and their application is in jeopardy of being denied (Jubany 2011, 85).[25]

Hence, there was a lot of pressure for Liberians living in refugee camps in West Africa to conform to the idealized images of victimized, vulnerable refugees (Fiddian-Qasmiyeh 2010; Malkki 1995) so they would be deemed worthy of being resettled (Dick 2002a). Liberians who were familiar with these expectations, possessed a certain linguistic maturity along with cross-cultural skills, and had enough stamina to relive past horrors and cruelties were the most likely to succeed. For example, Memba Wesseh, who had worked with the UNHCR and other international organizations in the Danané refugee settlement in Côte d'Ivoire, was well versed in the procedures and the "language of vulnerability and insecurity." He, unlike most other Liberian refugees who stressed the complexity of the process to be selected for resettlement, just described in a matter-of-fact way that after nearly ten years of displacement he approached the IOM, his employer at that time, because he "was not feeling happy . . . too secure with family . . . being in Danané." The same people also helped him to submit his and his family members' applications for resettlement, and he came to New York. But not everyone was so fortunate. Osiemeo Boye, who escaped from Liberia in the mid-1990s to the Buduburam refugee camp in Ghana, recalled that those who did not "pass" the RSD and thus were not selected for resettlement took the denial very personally: "Some . . . were not lucky to just pass . . . because after they question you . . . if they don't see any iota of truth in your story . . . they fail you. . . . Whenever people are denied, they want to kill themselves because they deny them coming here." Those who are not approved for refugee resettlement frequently take this "failure" very personally, as Mr. Boye described, and have to plan anew for the future, as there is no appeal process and that door to resettlement is forever closed.

Nevertheless, many refugees, including Liberians and the Somali Bantus in Jansen's (2008, 573) study, remain undeterred and come to believe that "resettlement . . .

[is] something that they could organize and achieve" if they presented their story in the right way. For example, some Liberian refugee women emphasized their special protection needs due to their gender during the RSDs. Here, they frequently built on knowledge that they had acquired from workshops and programing around women's empowerment, which often focus on combating gender inequality and domestic violence as well as attaining economic/financial independence, that the UNHCR and other international organizations provide in the refugee camps (Holzer 2015; Hyndman 2000; Rajasingham-Senanayake 2004). In addition, in all refugee situations women (and children) are typically considered more vulnerable and in more need of protection (e.g., "Women at Risk" program; Haffejee and East 2015).[26] However, this does not mean that they are always believed, as there have been accusations of "false claims of rapes" in order to better their chance at resettlement in a third country (Hyndman 2000, 79). While none of the Liberians whom I spoke with insinuated that they had resorted to this tactic, there were some Liberian women who presented themselves and their children as a single-parent household because, as Danny Gayflor, a Liberian UNHCR employee who worked in different refugee camps in West Africa, said, they felt that "this way they would move up in the list to come to America."

To some, including humanitarian aid workers, Liberian women's ingenuity and creativity seems perplexing since (African) refugee women are often assumed to be vulnerable, uneducated, and childlike, and thus have no or limited agency (Goodkind and Deacon 2004; Robertson et al. 2006), yet they have found ways to advocate for themselves and their families. While in this case some Liberian women deliberately emphasized certain aspects of their experiences and left out others to improve their chances of becoming one of the lucky few selected for resettlement, at other times Liberians felt that fudging some of the information was a necessity to ensure that their entire family remained together.[27]

The reasons for this can be found in immigration laws and the USRAP policies that are biased against African refugees. Not only, as already established, have resettlement quotas for Africans been significantly lower than for refugees from other geographical regions, but Africans have had more limited access to the more generous Priority 2 (P2) category of the USRAP. This category is reserved for groups of "special humanitarian concern" to the United States who are selected by the Department of State with or without the input of the UNHCR and NGOs. The important characteristic of P2 is that, since eligibility is based on group membership, thresholds to prove individual (fear of) persecution have been lower, and family ties do not have to be proven since everyone in the designated group is eligible for an interview (Esbenshade 2011).[28] In other words, once an applicant and their family in the former Soviet Union (FSU), for example, establish that they are evangelical Christian and "assert a fear of persecution" (Tyson 1990, 929), they can receive refugee status since the Lautenberg Amendment of 1990 and the Specter Amendment of 2004 presume refugee eligibility for certain religious and ethnic groups from the FSU, Southeast Asia, and Iran. In addition to the above-mentioned groups, at times, the P2 category has also been available to certain refugees from Burma, Bhutan, Bosnia, Afghanistan, Iraq, Syria, Democratic Republic of Congo, Sudan, Cuba, El Salvador, Guatemala, Honduras, and others.[29] More importantly, that renders them in the eyes of U.S. immigration staff who process these applications as "'clean cases' that can be relatively easily identified, processed, and resettled" (Watson 2023, 698).

This puts them into an extremely advantageous situation because they can rely on their family as they adapt in the United States. For example, one of the reasons why many FSU refugee families prospered in the United States is because they often arrived with extended family, which allowed the parent generation to pursue employment while the grandparents took care of the youngest generation (Kasinitz et al. 2008; Orleck 2001). There has been an additional benefit for some nationals processed under the P2 category. For decades, evangelical Christians, Jews, and ethnic minorities from the FSU, as well as Ukrainian Catholics, Cubans, Vietnamese, and Iraqis, and for a short time Bosnians and Haitians, have been eligible for "in-country" processing, meaning they can apply for refugee status while still living in their country and not having to cross an international border—very often a dangerous and costly process that causes families to become separated as it is difficult to flee as a large unit. Notably, African refugee groups have not been approved for this "in-country" processing, most certainly because their access to the P2 category has been limited.

Instead, African refugees are most commonly approved for resettlement to the United States as Priority 1 (P1) or Priority 3 (P3). P1, also referred to as "free cases," is for individuals from any country who have been officially identified (by the UNHCR, a U.S. embassy, or an NGO) as in urgent need of resettlement. Usually, this includes persons who are in immediate danger of violence or death and have no real chance of ever returning to their native countries. (For example, this extends to those identified by the UNHCR as "Women at Risk.") People of all nationalities are eligible to apply for refugee status under this category. And while a large number of Liberian refugees arrived in the United States within the P1 category, most Liberian refugees in Staten Island, as discussed in chapter 3, were processed under P3, which is the family reunification category of the USRAP.

Overall, African refugees have been more likely to be admitted to the United States under P3 than refugees from any other geographical region. For example, between 2003 and 2008, 95 percent of all refugees admitted under the P3 category were African (Esbenshade 2010). In order to qualify for P3, one needs to be a member of a designated nationality that is currently eligible to apply, as well as have an anchor in the United States. Like Mr. Boakai did, the anchors—who must have, or had at one point legal refugee, asylum status, or entered the U.S. as legal permanent residents—can file a petition for their legally married spouses, unmarried biological or legally adopted children (under the age of twenty-one), and parents to be resettled in the United States. Anchors also have to submit an Affidavit of Relationship with a VOLAG. In the refugee camps, at least one family member—the primary applicant—who is being sponsored by an anchor has to establish a refugee claim, based on the 1951 Convention, during the RSD.

Although numerous Liberians had family members in the United States, major complications arose from the discrepancy between how family is defined by U.S. laws versus Liberian culture. For example, common-law spouses, nieces, nephews, and adopted children whose official paperwork was never completed due to the war were not eligible to be part of the family reunification process through P3 (H. E. Brown 2011; Holland 2011; Waslin 2010).[30] This presented a conundrum for Liberians as they felt they could not in good conscience leave any of their family members behind, especially after the countless losses they had experienced during the war.[31] Further, in Liberian culture, nephews and nieces are often raised as one's own children, a practice that became only more common because of the loss of life during the war.

This was exemplified by Zaiway Paye who brought her young relatives (introduced in chapter 1) and also by Loko Pella, who lived in Nimba County prior to the war. Once Ms. Pella learned, just like Mr. Boakai had, about the possibility of bringing her family to the United States, she completed the paperwork with the assistance of a caseworker. She listed on the application not only her biological children but also some of her nephews, nieces, and grandchildren who were all refugees in Ghana. All of the relatives were presented by Ms. Pella as her "own children." She explained, "I . . . say 'my children' because in Africa, our sister's children is our children. . . . My sister's children, that's my children. They look at me like their mother. Not like here. . . . No, no. We don't do that. . . . I have more than ten . . . nieces . . . those are my children. . . . They call me their mother because when your sister . . . or relative pass away . . . you are so close, they take to you. They look at you as their mother." For her, this is not only a Liberian cultural norm but also her responsibility as the elder of the family. Varney Yarkpolo, her former caseworker in New York, confirmed, "Some of them brought their siblings' children as their own. They got creative . . . find solutions . . . to get everybody to America. . . . It was just important to get out . . . just leave."

But it was not just Ms. Pella's relatives who wanted to leave; there were many more who vied for the few resettlement spots allocated to African refugees. Some, as I shared in chapter 2, turned to prayers "to open the way for resettlement," while others pursued other routes, including distorting the truth. For example, a few Liberians who did not have relatives in the United States, were not granted refugee status under the P1 category, and/or were not in a refugee camp but in Liberia "bought spots" on the list of other families' resettlement applications. Danny Gayflor discussed—somewhat incredulously—this practice: "These guys sometimes used to . . . take money from people to buy a space. . . . Somebody will just say, 'I'm going to Ghana. . . . I've bought a space.' People going there with money try to get a space to go to the States. I don't know how they were using that system because . . . you have to be in the system, you go through the processes. And how would you just leave from Liberia and go there and your photo is not even . . .

included? They'll come by taking somebody's name." While U.S. authorities treat this as fraud, another possible way to see it is a practice "born out of desperation" (Holland 2011, 1674) given the very low quota for African refugees as well as the limited access that African refugees have had to the more inclusive and less stringent P2 program. One could also interpret Liberians' and other Africans' ingenuity as a demonstration of refugees' agency and their adaptation to a refugee system that has never been objective or fair. The structure's processes and setup have since its inception been characterized by modifications, "fraud," corruption, and abusive power dynamics (Agier 2011; Holzer 2015; Jansen 2008).

However, in the end, the government and the American public's view of Africans as fraudulent, "cunning" (Horst 2007, 93), and "manipulative" (Besteman 2016, 97) prevailed and ultimately led to the suspension of the P3 program between 2008 and 2012.[32] Notably, only African applicants were affected by the suspension of P3,[33] as individuals in other regions were continually eligible to submit applications for P3, P1, and often also for P2.[34] The consequences of this were dire for African refugees since none of their applications were processed during that time period. As such, fewer Africans were resettled, which has left more African refugees lingering in protracted refugee situations. Once the program resumed, it did so with an additional hurdle: requiring African applicants, but not others, to submit and pay for DNA tests to verify blood relations (Dove 2013). The practice of only imposing on African refugees to provide DNA samples "fits into a long history of medical testing on African Americans and Africans" (Esbenshade 2011, 189). Thus, this presents yet another example of a racist policy, since in the end not only were fraudulent claims dismissed but also credible ones, just because many African family situations do not correspond to U.S. laws. The use of DNA evidence to establish family relations is not only very problematic (because it forces individuals to reveal that they were raped) but also ignores cultural practices as well as logistical issues (e.g., unfinalized adoptions) (Dove 2013; Holland 2011). This consistent shifting of the goalposts of how, when, and where to apply for legal refugee status has required refugees, specifically African refugees, to respond with new strategies and agential maneuvering.

"Writing a Good Refugee Story": Applying for Asylum in the United States

While more Liberians who fled their native country have entered the United States as refugees (almost thirty-five thousand), there were also many who were granted asylum (just over eight thousand).[35] Unlike refugees who apply for refugee status overseas, asylum claims are filed either at the port of entry or when an individual is already in the United States. In order to obtain asylum, individuals are required to prove to USCIS or the Department of Justice (Executive Office for Immigration Review and Bureau of Immigration Appeals) that they individually have a credible and well-founded fear of (continued) persecution due to one or more of the five protected grounds defined in the 1951 Convention. Generally, there are two ways that individuals can seek asylum: affirmative and defensive. Affirmative claims are those made by individuals who are not in any removal proceedings. Often these applicants arrive in the United States on a tourist, student, or any other temporary visa.[36] While the vast majority of Liberians have obtained asylum status via this "affirmative" way, there is a smaller number who have been granted asylum after they had been put into removal proceedings, which is referred to as defensive claims.

Garsuah Janjay, who came to Kentucky to attend a church conference in 2000, exemplifies the affirmative scenario. While he was in Kentucky, he received calls from his family and friends in Liberia telling him that it was not safe for him to return because Charles Taylor's loyalists accused him of being against the current regime. These calls brought back memories of a previous time when Mr. Janjay had encountered the rage of Taylor's supporters, who subsequently arrested and tortured him and his wife. Shortly after he was released, he was detained again along with his daughter and his mother: "They took all of us. . . . Every time they come for me they grab everybody in the household." Remembering his arrest and subsequent torture, Mr. Janjay neither wanted to have to experience these cruelties nor put his family at risk yet again. He therefore had to decide "whether to take the risk to go back or whether to remain in the United States." Mr. Janjay chose the latter and filed for asylum, which he was granted a few years later.

Regardless of which way one seeks asylum, the process is complicated and lengthy.[37] But this is not the only similarity the asylum process shares with RSD; the approval of an application hinges on the evidence available and how it is presented. But since "'fear' is a subjective state of mind" (Wasem 2011, 4), the applicant is also at the mercy of adjudicators who "dissect and scrutinize . . . the claimant['s account] . . . in search for objective legal truth" (Sigona 2014, 374). In other words, the person who is reviewing and assessing whether an asylum seeker has a credible and well-founded fear or not is significant, as grant rates vary greatly by asylum officer, judge, and/or circuit (Ramji-Nogales et al. 2009; Transactional Records Access Clearinghouse 2007; 2016).

Several Liberians who were in the United States on tourist or other temporary visas were aware of this. They subsequently decided to move to Staten Island, where they felt their chances of obtaining asylum would be better than in other states.[38] They arrived at this conclusion after "doing some research," said James Paye, who was a human rights activist in Liberia and left for the United States when he felt his life was in danger. This included talking to friends and relatives and sometimes obtaining information from websites.[39] Varney Yarkpolo is a Liberian who pursued this route. Originally, he arrived in Texas on a visitor visa in 1998 and then worked in Georgia using the legal identity of a fellow Liberian. After he encountered difficulties with his application for asylum in the South, Mr. Varkpolo followed his friend's advice to "move to the East Coast." His friend's suggestion proved right; he was granted asylum shortly after. Once again, this demonstrates that forcibly displaced people often have to move multiple times and rely on their own agency to find an opportunity to apply and possibly obtain legal refugee status or asylum that gives hope for (permanent) protection.

Based on the evidence already presented, it comes as no surprise that grant rates also differ based on the asylum seeker's nationality (and thus, presumably, race). For example, asylum seekers from the FSU tend to have the lowest denial rates, between 10 and 27 percent without attorney representation and 2–10 percent with legal support. In comparison, denial rates for Liberians during the same time periods were 45 and 61 percent, respectively, which dropped to about half with attorney representation (Transactional Records Access Clearinghouse 2007; 2016).[40] The grant rates are even lower for other Black asylum seekers, such as Haitians.[41] So why are there these different outcomes for asylum seekers? There are several interconnected explanations; a dominant one is that asylum claims are evaluated by systems and individuals that (often) hold anti-Black racist biases.

At the outset, many of those deciding the fate of an asylum application are, for the most part, not experts in the particular contexts and country an applicant is fleeing, meaning that asylum officers and immigration judges frequently review applications from all over the world. They then evaluate a claim based on information obtained through U.S. State Department Country Reports on Human Rights Practices (Country Reports). Given that the U.S. State Department pursues certain economic, political, and, one could argue, at times also racial, interests of the U.S. government, it is fair to say that these reports can be biased. In addition, many asylum officers and judges are individuals who grew up in the United States surrounded by and exposed to stereotypes about racial groups, other countries, and continents.[42] Exposure to and internalization of these cultural stereotypes is a "crucial factor in the process that produces unconscious racism" (Lawrence 1987, 343; see also Ahmad 2002). Subsequently, asylum adjudicators and immigration judges who are not of African descent have neither spent significant time in Africa, nor have close relations with Africans, and then deduce who this African asylum seeker in front of them is. They do so by drawing (unconsciously) on stereotypical depictions of Africans (and other Black people) as lawless, violent, criminal (C. Abdi 2015a; Bashi 2004; Lennox 1993), and poverty-stricken (Besteman 2016; V. S. Johnson 2016; Mills 2012). In addition, conflicts in Africa are also viewed as not extraordinary but rather normal (Springer 2012) due to Africa's assumed "uncontrollable primordial tribalism" (Fair and Parks 2001, 36). Other refugees, such as Syrians (Janmyr 2021; L. Turner 2020) and most recently Ukrainians (Ray 2022), have been "explicitly position[ed] . . . as 'non-African' . . . and superior to 'African' refugees" and subsequently worthy of protection (L. Turner 2020, 138).

And so, African asylum seekers are less likely to be regarded as individuals fleeing persecution but rather poverty, thus rendering them ineligible for asylum status. Moreover, the success of asylum claims made by Africans is further hampered by the lack of familiarity that many people in the Global North (including asylum officers and immigration judges) have with different African nations. For example, immigration and asylum officers are frequently unable to distinguish between different ethnic groups or African languages and thus cannot confidently establish the legitimacy of who the applicant is; this is undeniably connected to the prevalent trope that "Africa is a country" (Aizenobie 2019; I. Berger 2015; Ngom 2015). This is something I also saw when serving as a country conditions expert. The initial asylum officer mixed up different ethnic groups and documented a nonexistent town in Liberia, with far-reaching consequences. The applicant was misidentified as being a member of an ethnic group that had participated in atrocities, which he was not. Nevertheless, despite presenting evidence during the appeal process, the judge remained firm that the applicant was "not credible," partially also because the Liberian asylum seeker was inconsistent in how he referred to his family members (e.g., not distinguishing at times between step and biological siblings or aunt and mother, which is very common in Liberian culture). Indeed, the final court decision noted that despite having "demonstrated past persecution," asylum was denied because "the respondent has lied" and thus "is not a credible witness."[43]

But it is not just an asylum seeker's nationality and race that affect how their claim is viewed. Other identity makers, among them gender, also matter in important ways; hence, the arguments presented earlier about (normative) gender performance during RSD (Llewellyn 2017; McKinnon 2009) also apply to asylum applications and hearings. For example, Gloria Adams shared with me how her lawyer, a Catholic nun, assisted her in crafting the statement for her asylum application, one that would ensure that she had "a good refugee story," as a fellow asylee, Sarah Beh, said. Concretely, the lawyer advised Ms. Adams to emphasize how her gender left her vulnerable in a country where girls and women experienced sexual assault at a very high rate during the war. Thus, Ms. Adams's plea for U.S. government protection from gender-based violence by Liberian fighters and soldiers can be understood in what Chakravorty Spivak (2010, 48–49) referred to as "white men saving brown [and Black] women from brown [and Black] men."[44] This demonstrates how "gender is racialized" (Nakano Glenn 2002, 7) and makes clear that (Brown and) Black refugee women in the asylum process, in comparison to (Brown and) Black men, are associated with more deservedness and vulnerability and thus worthy of protection (see also Gray and Franck 2019). Furthermore, while negative depictions about their fellow countrymen were beneficial to Liberian women's asylum claims, in the long run they reinforce "essentialist racial stereotypes" (that asylum officers and immigration judges may have) about Black men as more prone to (sexual) violence (Morgan 2006, 150; see also I. Berger 2015; Hanson-Easey and Augoustinos 2010). In other words, for Ms. Adams, being granted asylum depended on her ability to actively pursue asylum and craft her "story" in a way that others—namely the USCIS—saw her as in need of and worthy of protection. Subsequently, it shows that obtaining asylum requires agency, grit, and endurance; and while this is true for most forcibly displaced people, Black refugees face additional barriers due to systemic and individual anti-Black racism and stereotypes.

"RESETTLEMENT IS THE GOLD": ACCESS TO BENEFITS

For Liberians who obtained either refugee or asylum status, a new world of opportunities opened up. Their legal status granted them access to a number of services and programs aimed at facilitating their adjustment to the United States. Concretely, refugees—in contrast to immigrants—are immediately eligible for government benefits.[45] Liberians who came to the United States with refugee status frequently told me about RCA, access to affordable housing, and food stamps they obtained due to their status. Mr. Wright Talley, a single father of seven, explained, "The difference is that people who came as refugees like me, they have the advantage because upon your arrival at JFK you are given your permit to work, your Social Security card, an assistance for medical to start you off. But if you came as an immigrant, it becomes difficult for you, if not impossible, to get adjusted. So, the resettlement is the gold compared to the rest of the programs." Refugees receive more benefits than asylees, who often have to navigate their beginnings in the United States on their own. For example, VOLAGs either set up furnished homes for newly arrived refugees or support anchor families with securing larger apartments where they can accommodate their relatives who arrive via the USRAP. In this way, refugees are immediately connected with a caseworker who greets them, often literally when they arrive at the airport, frequently resulting in long-term relations.

These newly arrived Liberian refugees were not only glad to receive assistance from government programs but also praised the VOLAGs and caseworkers who assisted them and their families as they started a new life in the U.S.[46] Zaiway Paye, who eventually found refuge in Ghana, recounted her experience: "Lutheran [Social Services] is my mother. They are our mother, our father, because without them we wouldn't have been here. Working with [caseworker's name] was charitable. He's a man that cares for refugees. He was always there, calling us. Everything we want to do, he's there to spearhead it for us. Like getting your Social Security, doing this one, doing that. . . . It was profitable coming through Lutheran." Likewise, Desai Kpoe Monbello, a Bassa woman who was illiterate when she arrived in Staten Island from the refugee camp in Ghana in 2001, spoke of the legal refugee status's benefits: "I'm not working and they . . . give me free food, they . . . give me house . . . they pay the rent. . . . When you are here on your own with children, you don't have work; the government take care of you."

These advantages are not available to those with TPS/DED or immigrants (regardless of their legal status). In the Staten Island Liberian community, where people with different legal statuses live together, being excluded from the various programs assisting refugees and asylees can be a frustrating experience for immigrants, as in the case of Elizabeth Kamara, a mother of three who had found refuge during the war in Sierra Leone. She expressed her disappointment: "If you came here as an immigrant, you are not entitled to that program. In order for your child to be qualified for the program, he had to come here as a refugee; that's a big difference. . . . You come here as a immigrant, you supposed to have opportunity. . . . 'This program is not for you, it's for the refugees.' . . . One year, our children attended the summer program, but the next . . . year when they found out we came as immigrants . . . we were not entitled to it." Refugees and asylees are also eligible to receive assistance in their job search. Many Liberian immigrants like Philip Kollie, who came to the United States after he had "won" his green card through the Diversity Immigrant Visa Program, something he had done because he felt the war had destroyed his and his family's livelihood in Liberia, said that they would have liked to have had access to such programs as well: "With the IRC where my friend works, some things . . . I would want to do, she would say, 'No Philip, if you come as a immigrant, it's not for you, it's only for refugees.' For example . . . if you came here as a refugee, if you don't have a job, they can find you job. They help you go to school and all that kind of thing, but if you come as a immigrant, they don't. . . . I feel that's not fair. . . . You should have a program so that if you came as an immigrant, you have access to all those things." These examples highlight how individuals who arrived with legal refugee status or were granted asylum can receive numerous benefits from which other migrants, such as legal permanent residents who never had refugee or asylum status, undocumented immigrants, and individuals with TPS/DED are excluded.

While many undocumented Liberian immigrants fled for similar reasons as those with legal refugee status or asylum, they were not granted this protection due to timing or the place where they were when they needed refuge. Among them were many Americo Liberians who often arrived with temporary visas in the United States and who became undocumented when their visas expired.

Mr. Collins, whom we met earlier in the chapter, also "didn't have papers" when he came to the United States. He paints a picture of how he and his fellow undocumented Liberians' legal and economic situation differed from those arriving in Staten Island with refugee status:

> There were a lot of people who . . . didn't have green cards. . . . People were afraid . . . on Park Hill . . . in the early days. But as time went on . . . people were coming straight from Africa already with their papers. . . . These guys are getting off the plane already with their green card. . . . They can get a job and benefits. . . . They had all legitimate paperwork . . . because they came with refugee status. . . . But it was . . . more difficult . . . for most of the people that were here already. It took them so long to get it. . . . They struggled to become legitimate. . . . You had to probably get fake documents . . . marry somebody to stay. . . . They were here so long but couldn't move forward that easily . . . like they with the refugee status.

Given the advantages (e.g., international protection, chance of resettlement, access to U.S. government benefits) that the legal refugee status and, to some extent, asylum status has, it is clear why Liberians and other forcibly displaced people go to great lengths to pursue and try to obtain this legal status. However, once individuals have secured these benefits, they are often also eager to lose the informal label "refugee" ascribed to them. This is mainly the case for Black refugees, as the informal label is experienced as burdensome due to the racialized stigma.

"WIPE THE REFUGEE DUST FROM MY FEET": THE ONEROUS LABEL

While Liberian refugees and asylees readily pursued legal refugee status and took advantage of the different government benefits this status offered them, they did not embrace an informal refugee label. Put differently, when legally necessary, Liberian refugees identified as refugees, but they do not do so in their daily lives, as this informal label is not directly linked to real benefits (e.g., legal protection, government aid). Rather it represents a burden that holds them back by denying their individuality and agency, and, as such, continues to render them as objects "in need of assistance, training and a host of other resettlement services, though never to speak and act of their own accord in the public" (McKinnon 2008, 398; see also Gupte and Mehta 2007; Zetter 2007). This infantilizing of refugees, in particular Africans, on the part of refugee aid workers (Harrell-Bond 2002; Malkki 1995; Mfum-Mensah 2020) is in stark contrast to the demonization and criminalization they experience elsewhere, such as during RSD and asylum hearings.[47] At the same time, this ignores forcibly displaced people's strategic efforts to obtain legal refugee status and the countless hurdles they have had to overcome. More importantly, Black refugees become keenly aware that being labeled "refugee" does not afford them the same empathy that many other refugees are afforded. For Black refugees, the informal refugee label is yet—as I argue—another stigmatizing label that further complicates their lives and ability to succeed in their newly adopted home. This is an important distinction from other refugee groups, who at times have operationalized a "refugee identity" to (successfully) solicit empathy, open channels for refugee resettlement, and secure additional aid (García 1997; Zolberg 2005). Liberians and other Black refugees have abstained from a public "refugee" identification because for them this often evokes images of Black people as poor and frames their experiences as a flight from poverty but not an escape from political, religious, and other persecution, although that is the very reason they are forced to flee (Baranik De Alarcón et al. 2020).

Liberians in Staten Island also recalled how they felt when government and international aid representatives "managed" and placed them under their supervision in refugee camps and in the process, robbed them of control over their lives (Hyndman 2000; Agier 2011). Many Liberian refugees, including Zubah Kpadeh, remembered their lack of agency and how others made decisions for them and fellow Liberians, like they were children: "Refugee don't have too many choices like clothes, food. . . . It's what they give to refugees. . . . You can't . . . say, 'I don't want that . . . this is what I want'. . . . You got to eat what they give you." The lack of control and limited agency that Liberians experienced in their early days in the

United States brought back memories of the time when they were pushed out of their homes and into refugee camps or other living situations where they lacked control over their daily existence. The struggle to recoup their agency is, therefore, a chief goal and certainly, something they share with other refugees, regardless of race. The lack of autonomy was especially painful for male refugees because of their inability to fulfill their normative gender role as breadwinners (see also Buscher 2017). Wright Talley, who spent over five years with his children in the Buduburam refugee camp, gave insight into why he felt this way: "It's terrible. . . . The life . . . of refugees is not a good thing . . . because when you are in a refugee setting . . . you've lost your prestige. . . . Why? You've lost your income. . . . Once you've lost your income, your family does not . . . depend on you . . . for anything; others give them things. . . . So, at the end of the day, you no longer have dignity. . . . [*chuckles*] You've lost your pride, you lost your income, and your voices are not heard."

But the patronizing of refugees does not stop once they arrive in the United States. Frequently, refugees, including Liberians, have experienced that others, in particular VOLAG staff, treat them as passive victims in need of rescue, which undervalues their resilience—ignoring their past and present agency—and thus has the potential to perpetuate "social dependence and economic marginalization" and hinder their social integration (Portes and Rumbaut 1996, 85). Liberian refugees primarily felt that this accentuated their reliance on aid and in turn evoked images of them as a welfare-dependent economic burden, a common stereotype about Black refugees held by a significant portion of the American population, including the media, and several politicians (Charles 2006; Dawsey 2018). Furthermore, the view that Black refugees are a drain on public resources and the local economy is especially distorted since Black refugees have received significantly less generous resettlement benefits than the earlier waves of refugees from Cuba, Eastern and Central Europe, the FSU, and Southeast Asia (Congressional Research Service 2011).

The experiences of Liberians and other Black refugees is in contrast to many other non-Black refugees who have frequently been portrayed as deserving, honorable refugees (Gold 1992; Haines and Rosenblum 2010; Tang 2015) who are "ideologically American" (Perreault and Paul 2018, 91) and thus have gained an advantage from a "positive context of reception" (Portes and Rumbaut 1996) and more generous welfare benefits. These groups of refugees have benefited from what Tang (2015) calls "refugee exceptionalism"—the worthiness "to be continuously saved" and to receive welfare benefits in contrast to their native-born Black (and non-White Hispanic) neighbors in the "hyperghetto" (Wacquant 2008). However, Tang (2015) does not consider Black refugees when he invokes this term, overlooking their existence and the broader complexity of race within refugee communities.[48] Black refugees, because they are racially indistinguishable from native-born Black Americans who are deemed unworthy of saving, can thus not benefit from this "refugee exceptionalism." This not only highlights that Black refugees' experiences are distinct from those of non-Black refugees but also that they are often overlooked by refugee scholars.

For Black refugees, the overall stigma attached to being a refugee is very burdensome, especially if "every day . . . someone call me a 'damn' refugee,'" as Osiemeo Boye said. In other words, when Liberians are labeled "refugee" by others, such as neighbors, co-workers, or classmates, it is meant to insult them, not to highlight that they have overcome tremendous struggles or stand for "American ideals" as has been emphasized with and by those refugees fleeing Communism. Mr. Boye's experience was not an isolated one; all generations of Liberians have encountered that. Young Liberians, like Keisha Kole, who arrived as children in Staten Island, recalled how their classmates taunted them as "refugee" and "African" interchangeably. This is not surprising that American youth who grew up in the neighborhood thought that refugees were people "who seeked war on America" and thus "associated refugee with something bad," as Comfort Johnson, a grandmother of five, said. Older and middle-aged Liberians, such as Yassah Flomo, who spent fourteen years in different refugee camps in West Africa, described that at their places of work they were insulted as "Liberian . . . Black, African . . . the N-word . . . and refugee" all in one breath.

These experiences already show that for many Liberians, being called "refugee" by others can often feel like any other insult leveled against them. Thus, it is not surprising that they associate the label "refugee" with other stigmatizing labels and stigmatized people. For example, Cynthia Sherif, an Americo Liberian who fled Liberia via Switzerland and ultimately found refuge with an aunt in Staten Island, was vocal about her discomfort with the label refugee: "When I hear that word 'refugee,' I feel like an outcast, like somebody that had nothing. And most of us, we came, we had something but we lost it, but when they use that word, you feel worse than a homeless person, and I think that's kind of degrading for me if used . . . like you're putting somebody down." Her assertion that "refugee" is "worse than homeless" is significant not only because unhoused people are highly stigmatized but also because homelessness is racialized, especially for Black people (May 2015).[49] Furthermore, the term "refugee" reminded Ms. Sherif of another marginalized group: people with cognitive disabilities. This is not a random comparison, since she, like many other Liberians, is very familiar with people who have disabilities through her employment in group homes in New York City. Ms. Sherif articulated why she and other Liberians do not want to be called refugees: "I've worked with the mentally challenged. They've been lobbying for years for the socially correct word to use. . . . Like when I hear somebody call somebody a 'retard,' it takes something out of me, and I feel really bad because she's like labeling that person to be like a 'nothing.' I feel the same way when you call somebody a refugee or call me a refugee, like I'm a nobody. . . . It just sounds so degrading."

These experiences with the racialized stigma around "refugee" explain why many Liberians resent being labeled refugees. This is also reflected in that in over a decade I cannot recall a single event organized by a Liberian group in Staten

Island that had the term "refugee" included. Listen to what Memba Wesseh, who settled with his wife and eight of his children in Staten Island, had to say about his experience when he tried doing just that: "I'm organizing . . . an event for more than 350 Liberians that were living in the Ivory Coast and are now in America. . . . The first thing I called it 'Liberian Ivory Coast Refugee Association in America.' People took offense to that. . . . They talked, 'I'm not a refugee; I don't want to be reminded and . . . seen as poor.' . . . So . . . that's why . . . many Liberian people will not like to be called refugees."

In short, for most Liberians, "refugee" was a vehicle used to escape war and suffering in refugee camps for a better life in the United States. Hence, they concluded that "once they left Ghana . . . they became . . . settlers," as Juah Nimley, a woman of Kru and Americo Liberian descent said.[50] Janjay Waggah further illustrates this belief: "When I heard about coming to America . . . my conclusion was . . . all my suffering days are over. I am not gonna be walking all over with my bare feet no more, I not gonna eat . . . refugee food, I gonna eat American food now. I'm gonna wipe my feet, the dust, the refugee dust from my feet." This was also echoed by Sunday John, a young woman born in Buchanan, Grand Bassa's capital, who felt that Liberians like her "came as refugees" but stopped being refugees once they were in the United States and "stepped forward" by taking advantage of the opportunities this new lease on life presented to them (see also Clarke and Borders 2014). Saah Kandakai, who arrived in Staten Island in 2011, explains this further: "There are a lot of opportunities that the society offer. So, it's like a matter of mind, faith, what . . . you want to be. So, it's . . . about . . . how you want your life to be. . . . It's about your own determination and what you want. . . . If you . . . come over here and just sit and do nothing, that's fine for you, but once you're focused and you know you have an objective, that you have a job to accomplish at [a] certain point in time, you work towards it." It is therefore clear that the majority of Liberians sought to embrace the trope of the successful immigrant and distance themselves from the widespread stereotype of Black people, including Black refugees, as passive (and failed) individuals relying on government handouts.

However, while many Liberian refugees "came here . . . took the opportunity . . . and made something of themselves . . . becoming nurses . . . accountants . . . social worker," as Ms. Sherif stressed, this was not the case for all. There are a plethora of reasons why this occurred. From the outset, the odds have been against Liberian refugees. They found themselves in a place where a quick adaptation to economic self-sufficiency is expected, which is much more difficult to attain for Black, poor, and often illiterate refugees in a highly racialized society (Besteman 2016; Colic-Peisker 2005; Hadley and Patil 2009). VOLAGs and extended family often tried their best to ease the adjustment to their new lives in the United States, but not all Liberians had access to such resources, and these were often destined to fail and remain "suffergees" (a term I describe below). Varney Yarkpolo, who as a former caseworker was intrinsically involved with Liberian refugees' arrival and adjustment to the United States, explained why some prospered and others did not:

> It all depends on how they . . . got the opportunity to come to the States. If they had no relative . . . here . . . other families who felt sorry for them placed them on their list.[51] And . . . as soon as they came to the United States, they told them, "Now you're on your own." Because the agreement was, "I just want you to help me get to the United States; once I enter the United States, I'm going to take care of . . . myself." . . . But when they enter the United States, they found it very difficult. These people found themselves sleeping in hallways and stairways. . . . They had no direction, they had no guardians, they had no relatives to put them on the right path.

Thus, for this group of refugees, distancing from the stigmatized refugee label is very difficult.

"Successful" Liberian refugees who feared that this type of failure tarnishes the reputation of the entire community found harsh words for younger and middle-aged Liberians who remained on public welfare and "failed to succeed." "Suffergee" is one insult that has been used among Liberians. Bernice Richards, who was resettled from the Buduburam refugee camp as a teenager, stated that a "suffergee" denotes a person who continues to suffer and remains dependent on others:

> So, like refugee, "suffergee." . . . Everything negative about that. This is a way of just putting people down. I don't think that's a word people say to somebody's face, but if I say to a friend, "Look at this suffergee," he might laugh because we're friends, but that's a very bad thing to say. It's almost like I'm degrading him. . . . That's what they used to call people in refugee camps; they wouldn't say you're a refugee because everybody's a refugee. . . . I don't care what status you came on but to call somebody a "suffergee" is almost like if somebody was to say amongst Blacks, "Negroes" versus the "N-word." So, a "Negro" would be more, OK, we know we're Negroes, but then when you say the other one even though they might laugh with you, but they also find it offensive and maybe it's a joke because we're saying it to each other so it's OK, but it's that kind of negative word, and they used to say that because people were sick, no food, really struggling.

It should not be lost, though, that Ms. Richards creates an analogy between a term used to insult "unsuccessful" refugees and the most derogatory racist insult hurled at Black people. It indicates that she and other Liberians are keenly aware that they are doubly burdened as Black refugees in the United States.

Consequently, Liberians are very concerned with having too many "suffergees" among them, as they fear this will stigmatize the entire community. They are very cognizant of their usage of welfare benefits, whereas for other refugee groups the use of government support has often been an afterthought (Eckstein 2022; Kasinitz et al. 2008; Tang 2015). Furthermore, some Liberians worry that continued reliance on welfare puts Liberians into the same category as poor native-born Black Americans, from whom they—especially first-generation Liberians—sought to distance themselves at times.

Whether "successful" or "suffergee," most Liberians have another way they can—at least in a legal sense—cease being refugees. U.S. law requires refugees, after they have been physically present in the United States for at least one year, to apply for legal permanent residence—a status that does not expire—also referred to as "adjustment of status." Many Liberians, including Varney Konneh, viewed that in this process they traded in the stigmatized refugee status for "a good status." However, for Liberians who arrived with legal refugee status in the United States or were granted asylum, there is even a more superior status that they often strive for: U.S. citizenship. U.S. citizenship awards a number of benefits, including, but not limited to, voting rights, ease of travel, jury participation, greater protection from deportation, and, often most important for Liberians, avenues to sponsor close family members.

But the path to getting U.S. citizenship is lengthy, complex, and sometimes cost-prohibitive (Aptekar 2015) and fraught with racism (Ryo and Humphrey 2022). This is especially challenging for older illiterate Liberians, most of whom are women, who first have to learn how to read and write before they can even begin to study for the U.S. citizenship exam (Ludwig 2016b). Many have prevailed but then learned that their citizenship was neither the same as that of native-born U.S. citizens, and in particular those who are White. This is what Osiemeo Boye concluded about his U.S. citizenship status: "I am a refugee. . . . They gave me a green card; your status changed to a naturalized citizen, but that doesn't make you feel like . . . a birth citizen; they are not the same. People might say they are the same, but if my citizenship can be revoked and I could be sent home if I do things contrary to the law . . . I could be deported. But the real American, they won't deport them; this is their country." Mr. Boye, like other Liberians, is profoundly aware of his second-class-citizen status that still marks him as different and reminds him of his origins as a refugee and a perennial outsider.

This feeling of not belonging despite being naturalized U.S. citizens is not uncommon among refugees and immigrants (Haines 2010; Hing 2002), but it is intensified for Liberians because of their race. Citizenship in the United States is highly racialized, and Black people, regardless of where they were born, have their Americanness frequently questioned (Du Bois 1994 [1903]; Smith 2015; Treitler 2013). This circumstance, as I discuss in the next chapter, also shapes Liberian refugees' response to anti-Black racism.

BECOMING BLACK REFUGEES AGAINST ALL ODDS

At first glance, it appears that all individuals facing persecution based on the grounds listed in the 1951 Convention have an equal chance to obtain international protection and be selected for resettlement in a country in the Global North. Upon closer examination, as the chapter has shown, this is not the case. Recognition as a refugee often depends on location, including whether one is seeking refuge within one's country of habitual residence or outside. Furthermore, a person's race plays a significant role, as is evidenced by the different avenues (e.g., resettlement priorities and quotas) they have access to, as well as how their testimony and humanity are evaluated by others, namely mainstream society and the U.S. government through its fiduciaries—immigration and asylum officers and judges. These processes are shaped at every level by both structural and individual anti-Black racism with real consequences; African and other Black refugees have been among the least likely to be chosen to be granted permanent refuge in the United States, but even those few who are, are burdened with a racialized stigma that the label "refugee" carries for Black refugees. Exclusion for Black refugees has also been felt in other ways. Generally, Black refugees and asylum seekers have found their most steadfast supporters in the Congressional Black Caucus, which has advocated for increased quotas for African refugees and denounced racial bias in the resettlement policies (Boas 2006; Chisholm 1982); other groups have often remained silent, with a notable exception around the plight of Christian Sudanese refugees, including the "Lost Boys," that was taken up by evangelical Christians (Iversen 2007).[52] Overall, other refugees have received advocacy support from more diverse groups, including sometimes from conservative institutions (Enos 2022; Church World Service 2015; Sobolik 2021). Furthermore, at times other refugees' inclusion in the United States has been framed as beneficial, as they are depicted as and praised for having the "right" attributes and values: being anti-Communist, "ideologically American," and professional, as well as having paid their debt to the United States and, most importantly, not being Black. Thus, any analysis of refugee experiences must account for race and racist policies, as it shows that Black refugees have to overcome unique and additional hurdles and therefore have to assert their agency more in order to secure legal refugee status. At the same time, African and other Black refugees also must work hard to shed the informal label of refugee that is not aligned with any benefits but rather carries a racialized stigma. However, by doing so, Liberian and other Black refugees end up trading one stigmatized label—"refugee"—for another marginalized status in the United States—"Black"/"Black American"—which comes with similar, but also unique challenges and opportunities that are the subject of the following chapters.

5 WHITES ARE THE BOSS

One of the first times I met Maymay Bensing at the IRC's Staten Island office, where I was volunteering at the time, she complained to me about the New York City Sanitation Department. She talked about the citations she received for supposedly disposing of her trash incorrectly, over and over again. "These people are only after Blacks in Staten Island," Ms. Bensing vented, implying that sanitation workers are unfairly singling out predominantly Black neighborhoods. She had called various government offices to try to resolve the issue, to no avail. In the end, she was convinced that she was the target of an anti-Black racist agenda.

Shortly thereafter, she discussed her struggles with getting her daughter into a good middle school. She explained to me that she had been "given the runaround" every time she went to a predominantly White public school, where she was unable to secure a spot for her daughter. Hence, her daughter ended up attending a parochial school where the students are mostly ethnoracial minorities. At borough-wide after-school activities in which her daughter took part, Ms. Bensing frequently encountered White parents of students at the school where she was unable to gain entrance for her daughter. At these events, some of the White parents made snarky comments at the sight of the Black and non-White Hispanic students and their parents. Simultaneously, Maymay Bensing worried about her oldest child, a son, who was in his early teens when he arrived in the United States. He struggled to adjust to life in the United States, neither finishing high school nor fulfilling one of his mother's greatest wishes, for him to earn his GED. In addition, he had several encounters with the police, which Ms. Bensing and he felt were racially motivated.

But not all interactions with White people have been negative for Ms. Bensing and other Liberian refugees. On the contrary, there were times when she reported that native-born White Americans were very receptive to and supportive of her. Most often, Ms. Bensing interacted with these more caring native-born White Americans in the realm of refugee resettlement. For example, she worked for several years for a VOLAG where, like in most other VOLAGs, native-born White Americans held managerial positions. Over time, Ms. Bensing became very friendly with these managers. Whenever she faced an issue or problem, she turned to her White boss at the VOLAG. If this woman could not help her, Maymay Bensing "would try talking to somebody else. . . . Normally the next stop will be [a native-born White American immigration lawyer at the VOLAG] . . . because he's very . . . nice like that, and he . . . explain in details . . . what I should do." Ms. Bensing, along with many other Liberian refugees, concluded that certain White people were quick and willing to assist them because of their refugee status.[1]

Her interactions with native-born White American supervisors also shaped her preference for any potential boss at a job. For example, Maymay Bensing said on several occasions that she would rather be employed by native-born White Americans than others, citing her native-born White American boss at the VOLAG for whom she had worked for several years as the reason. Yet, with time this preference declined. Ms. Bensing now works as a full-time caretaker at a group home where she has frequently experienced racist treatment from both her supervisors and the clients. But up until recently, Ms. Bensing had taken these mistreatments in stride. For example, on weekday mornings when I met her on the Staten Island ferry as I went to work and she was coming back from her night shift in a different New York City borough, she lamented the long commute but quickly added that she had no other choice since she has to provide for her family both here in the United States and in Liberia and save for her retirement. Other times, she reminded me, "You know, I've been through much worse . . . during the war."

Ms. Bensing's experiences with discrimination and anti-Black racism show that she faces them because she lives in a racialized society that "has already subordinated" (Landry 2018, 135) Liberians because Blackness is generally stigmatized and devalued by mainstream (White) American society (Foner 2005).[2] While chapter 4 focuses on direct state racism through refugee resettlement policies, here I detail Liberians' experiences with interpersonal forms of anti-Black racism from landlords, employers, sales clerks, police, and so forth. (Although, as Hirsch (2019, 89) observed, these "interpersonal forms of racism . . . have a relationship with the racism perpetuated by the state.") Maymay Bensing's and other first-generation, and to some extent 1.5-generation, Liberian refugees' responses to and understanding of discrimination is informed by their experiences as refugees and having lived in Liberia. Put differently, Liberian refugees are not ahistorical figures who for the first time encounter discrimination and suffering. What is—to some extent—new for Liberians is their personal encounters with deep-seated, American anti-Black racism.

Thus, this chapter first details settings in which Liberians have experienced anti-Black racism and how this impacts their integration in U.S. society, and then describes and analyzes the varied responses that Liberians have to discrimination. Most discrimination that is targeted at Liberians is because they are Black, and thus they share many experiences that are akin to those of native-born Black Americans and, at times, other Black refugees. On other occasions, anti-Black racism directed at Liberians is intensified when other aspects of their identity (e.g., African/Liberian heritage and refugee status) are also identified. While in some situations Liberians address anti-Black racism head-on, they do not in others. To understand why this is the case, I lay out a theoretical framework—a refugee-specific dual frame of reference—that explains how Liberians contextualize and make sense of the anti-Black racism and discrimination they encounter in the United States. This refugee-specific dual frame of reference is an expansion of the "(positive) dual frame of reference" (Ogbu 1994, 379; Suárez-Orozco and Suárez-Orozco 1994, 130) that has been used to describe and understand why and how immigrants in the United States cope with different forms of discrimination. This extension accounts for experiences that are unique to (Liberian) refugees and thus helps explain why Liberian refugees', and potentially other (Black) refugees', responses to anti-Black racism are often muted.

EXPERIENCING ANTI-BLACK RACISM

Most refugees and immigrants experience animosity, discrimination, and hatred (Foner 2005; Fox and Guglielmo 2012; Ngai 2014). For Black refugees, discrimination must always be viewed through the prism of anti-Black racism. This is evident by evaluating U.S. government policies and immigration/refugee laws (see chapter 4) but also by how "individuals in the USA respond or react towards a refugee based on their skin color," resulting in the frequency of African refugees experiencing discrimination "consistently higher" than other refugee groups (Hadley and Patil 2009, 510–511). This occurs because Black refugees "are . . . placed in subordinate positions because of the unique . . . history of slavery, civil rights abuses, and continued discrimination in the USA" (511; see also Johnson 2016).

Their racialization exposes Black refugees and immigrants to anti-Black racism and discrimination that continue to shape their context of reception and daily lives (Arthur 2000; Nawyn and Gjokaj 2014; Portes and Rumbaut 1996). For Black refugees and immigrants, the other parts of their identities (e.g., ethnicity, nationality, gender) become subsidiary statuses to the master status of race in the United States (Foner 2018; Treitler 2015). Subsequently, Black refugees—from the outset—are saddled with stereotypes and prejudices against them because of their race, which most of the time precludes them from receiving empathy (and resources) that many non-Black refugees have gotten (Current 2008; El-Enany 2016; Tang 2015).[3] But such stereotypes and "discrimination counteract the very purpose of resettlement in the USA . . . [since] discrimination . . . acts to restrict opportunities for . . . general wellbeing" (Hadley and Patil 2009, 505) and have created systemic barriers that have limited Black refugees' "future social mobility" (510). Instead of the promise of refuge, Black refugees trade one "epic struggle" (of war and persecution) for another (anti-Black racism) (Mills 2012, 53). Black refugees and most other Black immigrants frequently encounter stigmatization and discrimination in the housing and labor markets, educational settings, criminal justice system, and public spaces similar to those of native-born Black Americans (Carbado 2005; Crosby and Brazelton 2017).

Being an African refugee in many instances intensifies discrimination and anti-Black racism, since African refugees (and immigrants) also have to deal with unique stereotypes associated with their African heritage. For example, popular images of Africa as the "dark continent" where people are seen as "barbaric," "economically and culturally backward," stricken by famine and poverty, and damaged by violence/war are omnipresent in U.S. media, school curricula, and many American minds (Achebe and Lyons 1998; Bonsu 2009; Traoré 2004). Black African Muslim refugees and immigrants additionally encounter Islamophobia (C. Abdi 2015b; D'Alisera 2004; Guenther et al. 2011). However, at the same time, emphasizing a religious identity has provided some African Muslim refugees and immigrants "an alternative to *Blackness* where identity is concerned" (Vickerman 2007, 156, emphasis in original text; see also Guenther et al. 2011). For example, research has shown that African Muslim refugees and immigrants, in particular women, have employed strategies, such as wearing traditional and/or religious clothing that mark them as Muslim to distance themselves from being part of the Black (American) community and the associated "punitive stereotypes" (Shaw-Taylor and Tuch 2007, 29; see also Abdi 2020; Fábos 2012). Thus, some African Muslim refugees and immigrants may perceive that being seen as Muslim carries less stigma than being Black, especially native-born Black American. Similarly, upper- and middle-class African immigrants and their children have emphasized their ethnic and national origins and class background to distinguish themselves from native-born Black Americans (Imoagene 2017; Kebede 2017), a similarity shared with many Black Caribbean immigrants and refugees (Etienne 2020; Clergé 2019).

For Liberians, accentuating their national origins does not come with the same benefits, as "being Liberian" is in the dominant narrative, especially in places where Liberians live in larger numbers in the United States (e.g., Staten Island, Minneapolis, Philadelphia), is equated with being of lower socioeconomic status, a barbaric and cannibalistic war, refugees, and child soldiers (Hylton 2019; Kamara-Umunna and Feeney 2011; Mullen 2009). In addition, for Liberians, Blackness is very much part of their identity. Recall how Liberia's origins are intrinsically linked to race, and Liberian citizenship is limited to only those who are Black. Thus, the experiences of Liberian refugees in the United States show that race is the modality through which refugeehood, nationality, ethnicity, and gender are lived (S. Hall 1996; Pierre 2004).

While there are differences in how Liberians respond to anti-Black racism and injustices, they all develop various coping mechanisms (Brondolo et al. 2009) and draw on comparisons that contextualize their experiences with anti-Black racism and insults. I theorize these responses in the context of the refugee-specific dual frame of reference, an expansion to the "(positive) dual frame of reference" (Ogbu 1994, 379; Suárez-Orozco and Suárez-Orozco 1994, 130) that immigrants employ to deal with discrimination through evaluating their lives in the United States in terms of the life they knew in their country of origin. When life in the United States becomes unbearable, the economic improvements immigrants experience in the United States and the option of possibly returning to their home countries are some of the main coping mechanisms for dealing with anti-Black racism (Vickerman 1999; Bashi 2007).

This is where Liberians and other refugees differ, since economic considerations are not the main push/pull factor for migration, and going back to their native countries, at least during and in the years immediately after experiencing persecution or a war, is not a viable option. Hence, refugees draw on different experiences to—consciously and unconsciously—contextualize the racism, discrimination, and xenophobia they are subjected to in the United States. Put differently, refugees have a distinct repertoire of experiences, compared to immigrants, that they use to cope with present-day discrimination. Among them are their positive encounters with "nice and helpful Whites"—as referred to by Maymay Bensing—like humanitarian workers whom Liberians and other refugees could call upon for assistance when they were in refugee camps abroad and/or during their initial time in the United States. This is quite different from most immigrants, whose interactions with native-born White Americans are often more limited, since many settle (and work) in immigrant enclaves or ethnic communities (Foner 2005; Iceland 2009).

Liberians, like other refugees, also compare their current circumstances with the intolerance, violence, and (ethnic, religious, political, etc.) persecution they fled (Colic-Peisker 2009, 109). Knowing that they are among the few fortunate ones who were resettled or received asylum while their families were or continue to be in danger contributes to survivor guilt (Potocky-Tripodi 2002) and a "significant and often . . . extensive expectation . . . [to] provide . . . extended family and friends . . . with financial and other forms of support" (Baldassar 2015, 86). Hence, resettled (Liberian) refugees have often felt that they should not complain about the anti-Black racism and hardships they contend with in light of what they regard as the greater suffering of their loved ones. Instead, they endure.

There are two additional comparisons that Liberian refugees make. While the first one is unique to Liberians, the second one applies to a lot of other refugees (and immigrants). Due to the unique history between Liberia and the United States, many Liberians were knowledgeable of past (and present) anti-Black racism, including, but not limited to, slavery, lynching, and Jim Crow laws, and thus expected that they would encounter anti-Black racism in the United States. Finally, Liberians and some other refugees and immigrants do not perceive the United States as their home, in response to a less-than-welcoming context of reception (Portes and Rumbaut 1996) and continued exclusion and, henceforth, do not regard racism in the United States as their fight to take on. While these perspectives shape Liberian responses to U.S. anti-Black racism, they do not protect them from going through it, as the following accounts make clear.

"I DON'T WANT NO AFRICAN . . . NO BLACK PERSON": ENCOUNTERING AMERICAN RACISM

Liberian refugees experience the effects of anti-Black racism, such as being denied better housing because they are Black, being abused at their places of employment because they are Black and Liberian/African, and being harassed by the police, private citizens, and retail clerks because they are Black. The following sections provide details of such experiences among the Liberian refugee community in Staten Island, but these accounts have also been reported in other areas throughout the United States where Liberian refugees and other Black refugees live (Besteman 2016; Reilly 2014; Stepick 1992).

"They Will Never Allow You in That Neighborhood": Housing Discrimination

Residential segregation, and for that matter, hypersegregation is especially felt by Black people in the United States, since this racial group, regardless of nativity or socioeconomic status, is most impacted by it (Clergé 2019; Iceland 2009; Sood et al. 2019). Residential segregation is the direct result of exclusionary discrimination: "*actions and practices that exclude an individual or family from obtaining the housing of their choosing*" (Roscigno et al. 2009, 52, emphasis in original text). These actions and practices are frequently interrelated with nonexclusionary discrimination, defined as "*discriminatory actions and practices that occur within* [or because of] *an already established housing arrangement*" (52, emphasis in original text). Liberians in the United States have experienced both because many of them have lived in the Park Hill neighborhood in Staten Island and in other predominantly Black neighborhoods in Philadelphia (Haddow 2015) and Minneapolis (Reilly 2014). The neighborhood stigma stems not only from the high crime rates in Park Hill that marked the 1980s, 1990s, and early 2000s, but also from mainstream society, which frequently views poor Black neighborhoods as hotbeds of violence and poverty (E. Anderson 2011; Wilson 2012) and/or "ghettos" (Ludwig 2016b).

These stereotypes then also inform how individuals from these stigmatized neighborhoods are treated by others, including, but not limited to, which services they (do not) provide for residents (Besbris et al. 2015; Roscigno et al. 2009). Oman Zumo, an informal community leader who arrived in the United States in 1986, described such an experience: "In the early '90s, I remember buying a carpet from . . . Fox Floors. . . . The guy said, 'Sir, we will deliver for you.' I said, "Good.' 'What's the address?' '____ Park Hill Avenue.' 'Are you kidding me? I'm never gonna deliver down there. . . . I don't want the business. . . . I may be mugged. . . . I can't deliver the carpet.'" Even though this incident dates back to the 1990s, similar instances still occur today.[4] For example, Lemon Angel, a young, native-born Black American woman who lives in Park Hill and works part-time for a Staten Island restaurant, shared how the management created a list of "no-delivery-zone neighborhoods," which included Park Hill and other predominantly Black neighborhoods in Staten Island.

Understandably, these nonexclusionary discrimination experiences coupled with the neighborhood's vices have compelled Liberians to leave Park Hill for more desirable and safer neighborhoods. Yet, moving from Park Hill is often not easy. In addition to other obstacles, such as limited financial resources, anti-Black racism is a main reason why Liberians have difficulty renting or buying homes in other parts of Staten Island, especially in the more prosperous South Shore. Most Liberian refugees are keenly aware that a lot of native-born White Staten Islanders will neither rent nor sell to them. For example, this is what Oman Zumo, who began house hunting in the late 1990s after living for years in Park Hill, which he called "the worst place in Staten Island," had to say about the process: "If you wanna buy a house . . . you're not allowed. God forbid! . . . How could you buy a land in certain parts of Staten Island being a Black guy? It doesn't matter you are African, Caribbean, African American. . . . Even the real estate man will tell you, 'I'm not going to sell you a house there. They will never allow you in that neighborhood.'"

Mr. Zumo is cognizant that anyone who is racialized as Black—regardless of their nationality or ethnicity—is likely to encounter discrimination in the housing market. Hence, it is not surprising that other Liberians who have been striving to secure better housing outside of Park Hill for their families had similar experiences. Zaiway Paye, a middle-aged single mother, recalled how she was received by White Staten Island landlords when she inquired about renting from them: "You go to a community to look for a place to live. You're Black . . . they have the place. They say, 'No, I'm not giving my place to this person.' And you know . . . you can tell . . . that they don't want you to be there. . . . They . . . look at me ugly. Or they will say, 'Oh this person is not of our type.'" Liberians have proof to back up these allegations, as several of them observed that after being told that the house/apartment was already rented, they called again "two weeks later," as Garsuah Janjay, a man in his sixties, said, only to find out "that the vacancy is still there." This was also echoed by 1.5-generation Liberian Americans, such as Sam Collins, who went to look at an apartment in the early 2000s only to be told by a surprised landlord that he neither has a Liberian "accent nor . . . even sound Black" and that he would not rent the place to him. In other words, had the potential landlord already detected that Mr. Collins was Black when he first inquired about the property, he would not have even met with him. Indeed, Massey and Lundy (2001, 466) found that rental agents discriminated against would-be leasees if they inferred based on "accent, grammar, and diction" that they are Black.

It is not just private landlords who discriminate against Liberians and other Black people; public housing authorities (Chandler 1992), including the New York City Housing Authority (Marwell 2009; Pear 1992), have a history of doing so. Sunday John experienced this firsthand when she sought to move out of her grandmother's crowded apartment in Park Hill, where many family members lived after arriving from the Buduburam refugee camp. She described what occurred: "I . . . experienced . . . housing discrimination. . . . You apply for an apartment . . . they look at your color and . . . decide where you should live. . . .

So . . . there're certain places that you—a Black person— . . . can't live. . . . I can remember when I applied . . . for—I think—Dongan Hill. . . . She said, 'Oh no only . . . Stapleton . . . is available for you.'" In the end, Ms. John had no choice but to accept an apartment in the Stapleton Houses in Staten Island's North Shore; its racial makeup and crime level reflect that of Park Hill. This is in stark contrast to the Berry Houses in Dongan Hills, a majority White area.

However, Liberians who succeeded in renting apartments or houses in predominantly lower-income White neighborhoods in Staten Island have endured anti-Black racism in different ways. Among them is Maymay Bensing, who was introduced at the beginning of this chapter. She now owns a house in West Brighton, a more ethnoracially diverse North Shore neighborhood, but prior to this she rented a home in a neighborhood with mostly native-born White Staten Islanders, who made her the target of their racist views and actions. Ms. Bensing remembers these difficult days: "We were like the only Black family. . . . The neighbors call the police and say that . . . my kids are sitting at home because they thought we used to leave our kids by themselves. So, constantly the police used to ring our door and say, 'Ma'am we got 911 call from this apartment stating that you got a sick . . . kid in the apartment.' And I'm like, 'We didn't call you, we didn't call 911, nobody is sick here.' The police come, enter the apartment, check the apartment . . . until I noticed that our neighbor was doing this."

"Customers . . . Say Bad, Hurtful Words": Employment Discrimination

Living in Park Hill not only limits the types of services Liberians can access but also their chances in the labor market—another nonexclusionary discrimination (Roscigno et al. 2009). Frequently, would-be employers discriminate against (Black) job seekers who come from disenfranchised and "bad" neighborhoods because they themselves "are viewed as possessing the moral liability of the neighborhood itself" (Sampson and Raudenbush 2004, 321; see also Neckerman and Kirschenman 1991). Liberians, such as Cynthia Sherif, who stayed with her aunt in Park Hill for the first couple of years after she arrived in the United States, are very much aware that living in a "high-crime neighborhood" means that employers stereotype them and question if they "can trust this person." Stereotypes about Park Hill and the people who live there are perpetuated by articles in the local newspaper, the *Staten Island Advance*, which has often portrayed the entire community as drug dealers, criminals, and welfare abusers. Online, such articles were usually accompanied by a slew of hateful comments that refer to native-born Black Americans and Africans in racist and vile language and characterize immigrants in the community as undocumented, despite the fact that the majority have legal status.[5] Generally no distinctions are made between native- and foreign-born residents, thus contradicting Holtzman's (1999, 86) claim that "African Americans [are] often . . . [portrayed] as a dangerous, criminal ignorant underclass. In contrast . . . Africans . . . are often seen as simple, pious people who are particularly in need, and deserving of our assistance."

Stereotypes have made it particularly difficult for younger Liberian refugees to find jobs. This is also something that Eva McGovern, a native-born White American who worked with refugee youth, including in Staten Island, for several years, observed: "An address in Park Hill, a lot of people are not going to hire you." Sam Collins encountered this when he was a teenager in the 1990s and sent out resumes that listed his Park Hill address: "I'm in high school . . . a sixteen-year-old kid trying to get a job. I go . . . everywhere and I can't understand why no one is hiring me. . . . It was frustrating not having a job, and that's the hardest thing. . . . Because of the racism or the segregated nature of the island."

But it is not just the Park Hill address that causes difficulties for Liberians in the labor market; some of this is related to obtaining a job, while other challenges pertain to the experiences on the job itself. As Black people, Liberian refugees enter a racialized labor market where they are discriminated against (Hadley and Patil 2009; Lamont et al. 2016). But unlike other Black immigrants, in particular English-speaking Caribbeans who are reported to receive preferential treatment over native-born Black Americans when they emphasize their national/ethnic/immigrant background (Vickerman 1999; Waters 1999), this is not the case for most African refugees and immigrants, with the notable exceptions of (upper) middle-class, (second-generation) Nigerian immigrants (Imoagene 2017). Actually, some scholars, such as Showers (2015a, 1817), have noted that an African heritage places African immigrants and refugees "at the bottom of the stratified racial systems at work," lower than Black Caribbean immigrants and native-born Black Americans. Thus, it is unsurprising that several Liberians, including Zaiway Paye, reported that they were treated worse than native-born Black Americans. Ms. Pay said, "Sometimes there are some bosses would treat you differently. . . . You know that they are treating you differently. . . . Because some things . . . Black American would do . . . would get away. When you do it, you get smashed up. Yeah. It happens."

Despite the heightened discrimination due to their Liberian heritage, race, and refugeehood, data show that Liberians, like Black African immigrants and refugees as a group, have higher labor force participation rates than both native-born White and Black Americans (Hamilton 2019).[6] Labor markets are not just racialized, they are also gendered, and thus employment outcomes for Black women and men—regardless of their nativity—are different.[7] Black men find it harder to secure employment (Nawyn and Gjokaj 2014; Pager 2007) for a variety of reasons, mostly related to structural anti-Black racism, normative gender expectations, and stereotypes. This also plays out in the Liberian refugee community, where women have higher employment rates than Liberian men (Capps et al. 2015; Hamilton 2019), a pattern that mirrors that of native-born Black Americans and several other Black immigrant groups (Hamilton 2019, 110, 121). However, employment does not mean equal wages. Overall, African refugees tend to earn less than African immigrants from countries such as Nigeria, Kenya, and Ghana (Elo et al. 2015; Hamilton 2019), a reflection of the fact that, generally, refugees arrive with lower human capital than immigrants (Elo et al. 2015).[8]

So, what explains this overall high employment rate of Liberian refugees? For many Liberians, including Saah Kandakai, Maymay Bensing's husband, "the assumption is . . . America is like bread and butter, all is good, all is honey," meaning that they "have a more favorable view of U.S. labor market opportunities than the U.S.-born" (Hamilton 2019, 139). But conceivably more important is that refugees have to accept jobs, including those that they do not like, in order to be economically self-sufficient—the cornerstone of the USRAP.

Most Liberians who have experienced anti-Black racism (and xenophobia) when looking for work are cognizant that they were discriminated against because they are Black and/or Liberian refugees (Hadley and Patil 2009; Ludwig 2016c) and that this is against the law. Wright Talley, who was resettled in Staten Island in 2003, illustrates this in his description of his forays into the job market:

> You go to a place of employment and you see a big sign, "Our agency is nondiscriminatory. We are here for everybody, whatever sex, creed." But deep down you realize three persons putting in an application and you are not the favorite, you're out, despite your qualification. . . . Take myself for example; I've been in America now for the several years, and you realize that there were some places I applied and people that applied along with me. When you look at their resume, you realize that I've an edge. . . . But at the end of the day . . . I'm not even called. . . . And then the next day, the person of their color will be . . . working. . . . I realize that I'm being pushed . . . aside. . . . So then, I consider it as indirect discrimination against me, you see. But because it's not open, I cannot prove it, make an issue against you.

Although, Mr. Talley notes, the potential native-born White American employers' actions are illegal, due to the covert nature of this discrimination, he feels he had no recourse because he would not be able to prove it in a court of law.

At times, Liberian refugees have not even tried to apply for certain jobs because either fellow Liberians had advised them against it or they assumed they would not be hired. Maymay Bensing was discouraged in this way. When she arrived in Staten Island, her mother and siblings assisted her in adjusting to a new society. Since they had been in the United States since the 1980s, they felt they were able to steer Ms. Bensing to jobs most open to hiring Black and African refugee women. Ms. Bensing said, "In the beginning . . . I didn't have any idea. I only depended on my family. In Liberia . . . I did airline ticketing . . . when I came I only wanted to work . . . as a agent. . . . I was told that only White people work with the airlines. . . . My mom, my sisters, they're like, 'Airlines? You just came. They . . . want White people, American people.' . . . And instead . . . [relatives' names] introduce me to the home health aide." When Ms. Bensing became a home health aide, she joined a profession in which Black women—compared to their percentage of the overall population—are overrepresented (Landes and Weng 2020). Indeed, jobs as caregivers have been held disproportionately by Black women—Americans, immigrants, and refugees alike (T. M. Brown 2011; Foner 2005).

Despite this, Liberian refugees still faced problems getting hired as home health aides. Enid Browning, who worked in the office of a home health aide agency in Staten Island and in the process—as described in chapter 3—helped a lot of Liberians obtain jobs, observed that Liberians were more commonly targets of discrimination than other immigrants because they faced anti-Black racism from both (would-be) employers and clients. Since there was no ethnic labor market/network that could have facilitated employment and protection from discrimination (Waldinger 1996), Ms. Browning intervened when she saw others who mistreated and overlooked Liberian job applicants: "Somebody else had interviewed . . . [a Liberian woman], and they wouldn't hire her because they said they couldn't understand her, her accent was so thick. . . . I personally took an offense to that because I see the Spanish . . . all come in and with very, very thick accent you can barely understand, but . . . they get hired."[9] Most likely, the "thick Liberian accent" was just a ruse to hide the employer's bias against Black (refugee) applicants, which is not surprising given that research has found that native-born White American employers often prefer to hire Hispanic (immigrant) workers of different racial backgrounds over Black employees (Marrow 2011; Waldinger and Lichter 2003).

At the same time, it is worth noting that while many Liberians speak Indigenous languages, almost all Liberians in the United States speak Liberian English and standardized English. Nevertheless, a large number of Liberians reported that they were discriminated against, as Ms. Browning observed, because of their accent. Creese (2011, 17) refers to this process as the "erasure of linguistic capital" for English-speaking African refugees and immigrants. For example, Beatrice Akoi told me how her Liberian accent kept her from performing certain tasks at her part-time job at a fast food restaurant in Staten Island when she was a college student. After experiencing insults related to the way she spoke, Ms. Akoi stopped operating the intercom in the drive-through and the cash register since she was "scared [when] customers get mad when they don't understand and . . . say bad, hurtful words" to her. When I asked her what these hurtful words were, she replied, "Monkey, refugee . . . n——, African, go back to Africa." Other African immigrants also reported having been discriminated against based on their "distinct African accents," which identify them as foreign and African, and this has "led to further discrimination in addition to their race" (Showers 2015b, 1822).

Just as Beatrice Akoi was subjected to racial and xenophobic slurs at her job, so have many Liberian refugees who work as home health aides for White and other non-Black Staten Islanders. Sometimes this occurs even before the Liberian home health aide is able to enter the home of a client, as Memba Wesseh, a former caseworker, shared: "Somebody just called me three days ago. . . . [Name of Liberian refugee] works as a home health aide. . . . This White lady . . . told her she didn't want . . . [name of Liberian refugee] in her house. . . . She didn't stop; she even called the cops. . . . They said, 'But the lady is helping you.' And she said, 'No, I don't want no African, I don't want no Black person in my house.'" This also frequently happens to Liberians who, like Garmuyou Dyemene, work in an assisted living facility. Mr. Dyemene started this job a little less than two years after he arrived in the United States. Since then he has had his share of racist encounters, which led him to conclude that "residents are very racist. . . . They say like, 'I don't like no Black person to touch me; I don't want to talk to you; I don't want you to come around.'" It is rather common for Black health care professionals to have been told that a non-Black patient/client does not want to be cared for and thus touched by them (Olayiwola 2016; Showers 2015a). However, it does not stop there. Discrimination and abuse take different forms. For example, Gloria Adams worked as a home health aide during her initial years in the United States while she was waiting on her asylum decision. She described how a native-born White American client's family assigned her "a chair . . . without the cushion" where she had to sit "for twelve hours . . . only to get out if the client needed . . . assistance for something." Furthermore, Ms. Adams was given her "own spoon and cup" so she would "not use theirs." She concluded that the "people treated" her like "a slave" because she was also "not allowed to sit on a good chair" like she is "not good enough."

Hence, Liberian refugees came to see that racial stratification in today's American society has not changed much and has kept "Whites," as Zaiway Paye said, "thinking they are superior . . . because they are the boss." As in the past, Black people today, including Liberians, are taunted by racial slurs, which include, as Garmuyou Dyemene and others said, being "called the N-word." Additionally, Liberians, as other Africans, are insulted with comments that target their African heritage, which others link to "the wild," "the jungle," "monkeys," and "running around naked" (Imoagene 2015; Kebede 2017; Showers 2015a).

"They Gonna Shoot You Right Here": Interactions with the Police

While many non-Black people only started to realize, as a result of the recent invigorated Black Lives Matter protests, the extent of anti-Black racism and police brutality (Embrick 2015), for Liberians this is something they either had already anticipated prior to arriving in the United States or quickly had to learn as they (were re)settled in the United States. Carbado (2005) refers to this process of learning and experiencing racial profiling (by the police) as "racial naturalization." In these encounters with the police, Liberians and most other Black refugees and immigrants "are included in the vortex of fear since they are placed into the racial category of Black" (Crosby and Brazelton 2017, 111). Subsequently, they are often treated similar to native-born Black Americans. Thus, it is evident that in these situations neither their ethnicity nor foreign-born status matters, as they are just seen as "Black" (B. H. Ellis et al. 2020; V. S. Johnson 2016). High-profile murders of African refugees and immigrants at the hands of the police just underscore this.[10] But there are also differences that are discussed in the following chapter.

Hence, it is not unexpected that many Liberians recognize the systemic nature of police harassment of and discrimination against Black people in the United States (Embrick 2015). For example, when I first asked Bernice Richards, who came to the United States in 1996, if she ever experienced racism, she replied, “Honestly, no . . . unless you wanna explore police brutality, but that . . . happens pretty much in every minority neighborhood.” She then proceeded to recount how her brother, a New York City police officer himself, had been profiled and stopped by White police officers in Staten Island. Ms. Richards was one of the few Liberian women who discussed police brutality, which otherwise was a topic that appeared to be more at the forefront of Liberian men’s minds. This, of course, is not surprising given the national discourse on police brutality over the last decade, which tends to focus on male Black victims, frequently overlooking female Black victims (Crenshaw 2011; Larson 2016).

Staten Island’s North Shore had several incidents of abuse by the police. The most notorious act of violence is the murder of Eric Garner in 2014. Another example is the native-born White Staten Island police officer who was caught arresting Black people on false accusations in 2011 (Donnelly 2012).

One afternoon early in my research, I had a chance encounter with some police officers. On that particular summer day, I was having lunch with Sam Collins in a North Shore neighborhood. While we were talking, his car, which was parked across from the restaurant where we were, was stolen. We called 911 and the closest precinct to report the theft, but it took more than two hours for a police patrol car to come. In the meantime, an acquaintance of Mr. Collins located the vehicle; however, valuables, including expensive technical equipment, were missing. When the police officers, both White, finally arrived, they slowly wrote down the information. I took the opportunity to talk with the reluctant officers about the Liberian community in Staten Island. It soon became clear that they had a very low opinion of Liberian refugees. Once they learned that Mr. Collins, whose case they were working on, is also Liberian, one replied perplexed, “But he does not have an accent and not a high-pitch screaming voice like they all do.” When asked about their impression of Park Hill, they said, “Stuff happens there all the time, shootings and things like that.” However, this does not reflect the reality of the decline in violence in the neighborhood in the past twenty years. But the continued perception of the neighborhood as a violent place explains why there were, as Liberian refugees reported, targeted frisking and policing of the residents of Staten Island’s North Shore, including Park Hill.

New York City Police Department data for the last decade indicate that the 120th Precinct (North Shore) has not only been among those with the highest number of stops (and frisks) but also had one of the highest proportions of innocent people who were stopped out of the entire city. Furthermore, in the 123rd Precinct, which encompasses the Whitest part of Staten Island, almost a quarter of all those who were stopped were either Black or Hispanic of any race (New York Civil Liberties Union 2019; 2022). Liberians have many tales about police harassment and brutality. Take the example of Wannie Jacobs’s brother, who is in his mid-twenties and no longer lives with his parents and siblings in Park Hill but visits them. When he does, he has to be mindful of the police.

Ms. Jacobs recalled, "Just about one month ago, the cop came and . . . beat on this door [points to the entrance door]. [Brother's name] . . . was coming . . . every day to eat because mom cooks. . . . They grab him . . . and asked whether he live here. . . . He was shedding tears; he was pissed off. . . . They saw his picture on the wall everything. . . . We tell them, 'He's family. . . . he eat here . . . come and watch TV, basketball game.' . . . They left him. They pushed him on the wall again; he got bruises all over him. . . . We didn't take no action against it. . . . So, that's how we live here."

Another example of police harassment involves Osiemeo Boye and his son, reflecting how young and middle-aged Liberian men are more likely to be stopped and interrogated by the police. One day, after Mr. Boye was picked up by his son from his job, they were stopped by the police:

> Sometimes the police see you in a car, they pull you over like my son, who got . . . dreadlocks. One night . . . I told him to pick me up. . . . It was raining . . . a cop drove behind us . . . he pull us over and . . . said, "Can I have the license?" My son gave him his license and then he's asking me for my license. I'm in the passenger seat. He said he want my license; I told him, "I'm not the driver, he's the driver, he gave you his license. Why you need my license?" I show him my job ID. He said, "No, I want your state ID." I give it to him and he went back in the car. . . . He asks me, "Where are you from? . . . Who is this? . . . You know what I pulled you over for? . . . Your taillight is not working." I said, "But how do I know my taillight is not working, it's behind me. So, even if you pull me over and tell me look, your light is not working, can you fix it, that makes sense." . . . He says, "Can I ask you guys to step down . . . check the car for drugs?" I said, "What drugs? . . . Since I was born, I never even smoke. . . . So, you wanna check it, you can check it." My son was mad. I tell him, "Look, calm down. . . . Don't . . . do anything because you have dreadlocks."

Fortunately, neither Mr. Boye nor his son was physically harmed during this encounter. This experience also reveals the different responses among Liberian refugees; while the older Mr. Boye was questioning the logic of the police officer, the younger Mr. Boye was understandably upset and also feared more for his life, since research found that police officers are more likely to use force against Black people who have dreadlocks, cornrows, afros, or braids (Dabney et al. 2017) and/or have more Afrocentric features (e.g., darker skin) (Eberhardt et al. 2006); the latter applies to most Indigenous Liberians. Knowing that police are even more prejudiced against Black people with dreadlocks, Osiemeo Boye had tried to convince his son to "cut that hair." Since his son does not want to do that, his father continues to remind him, "Be careful . . . dress good; when they ask you, don't hesitate, give them the ID, anything they say cooperate with them because they gonna shoot you right here and say you jump them; they will lie . . . and your life will be gone." However, as it is well documented, compliance does not mean Black people are safe from the police. In light of these occurrences, some parents, such as Winnifred Fassah, a Kissi woman who fled Liberia with her family, worry about their children and ask themselves, "Why did I come here? I think it was better I stayed back home."

But it is not just the police that Liberian refugees fear. Many also worry about immigration officials. Not only have I been witness to frantic calls that Liberian parents have had with each other after one of their children got caught up in a scuffle or with the wrong crowd and faced a deportation hearing, but I have also seen the outcome when I have served as a Liberia country conditions expert for deportation hearings throughout the United States. Liberians' fears are well-founded, as data show that "immigrants of African descent are more likely to be detained and deported than any other group" (McKanders 2019, 20). Furthermore, Black refugees and immigrants have a higher probability of being deported on criminal grounds than other immigrants.[11] Thus, when on a Sunday in August several years ago, the police, dressed in uniforms and plain clothes, entered the private premises of 55 Bowen Street, where community members, among them many older Liberian women, had gathered for a barbecue, they panicked. The police officers, who were all White, demanded to see everyone's ID. Shortly thereafter, rumors started to emerge in the community that the police had cross-checked their IDs with the U.S. Department of Homeland Security's data bank. And while in the end it was confirmed that this actually did not happen, it frightened Liberian refugees in Staten Island, especially since there was an uptick in arrests and deportations of Liberians during the first Trump administration, which only has intensified during the second term.[12]

Over time, some Liberians have become much more outspoken about racial profiling and police brutality, which is consistent with what the literature reports about the racial socialization of immigrants and refugees (Treitler 2015). Although many older and middle-aged Liberians, like Maymay Bensing, have at times felt that there is little to be done about it because, as she said, "The justice system is blind and rude" and rather supports and represents "another modern form of slavery." Her less-than-optimistic views about the state of American anti-Black racism and the chances for true equity and equality reflect that of the majority of Black people in the United States (Horowitz et al. 2019).

"You Aren't Supposed to Be There": Anti-Black Racism in Public Places

The nature of public spaces is also what creates the biggest danger for Liberian refugees and other Black people because there, they have "the least protection against overt discriminatory behavior, including violence" (Feagin 1991, 102). Liberians experience "street discrimination" when they "are . . . in informal situations in public spaces" (Colic-Peisker 2009, 179) and exposed to strangers who "react primarily on the basis of one ascribed characteristic" (Feagin 1991, 102), such as race, a foreign accent (Colic-Peisker 2009), and/or traditional African clothing. There is, of course, a direct link between the above-discussed racial profiling and police harassment and brutality faced by Black people on (and off) American streets (Crosby and Brazelton 2017; Embrick 2015).

In addition to discrimination by the police that may have been brought about when White or other non-Black people call to "report" Black people for simply existing (Gutsche et al. 2022; McNamarah 2018), racism and discrimination in public spaces occurs in many different settings and forms (Lamont et al. 2016), including on public transportation. Although it should be noted that, because of Staten Island's geography, demographic makeup, and limited public transportation, interracial encounters on public transportation occur less frequently than they do in other New York City boroughs. Nevertheless, they remain significant, especially for the many Liberian refugees who do not own cars. Desai Kpoe Monbello, who was resettled in Staten Island with several of her grandchildren, noticed that some White straphangers on New York City buses in Staten Island refuse to sit next to Liberians because "they don't want to touch Black skin." She was not alone in this observation. Love Juah, who joined her husband in 2009, detailed what transpires when she commutes to and from work: "There are a lot of people that still have . . . racism in them. Like . . . on the bus. . . . Certain people will not want to sit . . . or . . . stand beside you; they get up and walk off. . . . Or even on the train or on the ferry, certain people come, they sit, they look, they get up from there, and they go elsewhere." More often than not, Liberians try to ignore these racist behaviors. Other times, to cope, they may, like Annie Quide, who works as a home health aide, put a positive spin on it and rationalize, "I don't care. You can get up. I got the whole seat to myself. I can lay my head back and relax."

In addition to public transportation, Liberian refugees are often also subjected to anti-Black racism in places of consumption, such as the Staten Island Mall, where, from time to time, scribblings of racist slurs have been found on the bathroom stalls. On one of her trips to the mall, Wannie Jacobs lamented how she and her friend were subjected to racial profiling:

> We experience it every day, like when we walk into a store like we get followed because . . . they feel like . . . you know, the stereotype. There's so many . . . stereotypes . . . in America so . . . we get stereotyped as . . . to commit a crime. . . . We went into a store . . . are followed and the lady was acting like she wasn't following us, but . . . once we move to another rack the lady will follow and be like a rack or two away acting like she's like looking, you know through the clothes, but she was actually following us until we got out of the store. . . . She wasn't following anybody else in the . . . store.

Racial stereotypes that perpetuate Black people as shoplifters (and criminals) then lead to excessive surveillance (Alexander 2010; Lamont et al. 2016), like the one Ms. Jacobs described. She did not call out the person's racist behavior and just left.

More often Liberian women elect this type of response. Among men, the reactions vary a bit more; while many generally also walk away, Liberian men who are older, have more formal education, have been in the United States longer, or have some form of leadership role in the community report that they give a verbal response. Among them was Oman Zumo, who has decades of experience with anti-Black racism, including the example that I provided earlier about the carpet that was not being delivered to his home. Several years ago, he went to a pizzeria in an Italian American neighborhood in Staten Island and encountered what Feagin (1991, 105) labels a "modern discrimination," which, in contrast to "the 'No Negroes' exclusion of the recent past, [is a] rejection in the form of poor service" (see also Lamont et al. 2016):

> I was with two of my kids and two other kids, and that one hurt me more. I ordered pizza, I paid in advance. . . . More than six other people came after me; they were all served. . . . I walked to the desk and said, "I'm still waiting." "Sir, you have to wait some more; if you can't wait, take the money and buy it somewhere else." I said, "No, I'm here now, so I will wait." "You got a long time to wait," [the pizzeria employee responded]. . . . I got upset . . . said, "You will not serve another person till you give my pizza." I think he thought it was a joke, but I meant it. . . . I didn't leave that counter. I said, "You're not giving anybody food here and I'm not taking my money." . . . I continued to stand there. . . . He brought the food . . . and I didn't eat the food. . . . Racism has been very, very high here . . . on the island.

Whereas the pizzeria employee passive-aggressively conveyed to Mr. Zumo that he was not welcome in the restaurant, other White people are more vocal and forthcoming with their racist views. For example, Annie Quide and her Liberian friends have been told when they were in a predominantly White neighborhood that they should "know they aren't supposed to be there."

MAKING SENSE OF AMERICAN RACISM: REFUGEE-SPECIFIC DUAL FRAME OF REFERENCE

If we accept a normative argument of fairness, meaning that racism and inequality are unfair and unjust, many would expect Liberian refugees to respond by chastising and confronting those who have offended them. However, often this is not the case. The reasons for this vary but include cultural, gender, and class differences in how emotions are expressed (Hilario et al. 2019; Lamont et al. 2002) and are also influenced by English language skills, length in the United States, immigrant generation (first vs. second), personality, and when and where they are discriminated against. Other times, Liberian refugees contrast what they are now experiencing in the United States to past and present-day Liberia, relying on the refugee-specific dual frame of reference to cope with and make sense of what is happening.

This refugee-specific dual frame of reference shapes Liberians' responses along a range from direct confrontation to reluctant endurance of discrimination, as noted in the accounts in the previous section. Research has shown that withdrawal from racial harassment is very common as a "confrontation response is . . . costly in terms of time and energy" (Feagin 1991, 106). The cost may also extend to losing a job. For example, Liberian refugees working as caregivers have been, as Garmuyou Dyemene said, "taught by their bosses to be calm . . . not to take things personal." Liberians' behavior is also reflective of an "asymmetrical 'deference ritual' in which blacks . . . [are] expected to respond to discriminating whites with great deference" (Feagin 1991, 102) and which leads to a "resigned acceptance" (103) and realization that native-born White Americans continue to hold power, including withholding a paycheck—one that Liberians desperately need to support themselves and their loved ones near and far. So instead of "exchanging words" with such racist clients and supervisors that could jeopardize her job, Elizabeth Kamara, who supported her three children for years on a home health aide salary, simply thought to herself when her clients disparaged her by insinuating that as a Liberian/African she "sleeps in the tree . . . is a monkey," that "I know I'm not a monkey, I don't sleep in no tree." (Nevertheless, it should not be lost that anger suppression has been shown to have adverse health effects on Black people [Brondolo et al. 2009].)

"They Have Been So Nice to Us": Native-Born White Americans in the Refugee System

Often, the first White people, including native-born White Americans, many refugees encounter are members of the Peace Corps, teachers and staff in missionary schools, and/or aid workers in IDP/refugee camps and VOLAGs.[13] Bernice Richards's life story is exemplary of this. After spending several years in the Buduburam refugee camp, Ms. Richards was reunited as a teenager with her mother in Brooklyn through the P3 program and thus became connected to a VOLAG's youth program, which was managed by a native-born White American woman. After graduating with an associate's degree, Bernice Richards started an after-school program for Liberian youth in Staten Island. Her organization was one of two that received assistance from the VOLAG under a capacity-building grant that was managed by the same native-born White American woman whom Ms. Richards had met several years prior. She was grateful for the support her fledgling organization had obtained and said, "Caucasian people really love . . . Africans," and therefore, she personally "really do feel loved." At least she felt that this applied in this situation, as she, as detailed earlier, also acknowledged the widespread police brutality that Black people face.

Through experiences like Ms. Richards's, refugees often "created a positive image of caring, selfless, and generous [White] Americans" (Haddow 2015, 60). "American," for Liberians, like many others in the Global South, means White unless otherwise specified (Lipsitz 1998, 1). Subsequently, humanitarian aid, protection, nationality, and Whiteness become conflated, as often many Black, Indigenous, and people of color who work in these contexts are overlooked, and only White people are equated with being providers and protectors (Puar 1996). For example, Holzer (2015) details how Liberian refugees in the Buduburam refugee camp in Ghana blamed any misfortune on the Ghanaian UNHCR officials and credited the American UNHCR officials as sources of support.

Furthermore, the fact that the lines between those who deliver aid and those who review and decide on refugees' applications for resettlement are blurred complicates things. To make this more explicit, employees of the same organization, such as the IRC, provide food, shelter, clothing, and so forth in the camps and work alongside U.S. government officials to identify refugees eligible for resettlement in the United States. Such a setting creates an asymmetrical social hierarchy between refugees and humanitarian aid workers and, by extension, the U.S. government, making evident who "the saviors" with power are versus "the victims" in need of protection (Harrell-Bond 2002). Not surprisingly, many Liberian refugees express gratitude for having been resettled; among them is Janjay Waggah, who came with eleven of her family members to Staten Island in 1998. She exclaimed, "We want to tell God, 'Thank you . . . for America and the Americans.' They have been so nice to us. They did a very good job for the Liberians, the refugees. . . . I want to thank them so much for welcoming us in their country. . . . Oh my God, I don't know how to thank them; they did a lot for us. . . . The American government . . . they are very nice people."

Since, as just described, Americans are understood as "White," most Liberians believe that it was (exclusively) native-born White Americans who enabled them to come to the United States. This is not accurate, since the USRAP is funded by tax dollars, which are paid by all people living in the United States—regardless of their race.

In addition, only a handful of Liberians were aware that resettlement of African refugees to the United States has consistently been lower compared to that of refugees from all other geographical regions. Furthermore, it was actually the Congressional Black Caucus that lobbied heavily for U.S. military intervention in Liberia, Sudan, and Haiti in the 1990s (Eager 2011) and an increase in the number of African refugees admitted to the United States (Boas 2006). Despite this, a lot of Liberians, including Varney Yarkpolo, a former refugee resettlement caseworker, recalled that in his VOLAG, "White Americans . . . were very receptive . . . sympathetic to the Liberians' cause. They felt bad for them . . . coming from a war-torn country and all." But the emphasis of African refugees as "psychologically damaged by pre-settlement experiences" is problematic as it "goes hand in hand with paternalism that is motivated by 'good intentions' to 'help' Africans" (Essed 1991, 203 cited in Majavu 2017, 37). While there are certainly many White humanitarian workers who truly care, others can also be motivated by a "White savior" complex, "White guilt" (Bell 2013),[14] or "an obligation that 'whites' have towards 'blacks' [for] what they plundered from Africa" (Abu-Sada 2012, 45).

Concurrently, it is important to point out that these native-born White Americans in humanitarian organizations, including VOLAGs, hold supervisory positions and can rarely be found in entry-level jobs. I observed this myself when I worked in this area in Atlanta prior to undertaking this research as well as in my continued collaboration with VOLAGs in New York. In contrast, refugees and immigrants in these organizations are usually caseworkers and, as such, report to native-born White Americans. In fact, refugees and immigrants are expected to stay in these subservient positions; if they strive to acquire managerial posts, as I experienced firsthand, their credentials and fit will be publicly and privately questioned. When refugees and immigrants take on leadership roles, they assert power and agency, which not only makes it more difficult to "save" and/or control them, but it also threatens well-established power structures. Native-born White Americans, occupying positions of power in these organizations, make decisions about refugees' housing, employment, and other services, mostly with limited input from their refugee clients and refugee/immigrant employees (see also chapter 3). This setup reinforces the hierarchical (racial) refugee aid structure in which refugees, including Liberians, are recipients of aid and native-born White Americans are in a position of authority (Hyndman 2000; Malkki 1996; Ong 2003). Consequently, refugees come to understand and experience through these institutions the racial hierarchy in the United States, meaning "Whites . . . can either be your boss or . . . are in some way in control," as Annie Quide noted. Despite the stratified client-provider relationships, Liberian refugees frequently recounted how these first native-born White Americans they met were compassionate toward their needs and plight as refugees.[15]

While many of these sympathetic and supportive native-born White Americans are employees of VOLAGs, they can also be found among the sponsors that VOLAGs partner with. Usually, these sponsors are churches and synagogues with predominantly native-born White American and (upper) middle-class congregations who agree to assist refugees (see also Sackett and Lareau 2023). Members of these congregations provide additional support to that which the VOLAG offers; this includes donating furniture for the refugees' homes, tutoring children, and assisting with finding employment and overall cultural socialization to a new society. While such partnerships between VOLAGs and religious institutions are common, they did not exist for Liberian refugees resettled in Staten Island because the assumption was that their anchors who sponsored them would provide this type of support. However, some Liberians who now call Staten Island their home were resettled in other parts of the United States and thus remember their native-born White American sponsors. Among them is Yassah Flomo, who recalled her first days in North Carolina: "The White people were good. . . . I went to . . . a White church, and yes, they welcome me. . . . The pastor . . . came to our house, they brought me food. . . . One White lady and her husband usually came to pick us up every Sunday to carry us to church. . . . And one other old White man, he had a truck and took my dad for appointments and other things. They were very nice there in North Carolina." Liberian refugees also spoke about the interactions they had with native-born White Americans in VOLAGs. Garpu Garbleh, another former caseworker, fondly remembered a staff member at LSS who was pivotal in the resettlement of Liberians. Mr. Garbleh concluded that, despite being White, "she was more African than you can think" because she had "an African heart" that rendered her a "very, very nice woman." Thus, it was the "nice" native-born White Americans Liberians met in the refugee regime who temporarily shielded them from encounters with racist White and other Americans. At the same time, it is worth recalling that these were the same native-born White Americans who decided to resettle refugees in less-than-ideal neighborhoods.

Liberian refugees' positive experiences with native-born White Americans in administrative positions within the refugee system also inform at times their preference for native-born White American government workers. For example, one day when I was at the African outdoor market in Park Hill, I overheard a conversation between a Ghanaian market woman and a Liberian woman that represents this pattern. The Ghanaian immigrant happily told her friend that she had just received a letter from the USCIS inviting her for her naturalization interview. The Liberian woman congratulated her and said that she would pray that a White person would administer the test and interview. Due to her positive experiences with native-born White Americans working in the refugee camps, where her application for resettlement was processed, along with her (limited) interactions with VOLAGs, she, like other Liberian refugees, perceived native-born White Americans to be more lenient than other ethnoracial groups, especially in the realm of immigration-related issues. Although given the xenophobic and racist rhetoric and policies that are being pursued during the second Trump administration, Liberians are now less likely to hope for native-born White Americans to review their applications to become U.S. citizens.

"If I Can Live Among Tribalization, I Can Live with Discrimination": War in Liberia

While all migrants compare their present experiences in the new place of residence with those of their country of birth or previous residence, for refugees, this refugee-specific dual frame of reference often centers on painful memories that include war and persecution, the very push factors that caused them to flee. For many, it was armed conflict or discrimination based on ethnicity, religion, political opinion, and so forth that forced them to leave (Besteman 2016; Franz 2005; Gold 1992).[16] These experiences inform how refugees, including Liberians, interpret present-day discrimination. In other words, when Liberian refugees encounter anti-Black racism and xenophobia in the United States, it is not the first time they have been discriminated against. While in the United States it is their race,

Africanness, refugeehood, and in certain contexts their Liberian heritage that make them a target of discrimination, it was their (perceived) ethnicity and/or ancestry (Indigenous Liberian vs. Americo Liberian) that made them a (potential) target during the war in Liberia, where persecution, torture, and murder often took place along ethnic and/or ancestral lines. Compared to these atrocities, many Liberians conclude that they can "live with discrimination . . . if they can live and survive among tribalization," as Maymay Bensing said. In other words, when being a member of a certain ethnic group almost certainly meant death during the war, Liberians reason that the racial slurs and housing and employment discrimination they experience in Staten Island and elsewhere are comparatively minor (see also Franz 2005).

But even prior to the war, ethnicity and descent mattered a great deal in Liberia (S. Ellis 1999). This can be traced back to Liberia's origins, as detailed in chapter 2. This stands in contrast to the United States, where race overshadows ethnicity, especially for people categorized as Black. One could even argue that Black settlers from the United States brought with them American racism and disparaging views about Indigeneity when they arrived in what would become Liberia in the nineteenth century. Cynthia Sherif, an Americo Liberian who is married to a Kpelle man, is intimately familiar with how distinctions based on descent and ethnicity have shaped Liberia and its people: "There was prejudice in Liberia. . . . This is why the war came about because the Americo Liberians, most of them, looked down on the Indigenous Liberians. And like my husband always say, the same mentality that they came with from here, the way they were treated and suppressed, when they met these other people, they felt superior and suppressed them the same way." While discrimination based on ancestry started in Liberia as soon as the ACS claimed the land in 1820, it turned especially deadly during the country's civil war. Garpu Garbleh, an ethnic Krahn, explained that the boundaries between friend and foe frequently shifted during the civil war:

> The Americo Liberians were the ruling class . . . when Doe [a Krahn] took over in 1980 . . . the division reversed. So, the Indigenous . . . were . . . ill-treating the Americo Liberians. And in 1985 . . . the general [Thomas Quiwonkpa, a Gio] . . . who had staged the coup along with Doe . . . but when he [Quiwonkpa] defected . . . the Krahn and the Gio were not . . . getting along. And then the Mandingo . . . supported the Doe regime, and so the Mandingo also turned against the Gio. And then, when the Gio had the upper hand when Charles Taylor came to power, they started to kill the Mandingo and the Krahn people. . . . So, during the war a population [ethnic group] was targeted.

Thus, depending on the pan-ethnic coalitions the warring parties forged at particular times during the civil war, one was either protected or persecuted based on one's ethnicity. Wright Talley, a fellow Krahn, elucidated how this impacted him and his family: "There was senseless killings that caused thousands to die, millions were probably destroyed. . . . A senseless war because it was taking an ethnic trend in such a way that people went after my tribe. Because the late president Samuel Doe at the time was from the Krahn tribe, and so whatever he did during his tenure as president that people didn't like, they felt . . . the Krahn are collectively guilty . . . so really, I was affected; I lost a lot of family members."

Based on their experiences in the war, Liberian refugees often associate discrimination with the physical attacks and violence that many of them personally experienced. So, when Liberians are insulted by derogatory remarks at work or in public spaces in Staten Island because of their race, Liberian/African heritage, refugee status, or a combination, they feel hurt, but these insults pale in comparison to the atrocities they lived through in the war. Just imagine having to "hide in the forest . . . until the fighting was over . . . so they didn't get killed . . . seeing innocent people . . . pregnant women dying," as Janjay Waggah remembered. In other words, the war increased Liberian refugees' threshold for exclusion and suffering since these experiences were so harrowing.

"Everybody There Is Depending on Us": The Need for Remittances

Another reason why certain Liberian refugees have on occasion focused less energy on fighting anti-Black racism and injustices in the United States is the financial responsibility they have toward their loved ones in Liberia and other West African countries. Again, this does not mean that anti-Black racism is not detrimental to Liberian refugees' well-being, but the refugee-specific dual frame of reference puts their suffering, at least at times, in perspective in relation to what else is happening in their own and their family members' lives. The need to provide for multiple households in different countries pushes Liberians and other refugees, especially those from war-torn countries (Franz 2005; Villacres 2013), to accept jobs in which working conditions are less than ideal and that expose them to (anti-Black) racism and xenophobia. In addition, Liberian and other refugees do not have the luxury to resign from bad jobs because employment is essential to achieving the goal of economic self-sufficiency set forth by the USRAP.

Almost all refugees feel obligated to send remittances to their loved ones almost immediately after they arrive in the United States (Covington-Ward 2017b; Riak Akuei 2005).[17] I also observed this when I worked with different refugee groups, including Liberians, in Atlanta. This happens because most refugees regard it as their "most fundamental obligation . . . to support members of their extended family" (Weine et al. 2011, 39) who are either in their native country or in refugee camps elsewhere (Omata 2012a; Porter et al. 2008). Thus, it becomes clearer why Liberians in Staten Island feel that they must disregard the discrimination they encounter. Whenever Liberian refugees in the United States experience racism, they recall the needs of their relatives in West Africa and focus on their own access to "a little bit of heaven," especially in economic terms, as Mr. Baby, a father of four, said. They reason that their suffering in the United States, including discrimination, is a price they have to pay to mitigate their loved ones' plight, as "even the worst-paying jobs in the United States offer greater financial opportunities than the jobs available in their home countries" (Hamilton 2019, 139).

Zaiway Paye shows this need to continue to work so that she can provide for her family in the United States and send remittances to relatives in Liberia. On one of the occasions when we met, she discussed at length how one of the residents at the nursing home abused her, showing me the bruises on her hands. This reflects a wider pattern of discrimination and abuse of low-wage and low-skilled health workers (Jang et al. 2017). However, Ms. Paye stressed, "Everybody there is depending on us.... Liberia is from war, there's nothing good going on.... My mother... my kids are there. I have to work to support them.... Every month... I have to give them food money... take care of their medication; everything depends on me." Zaiway Paye has neither the time nor the privilege to worry about verbal and physical assaults and would not want to risk her job by complaining about abusive and racist residents because she is her family's financial lifeline, which is common among many refugees and immigrants (Porter et al. 2008; Riak Akuei 2005). Since Liberians in the United States know that every American dollar sent to their loved ones overseas makes a difference, they often concede to abusive working conditions (and low wages).

Osiemeo Boye, who was introduced earlier, had also been willing to endure a difficult work situation coupled with discrimination. This was particularly true after he had just escaped the war in Liberia, where his relatives were still in danger. At the same time, he remembered the strenuous physical labor he had had to do in Liberia before he fled. His reasoning exemplifies the refugee-specific dual frame of reference: "Over there when you shake... hands you feel their palm is rough [shows me the insides of his hands] because you work hard. But here, I go to work, I sit in the office... I give them medication... and assist... them.... I find it to be peanuts.... When I got here, the war was just advancing onto the capital city, Monrovia, so I told my cousin, 'Look, right now I just got the message that the rebels attack my mother's village and so... my family is leaving and they need money. I need to feed them and things, so give me anything.... I'm willing to do anything... even if it's two dollars a hour.'"

But even if Liberians in the United States tried to share information about the unpleasant working and living conditions in the United States with their relatives in West Africa, they feel they would not be believed. Flomo Yakpazua, a father of four young children, three of whom are in Liberia, elaborated on this: "Even when you tell them it's bad, they don't believe it.... I try to tell them... life here is not just bread and butter.... They think, 'Oh that man is in... America, he's enjoying now.'... But they depend greatly on you for... financial help, so if someone there has a problem and... need... cash... you have to provide it." While Mr. Yakpazua was willing to admit to his family and friends in Liberia that he faces difficulties in the United States, most refugees and other immigrants do not share details about the exploitative working conditions with their remittance-receiving relatives

(Hall et al. 2019). They, like many Liberians, believe that their situation in the United States is still better than that of those left behind. They also may not want to admit that they are not as successful in the "heaven-like" America as their relatives assume. Rather, they, as Beverly Coleman stated, "put up this impression that everything here is OK and won't tell them about the bad things."

Ms. Coleman, like other Liberians, delayed her return to Liberia until she could "come back big" and her homecoming would not go unnoticed, but, as she said, rather everyone "will know [she is] back . . . also . . . those in the hinterland."[18] Unfortunately, she passed away in her late 50s, before she was able to realize that dream. Osiemeo Boye has similar visions about his return to Liberia, which justifies for him the grievances he experiences in the United States: "When I am retired I'll be receiving my Social Security at the American embassy. . . . seven hundred dollars here it's nothing, but . . . in Liberia . . . a lot. So, if I have that money in Liberia, I'm the king. People come to me . . . to assist them. I assist them and I feel great that I'm helping other people. . . . So, when you suffer here, you enjoy there." While in his early days in the United States Mr. Boye accepted low-paying jobs in order to provide for his family in Liberia, who were still in harm's way, something else has helped him endure discrimination and anti-Black racism in the United States today: the prospect of a grand return to Liberia. Such a return for an extended visit or retirement is in stark contrast to the realities he and other Liberians currently face in the United States; in Liberia, they can—due to their financial status—expect to be admired and treated like royalty, as Mr. Boye said. With that as a consolation in mind, Liberian refugees often remain silent about everyday anti-Black racism and demeaning working conditions in the United States.

"I Anticipated . . . Racism": Prior Knowledge About American Anti-Black Racism

Whereas most of the literature contends that refugees and immigrants, including those who are racialized as Black, only learn about the significance of race, race relations, and racism in the United States once they are living here (Foner 2018; V. S. Johnson 2016),[19] this was not the case for the majority of Liberian refugees, especially those who grew up in urban centers and/or had some formal education. The reason for this is that the historic relationship between the United States and Liberia is very much part of Liberia's national identity, which is built on a collective memory of slavery (Ciment 2013; J. Levitt 2005). In addition, the history of U.S. plantation slavery is not only ever-present in institutions (e.g., the Liberian Constitution, the Liberian national motto, names of Liberian cities and counties), but it is also integrated into Liberia's educational curriculum and oral traditions. Thus, Liberian refugees, regardless of whether they are Americo Liberian or Indigenous, were somewhat prepared for the anti-Black racism they would experience in the United States. For example, Osiemeo Boye simply said, "Before coming here . . . we know that way back, people were slaves here. The White people don't like the Black people." Similarly, Love Juah who, as a college student in Liberia, read a book—the title of which she cannot remember—that provided her with insights about anti-Black racism in the United States that, unbeknownst to her back then, would prepare her for when she joined her daughter in Boston many years later. She said, "They talk about the Ku Klux Klan.... I read that book, and I knew that they had a problem with racism, but then I thought, over the years... Blacks and Whites are going to the same school, going to the same places.... I thought it was at a minimal level. But now... I don't think it's as rampant as it used to be before.... It hasn't been eradicated, but it has been minimized."

Liberians' familiarity with American anti-Black racism was also a reason why anti-Black racism was not discussed as part of the overseas Cultural Orientation, according to Memba Wesseh, who worked with the IOM in Côte d'Ivoire as part of the Liberian refugee resettlement efforts. He said, "No, we don't go into the discrimination aspect. We just say you gonna meet diverse... different people.... But nobody told them about discrimination because... Liberia people know... the slaves that were freed from here went and established our country." So, armed with this knowledge that anti-Black racism has existed in the United States since the beginning, Love Juah, Memba Wesseh, and other Liberian refugees arrived in the United States. Once they started to encounter anti-Black racism in their daily lives, they began to draw on their intimate knowledge of historical race relations and anti-Black racism in the United States and contrast present-day discrimination to it. Subsequently, they have contended that the anti-Black racism they and their loved ones have encountered in Staten Island and other places in the United States in the late twentieth and early twenty-first century has taken on a different form: still harsh and significant, but often less deadly and brutal compared to earlier eras.[20]

Some Liberian refugees have, through their Americo Liberian ancestry, personal connections to historical anti-Black racism that drove their ancestors to leave the United States. Among them is Mr. Boakai, whose reunification with his family serves as the opening vignette for chapter 4. His grandfather was born in 1895 in Arkansas and emigrated as a young child with his family to Liberia. Mr. Boakai remembered his father telling him and his siblings that they "should... in the back of our mind... know... what our position is... because... segregation and the slavery will be... here." Hence, these shared stories of ancestors escaping slavery and segregation for a free life in Liberia left no doubt in present-day Liberians' minds about what to expect upon arrival in the United States.[21] David Joe, an Americo Liberian who lives with his extended family in a two-family house in Staten Island, stated, "I anticipated it.... In fact... I expected racism every day.... I was taught that when you go America, they suspicious toward Black people. Therefore, if you're in a class with a White person, you must work harder than that White person... you must earn your respect through your work. You work twice... than the average White man to earn your respect."

But it was not just Liberians with Americo Liberian ancestry who arrived in the United States anticipating anti-Black racism. Garsuah Janjay, a member of the

Bassa ethnic group, came to the United States escaping torture in Liberia. He framed his expectations of race relations in terms of the Jim Crow era: "I read about . . . how the Black people were treated and how they were discriminated against. . . . How Black people were not allowed to go in certain areas, and Black children were not allowed to go . . . school with the White children. . . . A policeman would call a Black man maybe old enough to be his grandfather . . . 'boy' 'cause he's a White man." However, "Today," Mr. Janjay continued, "it is not as horrible as I pictured it . . . but racism still exists in America . . . but it's not at the level as it was before." Similarly, Osiemeo Boye discussed in which ways he felt race relations had changed since the end of de jure segregation, citing the example of the marriage of one of his sons to a native-born White American woman. He talked about how decades earlier "Black persons . . . were grabbed . . . jailed . . . back then . . . for going around . . . with a White girl. . . . This was a taboo; got you killed." But now, Mr. Boye feels that "you see . . . White girls . . . hanging with Black boys, and no one really care." Although, as well-documented, Black people still get "grabbed, jailed," and murdered in the United States, perhaps less so for being in an interracial relationship but for presumed minor infractions, or as stated earlier, for simply existing (Embrick 2015; Gutsche et al. 2022).

While Liberians at times have the impression that race relations have improved and anti-Black racism has declined, they also observe that this has been less so the case in Staten Island. Some would argue that blatant racism and xenophobia started to gain more ground with the 2016 election cycle. This can be especially felt in the most Republican borough of New York, where signs expressing support for Trump and "Blue Lives Matter" are widespread, leading Liberian refugees, including Sunday John, who joined her grandmother in Staten Island when she was in her early twenties, to feel that "there will always be racism." While Ms. John was quite clear that both young and old people held racist views, Liberian refugees such as Garpu Garbleh felt it is easier to explain why older native-born White Staten Islanders have these attitudes and tendencies: "The old . . . live in the '60s or in the '50s, practice discrimination; it's just part of them."

Hence, working for and living surrounded by people who are bigoted keeps them, as I have argued elsewhere (Ludwig 2017), in a continued "second exile" (Aleinikoff 2015), making it difficult for Liberians to develop a sense of belonging in Staten Island.

"This Is Not My Country": Feelings of (Not) Belonging

Many first-generation immigrants and refugees tend to identify more with their country of origin than with the United States (Haines 2007; Sorrell et al. 2019) and consequently focus predominantly on affairs there and less so on social justice issues here. Although there are some differences among genders, with male immigrants having an increased engagement with their country of origin to compensate for status loss in the new country (Arthur 2009; Binder and Tošić 2005; Guarnizo et al. 2003) and female immigrants focusing more on improving their own and their family's lives in the United States (Jones-Correa 1998; P. Levitt 2001). But despite these gendered differences, a good number of first-generation immigrants and refugees—Liberians are no exception—regard a lot of what is happening in the United States, including continued anti-Black racism, not as their struggle (P. Levitt 2001). They tend to be more occupied with achieving "migration goals" (V. S. Johnson 2016, 54), such as basic survival, creating better opportunities for their children, and sending remittances (Kasinitz et al. 2008; Portes and Rumbaut 2001). Hence, many Liberian refugees have come to see "America," as Maymay Bensing said, as a place of refuge from the war and "to work and make some money," but not a home—certainly not where they "wish . . . to get old," as her husband added, which also explains why they, compared to the younger generation, are less likely to take on racist institutions and practices.

However, there is another reason why many Liberian refugees have ambivalent feelings toward the United States and their position in this country: ongoing exclusion and anti-Black racism. Being constantly reminded that they do not belong or are not wanted here through discrimination, xenophobia, and anti-Black racism causes refugees and immigrants to identify less with the country of settlement and emphasize other identities and/or otherness (Golash-Boza 2006). Sometimes, that means that refugees and immigrants "may strengthen [their] . . . sense of belonging to the home country by manifesting itself in an ancestral identity" (Tezcan 2019, 192). In addition, not identifying as "American" allows Liberian refugees, including Garsuah Janjay, to create symbolic barriers between themselves and the painful anti-Black racism and discrimination that they are subjected to in the United States. Mr. Janjay is almost indifferent about his lower social status in the United States because he does not consider it to be his home: "Even if I'm treated as a third-class . . . or fourth-class citizen in America, I don't care. This is not my country. They don't hurt me. At least I got a job to do. . . . The good thing about America is that whether you're second- or third-class, there are opportunities. . . . And also, we always have in the back of our head that America is not our home." While he stressed the economic opportunities that the United States affords refugees and immigrants, he weighed them against the discrimination he faces in the United States versus Liberia and gives more importance to that in Liberia, a place that he considers his home. Mr. Janjay also thinks of a possible return to his "real home," where he will be an equal citizen now that the war has removed many of the stratifications that had existed along the lines of descent and ethnicity. In this way, "return migration" can be regarded as the "natural completion of the migration cycle" (Gmelch 1992, 284–285); although a "return home" for most refugees and asylees is often not possible for long periods due the continued threat that caused them to flee in the first place. Nevertheless, many first-generation Liberians I have encountered have held out hope that they would return one day, some for a visit and others to live. In fact, several of these older first-generation Liberian refugees have in recent years begun to dream of retiring in Liberia, and some even have started to build houses there.

Official U.S. immigration policies and laws, as well as many immigration scholars, suggest that becoming a U.S. citizen shifts one's allegiance (Aptekar 2015). While this does occur on paper when refugees and immigrants take the Naturalization Oath of Allegiance to the United States of America, it does not necessarily change how they (or we, as I am a naturalized U.S. citizen myself) feel or self-identify or how others identify them (us). Many immigrants and refugees, including Liberians, are motivated by other factors to naturalize, including, but not limited to, making it easier to travel between Liberia and the United States, sponsor family members to come to the United States, and have better legal footing in the United States, especially in light of increasing deportations during the second Trump term. Yet, Liberian refugees are also fully aware that neither their social status in the United States nor how people treat them would change once they are naturalized U.S. citizens. For example, Sunday John felt that being a Black refugee always means having fewer "privileges," and this implies that "there are certain things . . . such as racism that . . . you have to be . . . OK with." This also reflects that neither Ms. John nor other Liberian refugees "have a strong sense of social entitlement . . . [and have] accepted a degree of mainstream prejudice and discrimination . . . [instead of] full social inclusion" (Colic-Peisker 2009, 194).

This is informed by what Liberian refugees were told during the Cultural Orientation they attended shortly after their arrival in the United States. Varney Yarkpolo, who was one of the caseworkers who facilitated these orientation workshops, recalled how he and other caseworkers stressed to Liberians (and other refugees) that "they are in a strange country . . . must adhere to the rules and regulations . . . of the country. . . . Being in the United States is a privilege . . . not a right . . . that can be taken away." Consequently, Ms. John, like other Liberians, concluded that the only way her situation would be different is if she "was a real born citizen of this country . . . then, this is . . . [her] country . . . to pursue . . . [her] rights." At the same time, she was astutely aware that these rights are not granted to all natural-born U.S. citizens equally, citing how President Obama's accomplishments often went "unrecognized and not appreciated because he's Black" and the many times her native-born Black American husband has been discriminated against. Thus, it is evident that normative and legal bases of inclusion, like U.S. citizenship, do not necessarily extend social citizenship (Nawyn 2011). Subsequently, those who are othered based on race, ethnicity, culture, and so forth by the majority population are then both unable and reluctant to develop feelings of belonging (Abrego 2019; Ngai 2014; Yuval-Davis 2007). While many people may experience exclusion from being able to establish feelings of belonging, this is heightened for "black people [who] have been disenfranchised . . . and symbolically erased as subjects who have even the potential of national belonging," and thus "Black people in . . . the United States are legal citizens only in *sensu stricto*" (Smith 2015, 385, emphasis in original text), just as Sunday John observed.

It should also be noted that Liberia did not allow dual citizenship until 2022, and so Liberians who naturalized as U.S. citizens prior to this year felt that their Liberian identity is based on emotions and heritage but not the law. However, this makes little difference to Liberians and other refugees and immigrants who often continue to identify with their country of birth (Sorrell et al. 2019). The majority of Liberian refugees situated discussions of belonging and (national) identity in the context of what "home" means to them. This is what Everliner Ethridge, who joined her husband in Staten Island in 1995 after her mother was killed in the war, said: "I'm an immigrant. Liberia is my home. There . . . I was born; there is . . . my family. . . . Now I have my U.S. citizenship but . . . I haven't forgotten about my home, Liberia."

What perhaps is even more perplexing are the rare cases of Liberians who are, like David Joe, U.S. citizens through descent via their Americo Liberian parents yet do not identify as American. This is even more astounding given that Mr. Joe was—as described in chapter 2—flown out of Liberia during the war by the U.S. military because he is a U.S. citizen. Nevertheless, he identifies with the country of his birth and where he grew up: "I still feel more Liberian . . . than American because though I have my U.S. citizenship . . . [*chuckles*] . . . I'm born Liberian . . . so I still feel like a Liberian more than I do a U.S. citizen."

By emphasizing that Liberia is their home, these Liberian refugees not only try to distance themselves from what is happening in a place that they regard as a temporary refuge, but by doing so they also may find comfort that the anti-Black racism that they are confronted with is fleeting, until they "go home . . . when there is no more war," as Elizabeth Kamara said.[22] Subsequently, due to their (imagined) temporary time in the United States, and also because they do not consider themselves part of U.S. society, they conclude that they are not in a position to take on the fight against anti-Black racism.

COPING AS "TEMPORARY" BLACK CITIZENS IN THE UNITED STATES

Refugee resettlement is often thought of as a new beginning, away from painful memories, hurt, and persecution. But such an assertion is oversimplified and overlooks not only the many losses that refugees face (e.g., indefinite family separation; loss of culture, language, and familiarity) but also the fact that they are often near or at the bottom of the social hierarchy in the new society. This is especially pronounced for Black refugees in the United States, who "upon entering the United States . . . find a new racial categorization that is almost immediately imposed on them due to a longstanding history of racism, violence, and oppression toward . . . African Americans" (Magan 2020, 174). Consequently, as Black refugees, Liberians find themselves often confronting a similar and at times the same anti-Black racism that native-born Black Americans face. This means that Liberian refugees are stereotyped and discriminated against in all aspects of their lives: housing, employment, and encounters with the police and others in public places. In addition, their discrimination is exacerbated by the fact that they are Liberians, Africans, and refugees. This is in contrast to research about other Black immigrants that has purported that pan-ethnic and national identities, such as Caribbean or Nigerian in some instances, protect Black immigrants from American anti-Black racism and can lead to preferential treatment by native-born White Americans (Imoagene 2017; Waters 1999).

Liberians respond in different ways to the anti-Black racism they experience in the United States; often they do not challenge the racist individuals or structures, but this does not mean that they accept abuse. Liberians contextualize their current discrimination through a refugee-specific dual frame of reference. As refugees, Liberians met and benefited from knowing "nice and caring White Americans" who worked in humanitarian and resettlement efforts in West Africa and in the United States. In this context, Liberians directly experienced kind and supportive native-born White Americans, which subsequently complicates their views of this racial group. At the same time, racist native-born White Americans and other non-Black people are not the first people who have inflicted harm on them because of perceived otherness; Liberian refugees fled a war that exploited existing cleavages and inequalities due to descent and ethnicity. This very war and its aftermath compelled Liberian refugees in the United States to remain in exploitative and cruel jobs so they could send remittances to their families in Liberia and refugee camps in West Africa. While many of these circumstances also apply to other refugees, there is one important factor that sets Liberians apart from other refugees and immigrants. They, unlike most other migrants in the United States, were prepared for the anti-Black racism that they would encounter due to Liberia's genesis as a quasi-American colony. It was Black settlers from the United States and their descendants who retold the horrors of slavery, lynching, and Jim Crow laws that they escaped when they made Liberia their home. Over time these historical accounts became part of Liberia's collective memory and equipped Liberian refugees in the late twentieth and early twenty-first century for what they would experience as Black people in a racialized society.

Finally, Liberians, and certainly other refugees and immigrants, sometimes cope with racism and xenophobia by emphasizing that their stay in the United States is only temporary, and therefore this is just a place to work and make money but not a home. By doing so, Liberian refugees and other immigrants assert that fighting racism in the United States is not their battle, as they not only have other, more pressing concerns, but also because it will not affect them in the long term, as they envision a return "home." This disassociation with "belonging in and to America" is not created in a vacuum but in response to incessant reminders that they are not welcome here. With the exception of a few individuals like David Joe, described in the previous section, this is very different for second-generation Liberian refugees who are natural-born U.S. citizens and for whom the United States is home; their interpretations of and responses to anti-Black racism and discrimination differ from that of the first generation (Hirsch 2019; Portes and Rumbaut 2001), a theme that I discuss in more detail in the following chapter.

6 WE HAVE THE SAME SKIN COLOR

In 2018, Dan Donovan (R), the former district attorney of Richmond County (Staten Island), was running against Max Rose (D) in a bid to get reelected as a U.S. congressman. In the run-up to the election, debates took place among the Liberian community about which candidate they would support. Two months before Election Day, Donovan sponsored a resolution in the U.S. Congress that called for the implementation of an extraordinary criminal tribunal for Liberia to address crimes perpetrated during the country's civil war.[1] This move was appreciated by Mr. J., a Bassa man in his mid-forties, who voiced his support for Donovan in a public conversation with other Liberians.[2] Unconvinced of Donovan's intentions, Mr. B. another middle-aged Bassa man, countered that "he [Donovan] ain't gonna do shit for Liberians. . . . His ass watched Eric Garner choke on tape, and he still couldn't convict the guy [police officer] as a prosecutor." By doing so, Mr. B. called out the complacency displayed by then-District Attorney Donovan, given the overwhelming evidence that Mr. Garner died due to an illegal chokehold at the hands of a New York City Police Department officer. However, Mr. J. was not swayed and emphasized that "Eric Garner is not Liberian" and that a "cost-benefit analysis" was in order here. In other words, Mr. J. felt it was more important to deal with issues that pertained to injustices committed in Liberia than in the United States. This annoyed and angered Mr. B., who has experienced how the police have mistreated him and his son more than once. Thus, he replied, "My point exactly. If he couldn't do it for his fellow American, his constituent, what makes you think he will do it for a bunch of Africans?" Unperturbed, Mr. J. dug deeper and told Mr. B. and others who had been more passive bystanders to this conversation to "stop acting like you're Americans." To him, it only mattered what Donovan had to say about Liberia, despite Donovan's track record relating to immigration. In 2017, then-Congressman Donovan supported Trump's immigration ban that mostly affected predominantly Muslim countries in the Middle East as well as a number of African countries, and he had favored other anti-immigrant measures and legislation. But none of that seemed to matter to Mr. J., at least not at that time, as he believed that these things did not affect him as a Liberian. He identified as Liberian first and not so much as a Black man in the United States.

In the last few years since, this has changed, though. While Mr. J still actively participates and promotes Liberia-themed events around the country, he has embraced a more pan-ethnic Black identity. He has become vocal in support of the Black Lives Matter movement, for example, by posting calls to action on social media but also actively attending various events in and around Staten Island that have condemned violence committed against Black people while calling out performative and insincere public proclamations about commitment to social justice and ending anti-Black violence. Furthermore, Mr. J. has widened his cultural support of what he previously called "American" cultural icons. Now, he happily celebrates receiving an action figure depicting a member of the Wu-Tang Clan, finds joy and pride in Amanda Gorman's poetry, and states that Martin Luther King Jr. is one of the people he admires the most.

So, what occurred in the past few years that has led to Mr. J.'s transition in views about what he supports and what he considers himself part of? What roles did the decade-long interactions with his native-born Black American neighbors and experiences with anti-Black violence in the United States play? Are there generational differences between first-generation Liberian refugees, like Mr. J., and 1.5- and second-generation youth who grew up in a country that is stratified by race and less so by ethnicity, like Liberia? This chapter offers answers to these questions. Given the longitudinal nature of this study, I have had a front-row seat to observe how both individuals' and the community's perceptions about identities and racial belonging (Adjepong 2018; St. Louis 2005) in the United States have evolved over time.

It is in this context that I also discuss how Liberian refugees have positioned themselves as part of the larger Black community in the United States, a process that is dialectic and dynamic. It is often contextual, and not, as frequently portrayed, an either/or—distancing themselves from native-born Black Americans or embracing them as a group. Much of the distancing also draws on stereotypes that are rooted in misinformation and White supremacy (Asante et al. 2016). But the experiences with the manifestations of White supremacy (e.g., anti-Black racism) have led Liberians to develop a sense of "linked fate" (Dawson 1994)—the feeling that one's fate is affected by what happens to members of the same (racial) group—native-born Black Americans. In a way, due to how and why Liberia was created, there is a historical precedent for this connected fate between native-born Black Americans and Liberians.

Despite this connection and their consistently solid ideas of their racial identities as Black people, Liberian refugees began to realize that being Black has different meanings in these geographical contexts as they adjusted and began to incorporate themselves into U.S. society. Being Black in the United States means uniquely having to fear for one's safety and livelihood on an almost daily basis due to anti-Black racism. In addition, being Black has a different cultural and historical meaning in the United States, where the narrative around "Black" is often driven by the experiences of native-born Black Americans and their ancestors and connected to enslavement, Jim Crow, and continued alienation (Landry 2018). While there is some overlap in the importance of enslavement and Jim Crow for Liberian national identity, it has not been a daily lived experience until Liberians moved to the United States. Once Liberian refugees started living in neighborhoods like Park Hill, they have had to not only worry about meeting the USRAP's expectations about fast economic self-sufficiency but also find their place in the larger American racial hierarchy, a dialectic process that has involved engaging with both native-born White Americans and Black Americans. While Liberians quickly realized that native-born White Americans held power, their interactions with other Black people in the United States have been more complex. In their economically deprived neighborhood, diverging views with native-born Black Americans about Blackness and culture—at times informed by stereotypes as well as competition for limited resources—made for difficult early years. However, as time passed, Liberian refugees and native-born Black Americans got to know each other more intimately, as their children attend school together and share their inadequate neighborhood outdoor spaces, and they mourn together about painful experiences involving different forms of violence, including those fueled by anti-Black racism. As a new generation has grown up, friendships have emerged, and real and strategic coalitions, for example, in politics and around civil rights issues (e.g., Black Lives Matter movement), are being formed.

"I CHECK BLACK": BLACK IDENTITIES

Identities are contextual. The same holds true for the importance of race to one's understanding and life chances (Asante et al. 2016; Rodriguez and Cordero-Guzman 1992). While in some geographical contexts, such as the United States, race is of utmost significance (Treitler 2013), this is in contrast to the majority of African countries, where ethnicity is more important (Besteman 2016; Guenther et al. 2011), and thus "African identities are often tied more to ethnicity than race" (Clark 2008, 179). For the most part, this also holds true for Liberia, where ethnicity (e.g., Kru, Krahn) and/or descent (Americo Liberian or Indigenous) would frequently determine a person's fate, and during the civil war, chances of survival. But things changed when Liberians were resettled or arrived on their own in the United States; they had to learn about a new society, its cultures, norms, and expectations, including the enormous implication race has and what it means to be Black in the United States (Foner 2018; Pierre 2004) compared to Liberia.

For immigrants and refugees this also means that they are racialized, a process in which they are absorbed into existing groups "on the basis of physical characteristics into an ethnoracial hierarchy" (Agadjanian et al. 2017, 559; see also Bonilla-Silva 1996). This happens because it is not possible "to be without a race in a racialized society" (Bashi 1998, 966). Hence, Liberian refugees, like other Black refugees and immigrants, are racialized as Black (Carbado 2005; Asante et al.

2016). In other words, Liberians arrived with firm identities of who they are in terms of, as well as ideologies about, Blackness and Africa and then had to engage with dominant American ideologies of Blackness. This has not always been a smooth process, since Liberian refugees' views differed from those of native-born Black Americans with whom they find themselves lumped into one racial group and also sharing an economically deprived neighborhood.

"I'm Liberian. . . . You Will Know I'm Black": Blackness as a Cornerstone of Liberian Identity

Much of the immigration literature has documented that "being Black" has distinct meanings in different countries and hence also influences how individuals who are racialized as "Black" in the United States see themselves and are seen by others (Bashi 2007; Pierre 2013). Race, and in particular being Black, is integral to being Liberian. Being Black for Liberians is a given, since it is a prerequisite to Liberian citizenship (Pailey 2016). Specifically, the constitution stipulates that only those who are "Negroes or persons of Negro descent" are eligible for Liberian citizenship, both through descent and naturalization. The origins of this race-based citizenship in Liberia can be found in the beginnings of the country and the notion that Liberia would serve as the place where Black people from the African diaspora could (be) repatriate(d) to, as a symbolic nod to the vision that Africa has been "romanticized as a black space" (Kaj 2012, 3). Indeed, Black nationalist and pan-Africanist Edward Wilmot Blyden, who was involved in the ACS's effort to set up the Liberian colony, was motivated precisely by this belief of Africa as "the Black space." For Blyden (1856, 27), the "Black race" could only be vindicated through Liberia and the settlement's success project; "the object of Liberia was the redemption of Africa and the disenthralment and elevation of the African race, objects worthy of every colored man." Thus, it becomes clear, when Liberia was conceived as the place for the "redemption of the Black race" and a place where Black people had freedom, why the constitution was written to limit Liberian citizenship to Black people. Since Liberia's foundation coincided with the Scramble for and Partition of Africa, the Black settlers of the "Liberia project" were understandably extremely concerned that another predominantly White nation would come to recolonize them (Liebenow 1969). "This fear," as Baka Wehjay, a Bassa man who came to the United States on a student visa right before the outbreak of the civil war, said, motivated "the free slave or the Americo Liberians to put . . . in the constitution that no White should become a citizen. . . . When they become a citizen, they will buy the strategic land and begin to take over the entire country. . . . They do not want for their [former] slave masters to have complete control over the new country that they just formed." Hence, this is why Pailey (2012, para. 8) concludes that "Liberia's Negro clause . . . [is] not racist . . . [but] protectionary . . . to protect itself from foreign domination." The fact that Liberia's constitution bars people who are not Black from taking a stake in their country and lives has shaped Liberians' sense of self. For the last one hundred-plus years, they, unlike racial minorities in the United States, such as native-born Black Americans, had little to fear from other racial groups. To ensure this stays this way, the Liberian constitution limits landownership to Liberian citizens (Ludwig 2016a). This is the opposite of what has happened in the United States, where White people have consistently held power and ethnoracial minority groups have been subjugated. This fight for freedom, equality, and equity is very much part of what it means to be Black for native-born Black Americans (C. W. Smith 2014). However, this is not necessarily the case for Liberians, for whom Blackness is more a matter of fact.

For example, Beatrice Akoi, introduced in chapter 3's opening vignette, simply stated that being Liberian implies being Black: "I'm from Liberia . . . I'm Black. . . . If I say I'm Liberian and you know what color of people come from Liberia, you will know I'm Black."[3] This type of identification is present among different generations. For example, Maymay Bensing, a generation older than Ms. Akoi, uses the hashtags "#SimplyBlack #SimplyAfrican #Liberian" on many of the pictures she posts of herself, her family, and friends on social media.

Over time, though, Liberians have come to realize that their understanding of and identity as "Black" does not at all times align with what it means to be Black in the United States and in particular what being Black means to native-born Black Americans. For example, as I discuss later, Liberian refugees were not always fully aware of both the struggles that native-born Black Americans have had to overcome and how Black people in present-day American society have continued to be discriminated against, which at times was the source of tensions between these two groups.

"All Black Men Are from Africa": African Ancestry in the United States

Very often Black people, regardless of their ethnicity, nationality, and culture, find themselves lumped together in one group. For example, only in 2020 did the U.S. Census add different categories for Black people to identify their national and ethnic backgrounds, something that had been offered to most other ethnoracial groups for decades.[4] This perhaps not only reflects anti-Black racism but also "the power of race as a socially defining status in U.S. society [that] makes . . . intra-racial distinctions based on ancestry or skin tone . . . rather unimportant in interracial settings in comparison to the fundamental black/white color boundary" (Nagel 1994, 156).

However, categorizing these different Black people together is problematic since it flattens linguistic and cultural differences and also ignores the diverging ideas each group has about being Black and being of African descent. For Liberians, being Black is the norm and intrinsic to being Liberian, and accordingly, like many other Black refugees and immigrants, they do not have "reason to believe that they are inferior" (Appiah 1992, 6). This is in contrast to the United States, where in mainstream (White) society being Black is often linked to negative social stigmas (Pierre 2004) that have their origins in the dehumanization of Black people dating back to the institution of slavery (King and Adero 2020) and "the history of American racial oppression" (Landry 2018, 134). Therefore, most native-born Black Americans have an "exaggerated form of race consciousness" (Ekeh 2001, 89), which leads to high levels of solidarity and linked fate (Dawson 1994). While Liberian refugees, like other Black immigrants and refugees, may not have this "exaggerated form of race consciousness" during their early days in the United States, they share an African ancestry and a race with native-born Black Americans but have different views and expectations of what these common origins denote. After all, there is "no authentic or universal Black experience" (Asante et al. 2016, 369).

Prior to leaving West Africa, Liberians' views about Blackness and Black people in the United States were mostly limited to abstract ideas and historical and cultural ties to antebellum Black American cultures. Based on this, many Liberian refugees assumed that there would be a cultural affinity or similarity between native-born Black Americans and Americo Liberians. Often that meant that Indigenous Liberians, like Nyema Browne, who joined her husband in Oklahoma in 1987 before moving to Staten Island a year later, were wary of native-born Black Americans due to past persecution in Liberia at the hands of Americo Liberians. She explained why this was the case: "From my dealings with the Congos . . . I worried.[5] I don't trust them. They think they are better, have a better culture. . . . We see in history what they do to the real Liberians. . . . The Black people here are their brothers. . . . They come from the same place . . . so, I worry." And while others shared Ms. Browne's apprehension about native-born Black Americans, the vast majority of Liberians—regardless of ethnicity—envisioned that there would be connections and familiarity with native-born Black Americans due to shared ancestral ties and physical traits. Loko Pella, a Gio woman from Nimba County, illustrated this: "African Americans and Liberia people almost look alike . . . when you see some of them they're just like our people. They resemble so much. They look like somebody you know. So . . . we are all sisters and brothers." In fact, Liberians expected to be welcomed by native-born Black Americans like lost brothers and sisters (see also Covington-Ward 2017) due to a number of reasons, including, but not limited to, the perception of the United States as Liberia's "mother country" and shared historical ties between Liberian nationhood and Black people in the United States.[6] These anticipations were summarized by Varney Yarkpolo, a former resettlement caseworker: "Liberians . . . believe strongly . . . you see your kind . . . that you'll be accepted. They felt that . . . African American here was gonna be very receptive to them because we automatically see them as brothers and sisters prior to coming here . . . because . . . we were all from the same continent."

But despite these shared origins, finding a pan-ethnic Black identity in the United States that can accommodate different ethnic, national, cultural, and linguistic identities and experiences has taken some time, something that also occurs with other pan-ethnic groups (Okamoto and Mora 2014).[7] Developing this pan-ethnic identity as "Black" and/or "African American" for Liberians and native-born Black Americans has been challenging because of their different experiences and vantage points. For native-born Black Americans, the presence of Black immigrants, but in particular African immigrants and refugees, has "challenged . . . what constitutes Blackness" since the newcomers "do the cultural and social work of expanding what Blackness means in the American context" (Landry 2018, 127–128; see also Alao 2023). Some of this has played out in the daily interactions that Liberians have had with their native-born Black American neighbors. For example, Liberian refugees for the most part were affronted by native-born Black Americans' identification as "African American" while simultaneously rejecting "Africa." Loko Pella exemplified this when she said she didn't "understand" how "most of them say 'I'm not African' but . . . call yourself African American. So, how are you not African?" This was also echoed by Mr. Boakai, who is of Americo Liberian and Gola ethnicity: "As long as you're a Black man, you're an African. . . . Most of them . . . refer to you as African. So . . . I'll say, 'I'm African, yes, but who are you?' Then he'll say, 'I'm an African American.' I say, 'Can you define that for me?' But that's where the conversation stops. They start walking away because they can't define it, but I can; that's the difference. . . . But all Black men are from Africa. . . . And I accept myself being as a Black man." On the face of it, it is understandable why Liberian refugees reacted this way. However, if they knew more about the history of how "African American" as an identity and descriptor came about in response to anti-Black racism (Martin 1991), they most likely would have been able to better understand this seeming contradiction between identifying with and rejecting "African."

For many native-born Black Americans, the image of "Africa" represents "the motherland, the homeland [*chuckles*], where my ancestors came from," said Travis Rogers, a twenty-two-year-old, native-born Black American who has lived his entire life in Park Hill. However, others, such as Mac Willi, another native-born Black American, who moved as a child with his family to New York to escape anti-Black racism in North Carolina, pushed back on this idea. Mr. Willi said, "They say it's the motherland for us. But you know what? . . . This is my motherland. I was born here. This is all I know. I'm not getting on a boat to go to some place where I don't know anything about. . . . I'm not leaving this country to go to Africa. I know nothing about it." While Mr. Willi did not have anything negative to say about the African continent and its people, he made it clear that he also was not really interested in knowing more about it. However, other native-born Black Americans distanced themselves due to the negative images about Africa that have been omnipresent in U.S. society (J. Jackson and Cothran 2003; Okonofua 2013). This was something that Liberians came to comprehend over time. As David Joe, an Americo Liberian man, explained, "The Black American . . . didn't want . . . that connection with Africa . . . because Africa . . . is always portrayed to be a place [*chuckles*] that there's nothing good over there." In contrast, there were also native-born Black Americans who welcomed the arrival of Africans in the United States because, as Baka Wehjay said, "They wanted to be African. . . . They said instead of them going to Africa, Africa has come to them." He and other Liberians felt that native-born Black Americans who have these positive reactions are also those who "are more knowledgeable.... on Africans and African culture." And while Liberian refugees have generally welcomed it when native-born Black Americans are interested in exploring and embracing a shared heritage, they were skeptical of those native-born Black Americans who "overdo" it, as Sam Collins said. Mr. Collins, who has lived and traveled a lot in the United States, described some of his impressions: "When I went to Harlem... you go to people's homes and you see them walking around with Dashiki and that type of stuff. You clearly know that OK, these people are conscious.... I... respect the fact that they acknowledge their African heritage and they overdo it.... I run into African Americans that are more African than me." Whereas Mr. Collins was a bit critical of native-born Black Americans' embrace of their African heritage, others, including Annie Quide, who was resettled with her baby daughter, reasoned that this approach could potentially provide an avenue for native-born Black Americans to escape or at the very least, counteract discrimination and anti-Black racism. Ms. Quide said, "I always tell them... you have to accept yourself for who you are so you can... live your life. You can't live the life that somebody wants you to live. If you accept yourself as African, you will be free from everything, you will be released, you will walk with your chest up high regardless of what may happen to you in the past or whatever."

Yet retaining a connection to the African continent has been difficult. During slavery, plantation owners went to great lengths to sever ties that enslaved people had with their family members and others from their ethnic group and consequently robbed them of much of their cultural practices and languages. Today, Liberian refugees and their families struggle for different reasons. For example, several Liberians felt that U.S. bureaucracy did not provide any space to acknowledge their African, Liberian, or individual ethnic identity. This was voiced by Comfort Johnson, a Bassa woman who was resettled to Staten Island in 2003: "They don't have 'African'... I check Black... that is the only one... that match my race." Similarly, Maymay Bensing felt that becoming a U.S. citizen changed things for her. She said, "I am considered a Black American... because I already denounced my Liberian citizenship."

As much as Liberian refugees wanted to hold onto and claim their Liberian and African heritage, they knew it was sometimes an additional liability. They saw this in the negative views that some of their native-born Black American neighbors had but also in how racist native-born White Americans invoked someone's African heritage when they wanted to add insult to people they disliked. Everliner Ethridge, who is originally from Clay-Ashland, an Americo Liberian settlement, elaborated on this: "Some White Americans... think they are of a better caliber than you... because they... conclude... that my color, my country, and me being an immigrant... they will always want you to be under them." Ms. Ethridge noted that this was not only happening to Liberian refugees but also to others who had African parentage, including President Barack Obama, whom most Liberians admired. She discussed how he was perceived based on his race and African heritage:

> Look at what . . . they say about Obama! "He's not an American, he's not born here." . . . They tried to bring that racial discrimination to get people to turn against him. . . . They were bringing the name up, Barack Hussein Obama, so that it could affect him . . . a Muslim name. . . . They were doing that to keep him down because of his color. If they had a White young boy that was as brilliant as Obama, they would have shopping him a long time for president. I'm serious. But look at what they put him through. . . . They went . . . to Kenya and showed his grandmother's home, her traditional stuff, just to get the people to turn against him . . . show the grandmom . . . sitting by the fire pot.

Everliner Ethridge's observations reveal that she is keenly aware how birthers questioned Barack Obama's skills, ability, and eligibility to be the president of the United States because of his race and African parentage. Subsequently, it confirmed to her and other Liberian refugees, once more, in which negative light Blackness, but also in particular Africa and Africans, have been portrayed in dominant American culture.

"I CAME WITH PASSPORT; THEY CAME IN CHAINS": DISTINCTION AND DISCORD

Sharing a common ancestry and race does not mean that different Black groups forgo a desire to claim and be recognized as distinct ethnic and cultural groups, either vis-à-vis each other or non-Black people, in particular native-born White Americans. Much of the literature has argued that Black immigrants and refugees distance themselves from native-born Black Americans (Imoagene 2017; R. O. Jackson 2010) to achieve what Greer (2013, 7) refers to as an "elevated minority status" that would lead to economic and social upward mobility (V. S. Johnson 2016; Waters et al. 2014). Scholars have asserted that Black refugees and immigrants do this, since "one of the first things newcomers to America discover about their adopted country is that African Americans are a stigmatized group, to be avoided at all cost[s]" (Loury 2002, 90). Therefore, some Black immigrants and refugees pursue this "strategic disassociation" (V. S. Johnson 2016, 54) from native-born Black Americans, their assumed proximal host (Mittelberg and Waters 1992), through different avenues. Some African immigrants and refugees have embraced distinct non-Black categories, such as "Arab" in the case of some Muslim Sudanese (Fábos 2012) and Somalis (C. Abdi 2015a) and "Habesha" for some Ethiopian and Eritrean ethnic groups (Habecker 2012; Kebede 2017). Other times, African immigrants have emphasized their religious identities, specifically being Muslim, to convey separate identities (C. Abdi 2015b; Guenther et al. 2011).

Part of this distancing is motivated by a desire to employ a protective mechanism against anti-Black racism (Adjepong 2018; Guenther et al. 2011). While this most certainly is true in some instances, I posit that this should also be seen and understood as distinguishing themselves and claiming separate and specific ethnic and cultural identities, much in the way that, for example, Korean immigrants are afforded that in relation to Chinese Americans. They are Asian Americans but distinct in their cultures, languages, and histories.[8] The same ought to apply to Liberian refugees and native-born Black Americans, both being Black but unique in their historical, cultural, and linguistic backgrounds. By asserting their specific identities, they "are challenging dominant . . . conceptions about blackness as well as articulating the diversity of their black experiences" (Adjepong 2018, 251).

This desire for a distinct identity is not exclusive to Liberian refugees, as boundary-making between ethnic, religious, cultural, and linguistic groups is common (Barth 1998). Sometimes, this means that forging separate and distinct identities occurs by disassociating oneself from others, and in the process the other groups can even be at times viewed in disparaging ways (Nsangou and Dundes 2018). This has played out when African refugees and immigrants (Okonofua 2013; Traoré 2004), including Liberians, have emphasized their historical differences as it pertains to slavery. Indigenous Liberian refugees at times pointed out either among themselves or in interactions with native-born Black Americans that they were never enslaved.[9] Wannie Jacobs, a 1.5-generation Liberian refugee, exemplifies this. She was quick to establish that when she "got into altercation[s] with African Americans" she would "let them know . . . your ancestors were the one who were sold. They were slaves. . . . So, I mean I let them know that at the end of the day we weren't slaves . . . but you guys are the slaves and not us." Like Ms. Jacobs, Nowa Namo, a widowed, middle-aged Kpelle refugee who grew up in Bong County, believed that she was "better" than native-born Black Americans and Americo Liberians because her ancestors had never been enslaved. She recounted how her mother had told her that "during that olden . . . day when people sell people as slaves . . . from Africa," it was Africans who "had no respect" and an overall "bad behavior" who were sold and "brought to this country."[10] As described further below, she felt that these ancestral ties explained why Liberians have a superior culture compared to native-born Black Americans, something that was very hurtful to native-born Black Americans. Other Liberians, such as Baka Wehjay, observed that some native-born Black Americans "resented" Africans because "they felt that our forefathers sold them or sold their forefathers into slavery." However, not all Liberian refugees acknowledged native Africans' involvement in the transatlantic slave trade, asserting that they "are not responsible . . . and . . . got nothing to do with that," as Garsuah Janjay, an asylee originally from Grand Bassa County, said. In any case, Liberians almost unanimously pointed out that their own arrival in the United States was distinct from those of native-born Black Americans' ancestors. This was exemplified by Oman Zumo, a father of four, who noted that Black people in the United States "all came from the same root" but "got here through different medium. . . . I took the plane, they took the ship; I came with passport, they came in chains." By doing so, Mr. Zumo asserted that he chose to move, whereas Africans who were enslaved centuries ago did not have the choice. While this was certainly the case for him since he came to the United States as an international student before the outbreak of the civil war, Liberian refugees who were displaced and persecuted did not necessarily have a choice to move but were forced to do so in order to survive.

In addition to drawing on heritage to emphasize their distinct identities from other Black people in the United States, Liberians also highlighted how their culture made them different from native-born Black Americans, while not challenging their shared racial background. Some of this was not necessarily driven by animosity but rather by competition for scarce economic resources and social opportunities (Okonofua 2013) that manifests itself in assertions of cultural difference and sometimes claims of superiority.

For example, Enid Browning, a Monrovia native, said, "We're the same, we're one, but there's a difference of course in the cultural upbringing." This mirrors what many other Black immigrant groups have done. Some first- and second-generation Black Caribbean immigrants accentuate their ethnicity, as Haitians and Jamaicans, for example, to assert their cultural backgrounds in contrast to native-born Black Americans (Etienne 2020; Waters 1999). The same has been reported for African immigrants and refugees who use culture and religion to create intraracial boundaries (Nsangou and Dundes 2018; Sall 2022). In the case of Liberian refugees, their culture becomes visible to their native-born Black American neighbors mostly through the food they cook and sell at the market, the clothes they wear, and public celebrations of Liberian-themed events that are accompanied by West African music and dances. This public display of Liberian culture and traditions was not always supported by their native-born Black American neighbors and caused some intraracial tensions. For example, Brendan Mack, a young, native-born Black American who grew up in Park Hill, described the market and thus the Liberian refugees who went there as something "that made them different . . . them wanting to be closer to their people . . . and put their culture out there." And whereas Mr. Mack was polite when acknowledging that he never tried any of their food, others had harsher words, as Varney Yarkpolo, who was born in Lofa County, recounted when thinking of how some native-born Black Americans responded to the presence of Liberian culture, and food in particular: "Oh these Africans, What are you doing here? You smell. That food stinks." He noted that this made him and other Liberians "feel very bad." While Michael Lewis, a native-born Black American and long-term resident of Park Hill, did not disparage the food, indeed he noted how he eventually tried and liked "pepper soup, cassava leaf, and Torborgee";[11] he talked about how he was startled when he saw "late at night . . . Africans, Liberians . . . bring livestock into the building . . . like goats. I wasn't used to seeing . . . animals being slaughtered in the house." I should note that during all the time I spent in Park Hill I never saw that. However, I recall my co-workers at a VOLAG in

Atlanta telling me about other refugee groups in the 1980s doing similar things and that it was a time of adjustment for everyone. And while slaughtering of animals in residential areas is understandably a reason for concern in urban areas in the United States, cultural dress and other traditions should not be. But it was exactly this that Liberians, such as Baka Wehjay, recalled from their initial encounters with some of their native-born Black American neighbors in Park Hill. Mr. Wehjay said, "When they see the attire, they want to label you as inferior or some kind of African person who they don't... want. So, they look at you... down, especially the innocent African American, well, innocent in the sense that they don't understand... the African culture and... clothes." Relatedly, other Liberians remembered when native-born Black Americans used the same slurs and insults that native-born White Americans hurled at them. For example, Ms. Juah Nimley, who joined her mother in Staten Island in 1987, recalled her experiences in school with her native-born Black American peers: "I was called Kunte Kinte... Umfufu... Shaka Zulu.... This guy, Eddie [Murphy], got this show... where he talk about going to Africa and getting a wife with a big bone in her nose and sitting on a camel.[12]... Those kind of things.... They would say, 'She lives in a jungle, she lives in a tree,' you know... those kind of stigma.... Thought you live in hut because that's all they... see on television." Even decades later, when Beatrice Akoi, an ethnic Loma, first settled in the United States, she still encountered this type of teasing, which included insults such as "looking like monkeys... living with monkeys." Liberian refugees are not alone, as other African refugees and immigrants have experienced this discrimination at the hands of some native-born Black Americans as well (Imoagene 2017; Traoré 2004). Liberians I spoke with overall found the insults and rejections by native-born Black Americans more difficult to justify than those by native-born White Americans.[13] They had to some extent expected to be discriminated against by native-born White Americans, but hearing these slurs from other Black people was perplexing. Elizabeth Kamara, a certified nursing assistant, said, "Some of them will say those kind of mean things to me.... Then I say, 'We have the same skin color.... You calling me African, you calling me names, look at your skin color. You and I are Black. So, how can you call your Black sister names?'... They feel that they are... better than us from Africa. But we have the same skin color!"

But it was not just Liberian refugees who believed that native-born Black Americans "felt that they were better" than Africans. Native-born Black Americans, such as Dee Love who grew up in Brooklyn but raised her children in Staten Island's North Shore, voiced that Liberians and other Africans "look at you like they're better than you." Therefore, as her daughter Lemon Angel, recalled, her mother prohibited her and her brother from hanging out or playing with any of the Liberian refugees or other African immigrants in Park Hill. Ms. Love's feeling are supported by the disparaging views and stereotypes about native-born Black Americans that some Liberian refugees and African immigrants readily cited, describing them as "lazy" and "lacking respect and culture" (Arthur 2000; Roubeni et al. 2015) and thus different to how Zubah Kpadeh, who was resettled with his brother, aunt, and grandfather, described himself: "I am African, so I am humble and hardworking." In the end, these reciprocal insults and misgivings can be understood as symptoms of larger issues: the struggle to escape being placed or kept at the bottom rung of society and the fight for scarce resources (H. E. Brown 2011).

Liberians in Park Hill, like other African refugees across the country (Tesfai 2019), found themselves in a neighborhood that was not only resource-deprived but also ill-prepared to welcome and accommodate a group of refugees from a war-torn country. For the VOLAGs that facilitated the resettlement efforts, affordable housing and proximity to public transportation, as well as an assumed racial and cultural affinity between these two Black groups, were key determining factors for resettling Liberian refugees in Park Hill. The same pattern can also be observed for Liberian and other African refugees in cities such as Atlanta, Minneapolis, and Philadelphia (Besteman 2016; Reilly 2014; Sackett and Lareau 2023). During this intentional resettlement, none of the VOLAGs involved conducted outreach to the existing communities. Hence, native-born Black Americans were presented with a fait accompli. They only realized over time that they would now be sharing the neighborhood and already limited resources. This competition for scarce opportunities, including jobs and housing, is a big part of the story of the initial contentious relationship between Liberian refugees and native-born Black Americans, which has also been reported for other low-income neighborhoods where refugees and native-born Black Americans live (A. J. Kim and Bozarth 2021; R. S. Smith 2008). In the early years, most Liberian refugees did not grasp—or perhaps were too busy focused on rebuilding their lives—why native-born Black Americans perceived "these country people coming from nowhere . . . settling among them" as problematic, as Varney Yarkpolo, the former caseworker, said. But two decades later, Liberians, including Garpu Garbleh, who also had worked for a VOLAG, were able to voice an understanding of why some of the original residents of Park Hill were "hostile . . . and not very receptive . . . to the influx of refugees in their community," Mr. Garbleh said. Liberian refugees were seen as a threat to the scarce opportunities, including jobs.

Similarly, Bernice Richards, who for several years worked with youth in Staten Island's North Shore, was keenly aware of how many poor native-born Black Americans perceived the aid and support that Liberian refugees received when they first arrived in the neighborhood: "They never got resources that they needed for their community, so when the Africans came . . . because of the war . . . it was huge amount of aids in . . . Park Hill and that upset them. . . . At some town hall meeting . . . they said . . . 'We've been here so and so amount of time . . . we never got nothing, and you guys get everything.'"

The majority of Liberian refugees made the argument that they, as refugees, needed these resources after surviving a war to start a new life in a new country (see also H. E. Brown 2011). Cynthia Sherif, a mother of three, gave insight to this mindset when she said, "Liberians . . . needed a start. There were people that had twenty family members that came at one time. Food is expensive, medical is expensive. You can't put twenty people at one time on your health coverage, and these programs were here just to get people . . . on their feet. . . . A lot of the people just need it as a start because they want to do something, and this is a place of opportunity, and so people want that opportunity."

However, a good number of her native-born Black American neighbors also felt that they needed support, which they had been promised centuries ago and never received. It was hard to see newly arrived groups getting resources, as noted by Nigel Baba, a native-born Black American athletic coach: "We got to this point . . . saying . . . 'You guys are stealing all our resources.' . . . This psychological effect from us being slaves or the physical effect of us not getting our forty acres and a mule, or getting reparations or things of that nature." As Mr. Baba noted, for native-born Black Americans whose communities have experienced centuries of anti-Black racism, the incoming aid that they felt passed them by reminded them of past and present injuries and of overt and not-so-overt favoritism that the literature has documented for immigrants over native-born Black Americans, especially in the labor market (Marrow 2011; Waters et al. 2014).

I observed such competition over resources many times, including one spring day when I waited for a Liberian resident outside the SILCA office in Park Hill. While I was there, the New York City Food Bank was dropping off groceries for SILCA, and I got into a conversation with a Black man in his late twenties, who, based on his New York accent, I would identify as a native-born American. Upon the arrival of the truck, he commented, "They always get everything, but we don't," implying that the food donations were only for Liberians. While Liberians have assured me many times that their organizations and, by extension, services and goods, are available to all residents in the area regardless of ethnicity and nationality, it is easy to understand why others, including this Park Hill resident, thought this way. The name of the organization in charge of the food distribution clearly indicates a Liberian affiliation, thus possibly deterring non-Liberians from asking for assistance. Liberian refugees, unaware of this perception, often became defensive and felt that they were being singled out for naming an organization "Liberian" or "African." For example, Oman Zumo, who founded and operated an organization in Park Hill in the 1990s until the 2000s, noted that he received a call from the New York City commissioner for youth services about having "African" in the name of the organization, to which he responded that he is "an easy prey, easy . . . to pick on this way" because there is "not a problem with the Jewish Community Center that says 'Jewish' in their name."

Mr. Zumo felt victimized and singled out but at the same time did not—at least at that point—recognize the extent to which native-born Black Americans have been excluded and victimized in the United States. It is in this light that cleavages between Liberian refugees and native-born Black Americans, especially in the early days, must be understood. After all, their racial socialization was different;

whereas native-born Black Americans from a young age "learn about the influence of race on their lives . . . their racial group status . . . [and] relationships with other racial groups" in the United States (Nunnally 2010, 341), Liberians, like other refugees and immigrants, came to only comprehend the full extent of the dominant role of race and anti-Black racism as part of their incorporation into U.S. society (Treitler 2015, 159). While most Liberian refugees had expected anti-Black racism, time spent in the United States and the personal experience of this "systematically perpetuated . . . form of the state-sanctioned violence" made them slowly realize that they share more with native-born Black Americans than they had initially anticipated (Thomas et al. 2024, 395). Some Liberian refugees felt that they could have arrived at this point—understanding systemic anti-Black racism and the impact on native-born Black Americans—earlier had they engaged in more meaningful, and perhaps guided, conversations. This was illustrated by Sam Collins, who settled as a teenager in Park Hill. He bluntly said, "Ignorance and lack of education hurt the situation a lot."

Similarly, native-born Black Americans, such as Michael Lewis, recognized that they as a group had also failed to "take the time . . . to understand their new neighbors . . . their trials and tribulations" and thus had caused a lot of conflict and misunderstanding. But over time, as the groups started spending more time with each other, they learned about what makes the other unique, but even more so about their similarities and thus "gradually . . . absorb one another," as Varney Yarkpolo said. In particular, it became evident to many Liberian refugees, including Mr. J., who was introduced at the beginning of this chapter, that they had shared experiences due to the widespread anti-Black racism in the United States.

"IT REMINDS ME OF THE HARD WORK OF OUR FOREFATHERS": A FUTURE BOUND BY ANTI-BLACK RACISM

While the previous section was concerned on differences and distinct experiences of Liberian refugees and native-born Black Americans that at times have led to misunderstandings and tensions, here I focus on how these groups have come together at different times and for a number of reasons. One explanation is that Liberian refugees, like other Black immigrants and refugees, have had to deal with anti-Black racism in many, if not most, aspects of their lives in the United States. This is a similarity with native-born Black Americans, who over the past centuries have developed an outlook that their own lives are affected by what happens to other Black people in the United States. (Cox and Tamir 2022; C. W. Smith 2014). Dawson (1994, 77) defines this as linked fate, "the degree to which African Americans believe their own self-interests are linked to the interests of the race." Hence, the question arises if and when Liberian refugees come to see their experiences with anti-Black racism as resembling those of native-born Black Americans and feel that their fate is linked. As I describe below, much of this "coming together" is fueled by 1.5- and second-generation Liberian refugees' experiences. They have grown up in the United States and thus have been exposed to U.S. education and curricula while attending school and after-school activities with native-born Black Americans in their neighborhoods. The younger generation plays a crucial part in making visible to the first generation how Liberians' experiences with anti-Black racism are not isolated instances but part of the larger experience of being Black in the United States (V. S. Johnson 2016; Nsangou and Dundes 2018; Sall 2019). Recognizing the overwhelming control that anti-Black racism has over Black people's lives and well-being has also lead Liberian refugees and native-born Black Americans to join forces to amplify their voices for civil rights (e.g., Black Lives Matter movement) and elect politicians whom they hope would be advocates for them (see also Bunyasi and Smith 2019; Rogers and Kim 2023).[14]

"I Have the Experience of an American": 1.5- and Second-Generation Liberian Refugees

Growing up in the United States makes it harder for 1.5- and second-generation Liberian refugees to keep or develop strong ties to Liberia, which has in a sense facilitated processes of perceiving commonalities and building community with native-born Black Americans. Opposed to that, research shows that the majority of first-generation refugees and immigrants, regardless of their race, identify with their native countries and often also prioritize what is happening there (Gurung 2015; V. S. Johnson 2016). In an effort to strengthen cultural, ethnic, and national identification, (upper) middle-class African immigrant parents have used different strategies to keep their children part of transnational networks and exchanges, which in turn can lead to ethnic and cultural pride (Awokoya 2012; Kebede 2017). For Liberian refugees in the United States, however, maintaining and developing these transnational networks was, especially in the early days, not possible due to the war and widespread displacement. The majority of 1.5- and second-generation Liberians have either only visited their ancestral land once, recently, or not at all.

Therefore, the connection of younger generations to Liberia has been limited to what their parents and other family and community members have told them or the stereotypes they have been confronted with by their American peers, school curricula, and the media (Traoré 2004). Scholars have demonstrated that Black immigrants in general highlight their ethnic and parents' national origins at different times, for example, when they seek to evade a particular kind of American anti-Black racism (Chacko 2003; Etienne 2020). This was less so the case for 1.5- and second-generation Liberian refugees. In fact, they were reluctant to embrace Liberian identities, since for many of them "Liberia" and "being Liberian" has at times evoked shame due to distorted images and stereotypes that depict Liberia as a culturally backward place, the civil war, being poor refugees, and their (grand) parents' lack of or limited formal education and low-status jobs. David Joe, a father of six, witnessed this firsthand when his youngest child, who was three years old when she came to the United States, "didn't want to . . . accept that she was from Liberia, Africa . . . especially after she went to school." She was not the only 1.5- or second-generation Liberian refugee who did not identify as African or Liberian. Others, such as Samuel Black, who was resettled as a seven-year-old in Staten Island after his oldest sister had sponsored him, his mother, and his younger siblings, were also more comfortable with a non-African identity. While Mr. Black acknowledged that there were animosities and quarrels between Liberian refugees and native-born Black Americans in the neighborhood and in school, he explained that he was "never picked on" by native-born Black Americans because he "wanted to be with them, wanted to be close to them . . . wanted to be friends with them." He described that this was the natural choice for him since he "just want to see myself as an American and leave the past as the past." He further explained why this was the case: "I came here at a young age, so basically, I have the experience of an American. If I go back there, I am going to suffer myself. I don't have experience; I don't know nothing . . . if I go back to Africa." Identifying as "American" and/or with native-born Black Americans was an option for Mr. Black, who grew up in the early 2000s, due to the bonds that the generation of youth before him forged. Samuel Collins, who belongs to that earlier generation, elaborated on how these changes occurred: "So, there's a point where they started coming together because if you live next to somebody for twenty years in the same apartment, after a while you're gonna be able to determine, 'OK this guy is pretty good' because there was no gunfight next door, or they had a really cool party and knocked on my door and they invited me. . . . So, if you find the real people that understand and . . . have learned. . . . But there was a time where they were fighting, and like literally." Through spending time together at parties, in the neighborhood, and in school, friendships and romantic relationships between members of these two groups developed. Another very intimate relationship between some native-born Black Americans and Liberian refugees that I observed occurs in beauty care. I conducted several interviews in a barbershop operated by a Black Caribbean man who was in a relationship for a few years with a Liberian woman with whom he has two sons. All of the women working there were of Liberian ancestry. But the barbershop's clientele was made up of patrons from West Africa, the United States, and the Caribbean. Usually, their conversations about life in general, relationships, and family were accompanied by blasting reggae music.

Gerald Barclay, a well-known filmmaker and producer who was born in Liberia and came to the United States shortly after President Tolbert was executed, also exemplifies how professional collaborations have come about. Living in Park Hill, he grew up with members of the Wu-Tang Clan. As the Wu-Tang Clan began its rise to fame, Mr. Barclay was able to collaborate with them, helping his and their careers along. He explained, "I was becoming a filmmaker, and it was a no-brainer. . . . I am already in the community. So, they asked me to do stuff for them, and I did. It came out well." Until this day, Mr. Barclay continues to make films about the Wu-Tang Clan, Park Hill, and Liberia.

Just as Hip Hop is essential to American, and in particular certain segments of Black American culture, so is the Civil Rights movement. While, as discussed in the previous chapter, many first-generation Liberian refugees were keenly aware of past injustices such as the enslavement of Black people in the United States, the Civil Rights movement and the watershed legislations that followed were often less apparent to them. This is especially notable as they have directly benefited from these accomplishments (Imoagene 2017; Kasinitz 2008).[15] In contrast to Liberian refugees who arrived in the United States as adults, the 1.5 and second generations, who have attended school in the United States, have a more in-depth knowledge and appreciation of the struggles and achievements of native-born Black Americans. This exposure to U.S. education and curricula means that those who have come of age in the United States have a greater sense of how systemic discrimination and anti-Black racism affects all Black people in the United States. For example, after learning in school about the Jim Crow era, Israel Youkonjay Ways, who joined his mother after years of separation once she was granted asylum in the United States, took it upon himself to learn more about this particular part of history and race relations in the United States: "I wanted to know race relations. So, I got to know a lot of stuff and I actually cried . . . and I told myself I will respect every Black American person because they went through a lot. . . . Because I read that the Jim Crow era, the law was passed . . . how kids were killed for kissing other kids because they were White, children staring at young girls and they were killed for, and I also saw people being beaten to death. . . . I mean it's horrible, I felt horrible." As he pondered on what he learned and read, Mr. Ways reflected on the fact that had he been alive and in the United States at that time, this "would have been my status in history." He was aware that Jim Crow laws and anti-Black violence would have impacted him, too, as he is a Black man. This is why he did not "consider that some kind of gratification" when native-born White Americans told him that "people who come straight from Africa recently are . . . more well trained and have good behavior than the people who were born here." Instead, Mr. Ways was upset that native-born White Americans were not acknowledging the country's wrongdoings. Similarly, Sunday John, who is married to a native-born Black American man, discussed how she was grateful for the sacrifices that native-born Black Americans had made and their great achievements, which impacted her personally: "When I look back I say, 'Thank God for the Civil Rights movement.' Because when I look at some things, I didn't experience it, but I watch the movies. . . . If those things were still going on, I don't think some of them [Liberians] would have been here. . . . I wouldn't be here. . . . I don't think Black people could sponsor some people to come to America. . . . Thank God for people that fought." Therefore, once Liberian refugees, such as Annie Quide, who came as an older teenager to Staten Island, reflected on the sacrifices native-born Black Americans made to end slavery and bring about the Civil Rights movement, they expressed an understanding of why some native-born Black Americans were upset when newcomers, such as Liberian refugees, did not show deference for their or their ancestors' struggles but only just seized on the opportunities now available to all (Black) people.[16] Ms. Quide said, "For . . . African Americans . . . what happened to them back in the days. . . . Today the Africans have come and everything has been said and done. It's like I made the bed . . . I did this, I clean this place . . . finish sweeping the house . . . and now you just come and jump up on it . . . so . . . they will get mad." Learning more about these struggles and also personally experiencing anti-Black racism led many Liberians, but especially younger generations, to come to comprehend that they shared many experiences with native-born Black Americans because just like them, they have been racialized as Black.

"The Reality Is That You Are Black": Shared and Compounded Experiences of Discrimination

Personal encounters with anti-Black racism in the United States forced Liberian refugees to reassess the hopes and dreams they had for a better and safer future in the United States, as these are complicated by the systemic and historic role race, and in particular anti-Black racism, has played (Hadley and Patil 2009; Nunnally 2010; Guluma 2023). This has been evident in encounters that Liberians have had with the police and racist people who usually do not distinguish Black people based on their ethnicity but just see them as Black (V. S. Johnson 2016).

A good number of younger-generation Liberian refugees, like other second-generation Black immigrants and refugees (Sall 2022, Wallace 2018), have had dehumanizing encounters through widespread discriminatory policies such as stop-and-frisk in New York, leaving no doubt that race is the master status through which they are seen by others, in particular those in power (see also Asante et al. 2016). Given that most 1.5- and second-generation Liberian refugees have "the experience of Americans," as Samuel Black noted, they are, to outsiders most of the time, indistinguishable from native-born Black Americans. This was also not lost on their parents' generation, such as Nyema Browne, a Grebo woman, who said, "Most of our kids dress, they talk like the African Americans." These younger-generation Liberian refugees often lack ethnic markers such as a foreign accent and, at times, distinct West African names, since many Liberians have Anglo first and last names due to the historical ties of Liberia with the United States. Therefore, as Love Juah, a middle-aged woman who settled in Staten Island for almost two decades, observed, this shared race means that "when kids . . . go in the store, they are American Black, or maybe they are African . . . you don't know what . . . and they follow them." But regularly it was more than being followed. Baka Wehjay shared with me how he witnessed indiscriminate police harassment and violence in Staten Island's North Shore: "I have seen where cops . . . shot some Black kids because they . . . suspect them of selling drugs. And I have not heard or seen that in . . . White neighborhoods. . . . In Park Hill, there is always . . . something going on like that. . . . The White kids . . . may behave the same way like the Liberian . . . or the African American kids. . . . The police have a job to do and some of them . . . have to meet their quota, so it doesn't matter whether you are African or you are African American." These observations left no doubt for Mr. Wehjay and other

Liberian refugees that they, and in particular their children, were experiencing anti-Black racism similar to that of other Black people in the United States, which included being stereotyped as "immanently and exceptionally violent" (Smalls 2018, 356).

However, there has been an added layer for Liberian refugees: the intersection of being Black and being a refugee from a country with a lengthy civil war. In other words, Liberians, in particular (young) men, have been burdened with not only "general" stereotypes of Black men but also those about African men who experienced war. The glaring images of the brutality of the Liberian civil war, with its use of child soldiers in the media, have nurtured views among a number of non-Black Staten Islanders that Liberian men are innately violent (Quart 2007). The following conversation in a teacher's lounge at a Staten Island middle school—overheard by Eva McGovern, a native-born White American who worked for a VOLAG—demonstrates this vividly. She described hearing several teachers discuss the behaviors of students who included 1.5- and second-generation Liberian youth. She called one teacher, saying, "Oh, don't you know that the Liberians . . . can come to this country for free . . . because they took people out of the jails in America and sent them back to found this country [Liberia]. Haven't you guys read your history about this?" Another educator responded, "Maybe that's why the boys are so violent." This notion of "violent Black men as brutes" is deeply rooted in U.S. society (Ferber 2007) and especially its discourse about refugees, where Black refugee men "are assumed to be incapable of controlling their animal instincts . . . including violence" (S. Turner 2017, 54). This is also a common narrative used by police officers around the country who, when using (deadly) violence against Black people, claim to have feared for their own lives (C. Lee 2004). But it took the Liberian refugee community several years of living in Park Hill to fully grasp the extent of the danger they were facing as Black people in the United States, since they "are not educated . . . about police. . . . Police who . . . just shoot Blacks," according to Varney Konneh, who came to Staten Island when his children were in elementary school. These sentiments have been echoed across the country in other African refugee communities. For example, after Patrick Lyoya, a Congolese refugee, was killed by a police officer in Michigan, Robert Womack, a representative of a local Black Leadership Advisory Council, noted that Black refugees "never really got a chance to get briefed by us of our experience as Black people with the police" (Shammas 2022, para. 11). Just as Patrick Lyoya and his family never received a warning about anti-Black racism and its potential lethal outcome, neither did many Liberian refugees in the early years of their resettlement to the United States. And indeed, it did not take long for the first person of Liberian descent to lose their life by police force. One of the first cases was Lucia Roberts, who was killed in 1982 when she was sixteen years old. She was the aunt of a young 1.5-generation Liberian woman who participated in this study.[17] The niece recalled how decades after "my mom's younger sister . . . in Boston . . . was murdered—raped and murdered by cops," her family "has been trying to get justice . . . for so many years." But as of the writing of this book, the White police officers implicated were not found guilty despite a Boston police detective alluding that this was a police cover-up (Marie 2021). A decade later, police violence also took the life of a Liberian American in Staten Island. Ernest Sayon, a second-generation Liberian, was killed in a police encounter in Park Hill in 1994 (Bernstein 1994). What followed were joint protests by Liberian refugees and native-born Black Americans against police brutality, which in turn brought these two communities closer to address police violence and intraracial violence in the community (Auer 2008). Beverly Coleman, who had moved to Staten Island in the 1980s, remembered these days: "It was about time that the African Americans and the Africans work together because the killing was so high on Park Hill. . . . We had three meetings with 120 [police precinct] . . . in a month." Despite these efforts to work with the local police precinct, the attacks on Black lives have continued. For example, a 1.5-generation Liberian teenager, who had only arrived eight years before, became the victim of a hate crime the night Barack Obama was first elected president of the United States in November of 2008. The assailants did not target him because he was Liberian but because they were on a mission to "beat up n——" (Hauser 2009, para. 12).

Whereas the U.S. Department of Justice report states that another victim that night was "an individual whom the defendants mistakenly believed was African-American" (U.S. Attorney's Office, Eastern District of New York 2009, para. 7),[18] it identified the Liberian refugee as an "African-American man" (para. 5). This is an indication that ethnicity and nativity for Black immigrants and refugees are often ignored (V. S. Johnson 2016; Pierre 2004; Thomas et al. 2024). Hate crimes have continued through this decade as well. In 2020, campaign signs for Kelvin Richards, candidate for City Council, who had spent his teenage years in the Buduburam refugee camp in Ghana, were vandalized with "no n—" and "f—you n—" scrawled next to his picture (Donnelly 2021).[19] To the offender, a White Staten Islander with a history of leaving anti-Black racist messages in Staten Island's North Shore, Mr. Richards was just Black; his Liberian/refugee background was irrelevant. This was not lost on Kelvin Richards, who invoked the sacrifices native-born Black Americans had made and how he identified with them in his response to the hate crime: "I'm surprised that we still have to go through this. . . . It reminds me of the hard work of our forefathers and our civil rights leaders. . . . I want to be judged by the contents of my character, not the color of my skin" (Moore and Cassady 2020, para. 4).[20]

While these particular hate crimes "only" led to bodily harm and emotional duress, Liberians became more and more aware that hate crimes and other forms of violence against Black people often turn deadly in the United States. High-profile murders such as those of Eric Garner in Staten Island and George Floyd in Minneapolis—both areas with large Liberian refugee populations—made this more evident. Subsequently, an increasing number of first-generation Liberian parents have been educating their children, in particular their sons, about the deadly reality of anti-Black racism in the United States. These parents included Thomas Bono, who for a long time held a leadership position in the community and was thus even more attuned to what has been happening. Mr. Bono summarized coming to this realization and how the community tried to prepare their children for anti-Black racism: "We educate, we try to tell our children . . . that the reality is that you are Black . . . especially . . . a male child . . . have a disadvantage, you fit a lot of negative profiles. So, we tell them these things when they get in the street. . . . They are not a regular White kid living in some suburb. No, we tell them that's not the reality. The same for us, the older folks. . . . We were not used to it; we are now used to the idea there's a second class . . . a second color." Experiences with anti-Black racism tend to make Black immigrants more sympathetic to the plight of native-born Black Americans and to subscribe to the concept of a linked fate (Apraku 1996; Rogers 2004). Given these real concerns and racialization experiences (Kasinitz 1992), Liberians started to more actively seek alliances with native-born Black Americans and to some extent, join the Black Lives Matter movement, a similarity shared with other Black immigrants (Imoagene 2019; Thomas et al. 2024). This has also been supported by the Liberian community's leadership. For example, Abraham Tucker, then-president of SILCA, reasoned that different Black groups were in this fight together and concluded that "what affects one, affects the other. . . . Racists and the police are not targeting African Americans alone, they are targeting blacks" (Kamara 2020, para. 9).[21]

Despite coming to these recognitions of shared fate of being targeted as Black people in the United States, native-born Black Americans and African refugees and immigrants in Staten Island held separate virtual meetings with local politicians and the local police precinct after the murder of George Floyd in the summer of 2020.[22] Perhaps this reflects not only how Liberian refugees, especially the first generation, generally have held on to their Liberian identities but also the way that they find themselves vulnerable to law enforcement. Many Liberians, like other Black immigrants and refugees, occupy a "double stigmatized status" (Layne 2021, 3) and thus are in "double jeopardy" (Ibe 2021, para. 11) due to being Black and their noncitizenship status.[23]

Racialized policing that singles out Black people through stop-and-frisk and similar policies has the potential to have specific consequences for Black refugees and immigrants, since they are not native-born U.S. citizens. Whether they are refugees, legal permanent residents, or undocumented immigrants, any kind of felony conviction frequently leads to deportation. Data and research (McKanders 2020; Morgan-Trostle et al. 2020) bear out what I have seen and read firsthand in Staten Island and as a country conditions expert for several deportation hearings across the country. The scenario is frequently the same: a male 1.5-generation Liberian refugee who arrived in the United States as a young child or teenager, often highly traumatized, was resettled in a neighborhood similar to Park Hill: violent and underresourced but overpoliced. As the young person grew up, he got caught up with the wrong crowd or, based on past experiences in the war or in a refugee camp, chose to protect himself or his family with an illegal firearm.[24] That weapon or another illicit activity was uncovered by the police following a targeted, racialized stop because, as James Paye, a former community organizer, said, "The police . . . do that all the time to Black men in this country. . . . At the root . . . is Black suspicion." In other words, Black immigrants and refugees, especially men, are caught up in the criminal system foremost because they are Black, not because they are immigrants and/or in violation of immigration laws. Data show that "Black immigrants are nearly three times more likely to be detained and deported because of an alleged criminal offense" compared to other immigrants and refugees (Ibe 2021, para. 14). Furthermore, Black immigrants are overrepresented among immigrants facing deportation based on criminal grounds and also more likely to be deported than immigrants and refugees who are not Black (McKanders 2020; Morgan-Trostle et al. 2020). Nopper (2008, 204–205) describes these facts as "reflect[ing] the growing intersection between immigration enforcement and the forms of crime control to which Black populations in the United States (both immigrant and native-born) have been historically subjected." This implies that Liberian refugees, like most other Black refugees and immigrants, have had to come to the realization that acculturation and incorporation into U.S. society results in being affected by the same systems of racial profiling, overpolicing, and unjust application of U.S. criminal laws as native-born Black Americans (McKanders 2020; Palmer 2017). Living in a sanctuary city like New York does not protect Liberian refugees, as they are caught in the racially targeted dragnet policing that focuses on (alleged) crimes that are part of the federal crime register, which is tied to immigration enforcement. It is then these shared experiences with criminalization based on their race, as well as newfound appreciation for the political struggles of native-born Black Americans, that have led Liberian refugees and native-born Black Americans to join forces for political causes.

"At Least We Have Somebody of Color": Political Representation

Liberian refugees and native-born Black Americans' strategic coalition, especially in the political realm, builds on a rich tradition of alliances that have existed between Black immigrants and native-born Black Americans dating back to the early twentieth century. While in the beginning Black Caribbean immigrants did not claim separate ethnic identities in politics, they have done so starting in the late 1960s as their numbers increased (Bryce-Laporte 1972; Kasinitz 1992). Subsequently, they began emphasizing distinct identities and different priorities, which sometimes fractured existing relationships between this immigrant group and native-born Black Americans (Greer 2013; Rogers 2001). Given the sheer size of the Black Caribbean immigrant community in major cities such as New York and Miami, it has been feasible on occasion to have their "own" candidates and initiatives. This is less the case for African refugees and immigrants, since their numbers are smaller and there are larger linguistic, cultural, and religious distinctions within the group. African refugees and immigrants, like Liberians in Staten Island, at times pursue specific concerns (e.g., immigration, issues in their country of birth) and strive to have their own political candidates, but in the end, they often join ranks with native-born Black Americans to address anti-Black violence and racism and get a Black candidate elected.

Liberians and the leadership of the Liberian community have also expressed solidarity through public celebrations of Black lives and accomplishments. For example, they have participated in borough-wide Black History Month events and celebrations, where they also occasionally received awards in recognition for their work in the community. In addition, several North Shore churches that have Liberian pastors and large Liberian congregations have organized Black History Month–inspired events. Other times, Black residents from diverse backgrounds (Africa, Caribbean, and the United States) have come together to celebrate the African diaspora and its people during the Black Heritage Family Day Parade, the Staten Island African Heritage Cultural Festival, and/or Staten Island Black Heritage. The names of these events reflect changes in the leadership and collaborations—alternating between close and nonexistent—over the years. For example, Beverly Coleman, a Liberian community activist, shared that the initial name "Staten Island African Heritage Parade" was not supported by native-born Black American organizers because "the name . . . centered Africa." With that name in place, the native-born Black American support "faded away," and "no American attended the parade," as she remembered. Not ready to give up on this shared programming, Ms. Coleman invited all constituents back to the table to "look for something we have in common and that . . . African Americans will have interest in . . . our common heritage in Africa." Consequently, the name of the event was changed to Black Heritage Family Day Parade.[25]

Whereas these celebratory coalitions have not been without disagreement, there has always been more unity as it relates to supporting and electing Black politicians representing Staten Island's North Shore because most Liberian refugees and native-born Black Americans recognize what is at stake for Black people. Concretely, "linked fate is the linchpin to their solidarity in politics" (Rogers and Kim 2023, 290).

Over the years, the larger Black community in Staten Island has turned its attention to hyper-local political races, such as city council and state assembly members. This is where Liberians and other Black residents in Staten Island's North Shore have had the biggest political impact. Beginning in 2009, when native-born Black American Debi Rose was elected as a city council member, this seat (49th District) has continuously been held by a Black person. During all three campaign cycles, campaign ads for Rose could be found all over Park Hill. Several Liberians also actively campaigned for her, often with the hope that with her leadership things would improve for Liberian refugees and other Black people in the North Shore. Oman Zumo summarized his support during the last years of her tenure on the city council: "Thank God for Debi Rose. . . . At least we have somebody of color on the stage of electoral official on Staten Island. . . . When she was running, I invited Debi to the Liberian community; I wanted her to see the problems we have. . . . Debi . . . has been in the community; she knows about the bad funding situation for Black-run organizations in Staten Island. . . . She understands . . . she use her office."

Over the years, I observed that Debi Rose attended events organized by the Liberian community and also advocated for several projects that supported the diverse Black communities in the North Shore. For example, she stood by the Liberian community when they experienced discrimination due to being linked to Ebola or feared deportation when Trump announced that TPS would not be renewed. She also spoke out for justice in the aftermath of Eric Garner's murder and secured funding for parks and a recreation center in the North Shore. Debi Rose was succeeded by Kamillah Hanks, another native-born Black Staten Islander, in 2022. Hanks won the Democratic primary after the Black immigrant vote split among three Black candidates with immigrant/refugee backgrounds (Jamaica, Nigeria, and Liberia). The emergence of 1.5- and second-generation Black immigrant/refugee candidates in local Staten Island primaries mirrors what scholars have observed in Black Caribbean immigrant communities across the United States (Rogers 2004; C. W. Smith 2014). Whereas Greer (2018, 20) asserts immigrant candidates have run due to "weakened coalitions," the reason could also be that African refugees and immigrants are growing in numbers and have come to understand that they can be and are an important voting bloc. Case in point, several Liberians, including Beverly Coleman, noted that Debi Rose was elected because Liberians came out to support her. Based on the frequent visits that Rose made to events in the Liberian community during her tenure, it can be assumed that she also understood this group's collective power.

Rose's election in 2009 served as a catalyst for the ethnoracially diverse North Shore to elect a Black state assembly member starting in 2018. Charles Fall, a second-generation Guinean immigrant, won the Democratic nomination (over a native-born White American and a second-generation Nigerian immigrant) and has been reelected since then. Both political positions are now held by Black people, demonstrating that when Black people of different ethnic backgrounds "put aside their differences and form alliances" in favor of racial solidarity, they are able to elect Black politicians (Thomas et al. 2024, 395). Thus, the larger Black community in Staten Island appears not to be following a path scholars have observed regarding some political contests between native-born Black Americans and Black Caribbean immigrants who "elevate their competing ethnic interests over the prospect of racial solidarity" (Rogers and Kim 2023, 295). Instead, currently the larger Black community of Staten Island's North Shore seems to be leaning on their pan-ethnic coalitions, which have the potential to draw attention to issues that all Black people face and hopefully also secure government funding for these (Humphries 2009; Rogers 2001).

BEING BLACK AND LIBERIAN IN AMERICA

One thing has always been clear for Liberians: that they are Black. This was true in Liberia and is now true in the United States. However, the implications of being Black differ in these geographical contexts. Being Black is the prerequisite to being Liberian. Hence, while in Liberia, they paid very little attention to this part of their identity on a daily basis. Other aspects of identity, such as ethnicity and/or descent, have mattered, especially during Americo Liberian rule and much more during the civil war. Upon arriving in the United States, they experienced directly that anti-Black racism, which had provided the impetus for the creation of Liberia in the first place, is not something of the past. Simultaneously, their resettlement in a predominantly native-born Black American neighborhood forced Liberians to reckon with the notion that native-born Black Americans have different views of what it means to be "Black" and/or "African." These diverging viewpoints, coupled with limited resources in a neighborhood fraught with violence and crime, made this new beginning difficult for Liberian refugees. Only after years of living side by side, having children grow up together, and foremost, encountering the full brunt of anti-Black racism (e.g., through brutal and deadly encounters with the police and racial slurs) have these two groups forged some alliances in the political realm. Given the experiences of 1.5- and second-generation Liberian refugees and their identification as people who have "the experience of an American," the question arises of what happens as this generation continues to live here and has children. Will there be a renewed interest in a (symbolic) Liberian ethnicity akin to Hansen's law of "third-generation interest"? At the very least, from what I have been able to observe, their grandparents are eager to keep them exposed to and embedded in Liberian culture and traditions (e.g., through religious ceremonies, food, and music), while their parents are simultaneously concerned with transmitting the significance of being Black in a society shaped by anti-Black racism and how to protect and stand up for oneself.

7 THERE ARE LIBERIAN REFUGEES IN THE FUTURE

More than ten years ago, when I began this research about the Liberian refugee community, many people, inside and outside of academia, felt that this was an obscure topic. Simply put, the topic was not "sexy." Research about refugees in the United States had its heyday in the 1980s and 1990s, following the resettlement of thousands of people from Southeast Asia, Cuba, and the FSU, and the passage of the Refugee Act of 1980, which brought the U.S. definition of refugee on par with that of the UNHCR. Then, for almost fifteen years, refugees were not the subject of many academic studies. That does not mean that there was no mass-scale displacement of people; in fact, there were many, but they did not seem to resonate as much with either the public or scholars until events of the mid-2010s: the Syrian refugee crisis starting in the summer of 2015;[1] Executive Order 13769, which was the first iteration of the so-called Muslim ban, which in many ways was also an "African ban"; the temporary suspension of the USRAP in 2017; and the ongoing crisis around the treatment of Central American and other asylum seekers at the southern U.S. border.[2] The displacement of Ukrainians and Palestinians has also continued to capture the attention of the public, scholars, the media, and policymakers. Less prominent in the media and scholarship are the millions of African refugees who have lingered in protracted refugee situations for decades, such as Somalis, (South) Sudanese, Congolese, Central Africans, and the millions of IDPs around the globe. Roméo Dallaire (2009, 6), who served as the force commander of the U.N. Assistance Mission for Rwanda, concluded that "the root of it all . . . is the fundamental indifference of the world community to the plight of . . . black Africans in a . . . country that had no strategic or resource value to any world power."

This book seeks to shed light on this indifference toward Black refugees and thus is also a reminder that there is not one singular refugee experience, but that refugees are from different backgrounds and subsequently have very distinct experiences (Dutt et al. 2022), often shaped by race. I have documented how official immigration policies and systemic anti-Black racism have impacted if and how Black people can find refuge in the United States. Refugee and immigration policies are not, and never have been, race neutral; rather, they reflect the priorities as well as the history of a nation. The U.S. immigration and refugee policy is no exception. Many scholars have documented how nineteenth- and early twentieth-century immigration (and citizenship) laws targeted certain national groups from Asia and Southern, Central, and Eastern Europe (Ngai 2014; Roediger 2005). Yet present-day refugee laws have also favored some ethnic and national groups and thus, by extension, racial groups, over others, with the most blatant case being Trump's designation of White South Africans as "refugees." By examining policies and the everyday experiences of Liberian refugees, I make the case that any analysis of refugee and immigration policies and subsequent integration must be done through a racial lens. How refugees are selected and asylum claims are processed is deeply shaped by anti-Black racist views that have been part of U.S. society since its inception. Obtaining refugee and asylum status is difficult for most people seeking to escape persecution or the fear of persecution. They are often met with suspicion regarding whether their fear is well-founded and can be substantiated by objective documentation. In addition to this generalized suspicion that many refugees and asylum seekers must overcome, certain stereotypes are applied to particular individuals based on their nationality, race, gender, religion, age, and intersections of these. For many African refugees this means they have to prevail not only in the face of stereotypes about Africans but also anti-Black racist stereotypes that are part of American mainstream society at every turn.

Even when Black refugees, including the Liberian refugees in this study, are among the very few lucky ones who gain lawful admission to the United States, their worries are far from over. They encounter labor and housing markets that are highly racialized and in which Black people of all geographic origins have experienced uniquely difficult hurdles and discrimination. In addition, due to their race, Black refugees, like other Black people in the United States, often fear for their lives during encounters with police. Taken together, it is clear why King and Adero (2020, 37) conclude that "in the experience of Black immigrants, Blackness often serves as a master status marking and differentiating Blacks from non-Blacks." In this sense, it is perhaps questionable whether in a society that has yet to address the causes and consequences of anti-Black racism, Black refugees can ever find true refuge and safety. Realizing that their own sense of safety and belonging is connected to that of other Black people, 1.5- and second-generation Liberian refugees have sought alliances with native-born Black Americans that at times have also been joined by first-generation Liberian refugees. Other Liberians cope with anti-Black racism by contextualizing it through a refugee-specific dual frame of reference where they consider past discrimination in Liberia, especially during the fourteen-year civil war; positive encounters with native-born White Americans they met as part of the USRAP; the need to send remittances to family members and friends in West Africa; an expectation of anti-Black racism in the United

States; and acceptance that the United States is "not their country" and thus a fight against anti-Black racism is not something they can or always want to take on. However, as the experiences of Liberian refugees show, a desire not to engage in combating anti-Black racism does not mean that it does not affect them. Indeed, anti-Black racism is the very reason why Liberia exists.

FOR A BETTER REFUGE: POLICY AND PROGRAMMING SUGGESTIONS

As discussed in the introduction, my inspiration and motivation for this research are firmly grounded in my work experience with refugees and immigrants in Atlanta. There, I saw firsthand how policies and requirements of the USRAP played out on a daily basis. On many days, they created more challenges than help for those of us trying to support refugees and asylees. More than once, especially when I had to enter data for the ORR, it felt that those who had created the guidelines were out of touch with what had been happening on the ground. Hence, true to the origins of the field of refugee studies to contribute to policy (Jacobsen and Landau 2003; Turton 1996), I present a number of policy and programming suggestions that could go far to not only address anti-Black racism within the USRAP but also provide better outcomes for all refugees, regardless of their race, as well as the communities where they are being resettled. Specifically, my suggestions address two main areas: admittance to the United States as refugees and resettlement (reception and placement). These suggestions are intended for both the U.S. government, which creates policies, priorities, and programs, and VOLAGs, which are responsible for the implementation of said policies and programs. This, of course, assumes that there will be again a USRAP, which as of writing this book has been suspended with the aforementioned exception of Afrikaner's resettlement.

Evaluate and Revise the U.S. Refugee Admissions Program

As demonstrated throughout this book, not every refugee has the same chance to obtain refugee or asylum status in the United States. To begin, only a tiny fraction (less than one percent) of the millions of displaced people around the world are resettled to other countries. Certain factors loom large when a person is considered for resettlement to the United States. These include the priorities and quotas set by the U.S. government, which are influenced by national interests, racial and religious preferences, at times lobbyists for certain groups (Lazin 2009; Trudeau et al. 2023), and presidents. The consequence has been that for most of the USRAP's history, African refugees have had a low chance of being resettled compared to other geographical groups.

One way to address this inequity would be to reassess how P2 categories are created and open them up to more national groups, in particular those from Africa. As described in chapter 4, the threshold to "prove persecution" is lower for national/ethnic/religious groups declared eligible for the P2 category than for P1 and P3; P2 applicants gain access to the resettlement program because of being a member in a particular group that has been persecuted or has a well-founded fear of persecution in the future. This has far-reaching consequences, since establishing family ties is not always necessary, and all members of a household and/or family can be resettled. Furthermore, when certain refugees are resettled under the P2 category through in-country processing, they are in some instances able to avoid a traumatizing, dangerous, and expensive flight across international borders, which also increases the chances of the family and/or household staying together. Refugees processed under the other categories (P1 and P3) are not afforded these privileges, but this should change. Systemic change and investment in new geographical hubs need to be made, adding pipelines to those already well established for refugees from the FSU, the Middle East, and Asia (Watson 2023), which would then open up resettlement opportunities for African refugees. Under the Biden administration, regional processing centers, or Safe Mobility Offices, were created in Central and South America, which built on the earlier Central American Minors Refugee/Parole Program and show that this is a way to facilitate migration (Selee 2023).

The inequities are exacerbated as refugees begin to integrate into their new U.S. communities. Arriving as part of an incomplete family or household is not only psychologically difficult but also financially straining, as those with family members left behind will continue to send remittances and seek ways to be reunited, all at a very high cost (Holtzman 1999; Riak Akuei 2005). Despite the different starting positions, all refugees are eligible for the same kind of aid (e.g., Refugee Cash Assistance, employment services), although different groups need different levels and lengths of support. This one-size-fits-all approach calls for change. Equality is not the same as equity. In order for all refugees to have the opportunity to thrive, equitable solutions are needed. The circumstances of a refugee necessitate distinct services in the first ninety days after arrival in the United States and beyond. The following examples bear this out. A refugee who is literate in their native language, has English language skills, and has a high school education will be able to navigate American society faster than a refugee who has neither literacy nor English language skills. The first refugee may need less support to understand how to move around, read their mail, and so forth, whereas the second refugee will need more assistance and also will have much more limited job opportunities. Similarly, multigenerational households often are able to rely on the grandparent generation to provide childcare, whereas single-headed households do not have this option. Some of these grandparents in the first household may even be eligible for Supplemental Security Income, which increases the overall household income (Kasinitz et al. 2008; Orleck 1999). In addition, the ninety-day requirement for economic self-sufficiency does not account for the fact that a refugee's race, gender, age, religion, formal education, and (dis)ability—and the intersections of these—impact how they engage in the labor market in the short and long term, undeniably trapping those with less desirable human capital in permanent poverty (Lumley-Sapanski 2021; Minor and Cameo 2018).

The USRAP would also do well to provide additional support as it relates to refugees' employment. Its mandate of early economic self-sufficiency pushes refugees to accept jobs that are often below their qualifications. However, this has not always been the case. When Cuban refugees first started arriving in the 1950s, the United States provided extensive job and recertification programs for those in the medical professions, teachers, and lawyers (Chommie 1963; Moncarz 1970). In the past two decades, there have been small-scale projects (e.g., Lutheran Social Services' Refugee Recertification Program in Baltimore; Higher, formerly known as RefugeeWorks; Upwardly Global) that have sought to assist refugees and immigrants with recertification, but efforts remain negligible and limited in scope. While I met many Liberian refugees without transferable job skills, there were also others who worked in managerial positions at banks and for the government in Liberia prior to the outbreak of the civil war, and they had great difficulties finding a job that matched their qualifications. Some of them were, like other refugees, pushed to accept jobs for which they were overqualified by resettlement caseworkers, themselves under a government mandate that prioritizes refugees' early economic self-sufficiency (Capps et al. 2015; Nawyn 2010). This is not only a waste of human capital (Boas 2006; Sienkiewicz et al. 2013) but also shows a lack of respect for refugees' agency and right to self-determination. To match the diverse needs of resettled refugees, employment services should be expanded to include more recertification programs, job-specific employment training, and extended English language and literacy training. This will lead to increased job satisfaction, which is good for refugees' successful integration (Colic-Peisker 2009; Kelly and Hedman 2016) as well as the U.S. economy and larger society. However, these trainings and recertification programs need to be sensitive to the realities of a gendered and racialized labor market and thus provide mentoring programs and other kinds of ongoing support for refugees so that they can truly thrive in their careers.

Provide Real Information About Anti-Black Racism and Other Forms of Discrimination

Prior to and after their resettlement, refugees are expected to attend a Cultural Orientation as part of the USRAP.[3] Its length and content depend on a number of factors: the time between when a refugee is selected for resettlement and their actual departure, geographical location, and the staff in charge of delivering the Cultural Orientation. Not too long ago, the curriculum for this Cultural Orientation was evaluated and updated by the Cultural Orientation Resource Exchange, the technical assistance program that provides the resources for this government-funded Cultural Orientation. However, the topics labeled in the "objectives and indicators" of both overseas and domestic Cultural Orientation materials remain very much the same as before. They include budgeting and personal finance, cultural adjustment, health and hygiene, employment, safety, and U.S. laws, among others. The issue of discrimination is only mentioned in two contexts: "Participants can list at least two rights in the workplace (e.g., to be paid for their work, work in a safe environment free from discrimination and harassment)," and "participants can articulate three ways U.S. federal law prohibits discrimination (e.g., race, religion)" (CORE 2019, 5, 12). While knowing about these rights is useful, it does very little when refugees must achieve economic self-sufficiency and are compelled to send remittances; it pushes them to endure discriminatory and racist workplace situations (Hess et al. 2019).

The orientation materials make a "supplemental lesson plan" on "public safety and police interactions" available, but using it is not a requirement. This lesson plan is also void of any language around systemic anti-Black racism in the U.S. justice system or any other form of discrimination. Rather it notes, "The role of the police in the U.S. is to maintain public order and safety, enforce the law, and protect the civil rights of individuals in communities across the country" (CORE 2020b, 1). Not discussing discrimination and systemic (anti-Black) racism with refugees is a disservice to their well-being and potentially also their safety. As the examples of murdered Black refugees have shown, many Black refugees were unprepared for the intensity of anti-Black racism they would encounter in the United States.

Only after George Floyd was murdered did the wide reckoning among many non-Black people about the deep-seated nature of anti-Black racism in the United States reach VOLAGs. In the aftermath, these organizations acknowledged that the "current resources do not cover the full scope of need at this time" (CORE 2020a, para. 2) and facilitated a few workshops that discussed (anti-Black) racism and inclusion, diversity, equity, and accessibility ("Talking About Race and Racism: Tips for Participating in Introductory Conversations" 2020; Tholen and Church World Services 2020). Most of the time, the target audience was VOLAG staff. As noted in chapter 4, many of the leadership positions in VOLAGs are held by native-born Americans who are often White, and it seems appropriate to educate them more about the experiences of the populations with whom they work. However, very little changed in regard to the type of information that is delivered to refugees. Switchboard, which is implemented by the IRC, has a blog post titled "Talking About Race and Racism: Tips for Participating in Introductory Conversations," which predominantly focuses on how providers should prepare for conversations with their refugee clients about race and racism.[4] There are a number of questions listed that VOLAG staff can broach with their refugee clients while "prioritiz[ing] clients' autonomy and choice, both principles of trauma-informed care," but there are no real tools (e.g., how to go about reporting racist behavior in a workplace or housing) provided that they could share with their refugee clients (Switchboard 2020, para. 8). Put differently, here the focus is on non–refugee service providers and "prompts . . . designed as a starting point for . . . making a long-term commitment to incorporating topics of race, racism, and anti-racism into their work."

While these are laudable and important steps in ensuring that refugees are supported by VOLAG staff who are better informed about various forms of racism and discrimination, it is not sufficient. Hence, I propose that VOLAGs should offer supplemental trainings that educate refugees about both current and past forms of anti-Black racism in the United States as well as other forms of discrimination. These trainings would be separate from the government-sponsored (overseas and domestic) Cultural Orientation, since it is very unlikely for materials funded by one government entity to criticize another government entity. Indeed, the materials of the Cultural Orientation do not acknowledge any of these injustices but rather offer basic and superficial statements that emphasize that "the U.S. is a nation of diverse communities and individuals" (CORE 2019, 2) and "all people are created equal under American law" (Kawahara et al. 2022, 21). These assertions are, as this study and others have documented, far from reality. Hence, this additional training facilitated by VOLAGs should focus on race, racism, and discrimination in the United States. The purpose would be twofold. First, it would create (more) realistic expectations about how certain refugee groups will be received as they settle in the United States. Second, educating refugees about historical and present-day (anti-Black) racism and other forms of discrimination in the United States will ideally nurture empathy for others, including historically excluded and marginalized native-born Americans. This would also be an opportunity for an early intervention to address anti-Black racist views some non-Black refugees harbor about Black people, often stemming from stereotypical depictions of Black people in movies and (social) media (Ernyes and Pulleyblank Coffey 2006; Kawahara et al. 2022). The orientations should be conducted by people who themselves were refugees at some point and are able to speak from their own experiences. While this study gave examples of how some Liberians were frustrated when Cultural Orientations were conducted by people who themselves were not familiar with the United States and the USRAP, it also showed how Liberian refugees, and presumably others by implication, continued to trust their former caseworkers, who were like them Liberian refugees, for years after they were resettled. Very important aspects that these trainings should include are tools and information that would help refugees to protect and defend themselves. Honest conversations ought to be had, in particular with Black refugees, so they are aware of continued anti-Black racism and have resources (e.g., contact information for local and national civil rights organizations) that allow them not only to thrive in their new homes but actually survive.[5]

Recognize and Educate About the Diversity of Refugee Experiences

Although VOLAGs work with community organizations, health care providers, schools, and other entities to prepare for the arrival of refugees, very often these entities do not know how to serve diverse refugee and immigrant communities. One of the areas where I have noticed this shortcoming is in terms of language access rights. Frequently, organizations, schools, and hospitals advertise that they have bilingual staff; in reality, most of the time that means that people who speak Spanish and English work there. But bilingual is not synonymous with Spanish-English and should not be treated as such.

While there are many Spanish-speaking immigrants and some refugees in the United States, millions of people have different linguistic needs. For example, when the U.S. Customs and Border Protection (CBP) first launched the CBP One app, it did not include a Haitian Creole language option even though a record number of Haitian asylum seekers were trying to enter the United States via the southern border, and it was the only way to schedule an appointment with CBP (Forrest and Gassama 2023).[6] Another example is Liberian refugees. None of the Liberians I spoke with in Staten Island or Atlanta in the past two decades had ever been asked at any agency or school appointment if they would like to have an interpreter who spoke their Indigenous language.[7] This is despite the fact that Title VI of the Civil Rights Act of 1964 requires institutions (e.g., schools, medical service providers) that receive any federal funding to provide language access (interpretation or translation free of charge).[8] Indeed, not even when the focus shifted to West African immigrant and refugee communities in the United States during the height of the Ebola epidemic in West Africa in the fall of 2014 (Ludwig 2016c) were their linguistic needs considered. For example, New York City health officials organized an informational event in Park Hill and apologized to the audience that they did not have a Spanish language interpreter. They never acknowledged that the audience was almost exclusively made up of refugees, asylees, and immigrants from Liberia, Sierra Leone, and Guinea. Some of these attendees could have benefited from having interpreters who spoke Kru, Crio, Bassa, or another Indigenous West African language. The absence of interpreters who speak Indigenous languages can also be felt in the health care and court systems and in parent-teacher conferences, as I saw when working with different refugee and immigrant communities in Atlanta but also in Staten Island (Ludwig and Reed 2016). This also requires providers and government officials to rethink their assumption that most African refugees and immigrants are fluent in the colonial languages of English, French, or Portuguese. While many African refugees and immigrants speak these languages, it is often not as a first language, putting additional strain on vulnerable populations in high-stress and high-stakes situations (e.g., as related to their or a relative's health or an asylum application). The outcome can be confusion and misunderstandings that lead to denial of asylum applications, which I have observed while serving as a country conditions expert, when ethnicity and language were mixed up by the immigration officer, which directly impacted the outcome of the case (see also I. Berger 2015; Ngom 2015).

But it is not just linguistic barriers that refugees, asylum seekers, and immigrants from smaller national and ethnic groups have to overcome; there are also cultural ones. Service providers and government agencies, including immigration and asylum officers, are often less acquainted with refugee and immigrant groups that are not frequently talked or written about. The consequences are more significant than a lack of culturally and linguistically sound services. As this study and other studies have documented, these gaps in understanding can make it very difficult for individuals from these groups to be granted asylum, as they have to overcome a litany of hurdles, including stereotypes (Aizenobie 2019; I. Berger 2015). Thus, I propose that VOLAGs and other organizations that serve refugees and immigrants offer schools, health care providers, local government entities, police departments, and so forth training and/or written materials that provide basic information about the newest community members. For several decades, the Cultural Orientation Resource Center created "Cultural Backgrounders" about different refugee populations; now some of this work is continued by the Cultural Orientation Resource Exchange. These backgrounders, intended for those working with refugees, are not without issues but are a very good starting point. Similarly, the U.S. government should familiarize asylum and immigration officers, as well as immigration judges, with the various countries asylum seekers are coming from. They often heavily rely on information found in the annual Country Reports that are published by the U.S. Department of State. These Country Reports focus on human rights issues but less on the history of a country, demographics, and so forth. Even if it proves impossible to educate government officials working in the immigration enforcement realm, VOLAGs, organizations serving refugees, and scholars conducting research about refugee populations can still provide immigration attorneys and immigration clinics with up-to-date information on various national and ethnic groups to give members of those groups a better chance to obtain asylum.

Collaborate with and Include Receiving Communities

Given that most refugees are resettled in disenfranchised neighborhoods (W. Lee and Disney 2024; Tang 2015; Besteman 2016), it is of utter importance for the resettlement efforts to educate and include those already living in them. However, this usually does not happen. Communities where refugees are resettled are selected by VOLAGs based on a variety of factors that include, but are not limited to, affordable housing, access to services and public transportation, availability of (low-entry) jobs, existence of a conational/coethnic group, and at times, a native-born population that shares the same race as newly arriving refugees. VOLAGs spend a tremendous amount of energy and time working with landlords, employers, schools, health care providers, and other organizations providing services to refugees and immigrants, as I observed when I worked in Atlanta (see also Hinkle 2023). Missing in the process are residents in these neighborhoods. These immediate neighbors are most often refugees who were resettled months or years before, immigrants, and lower-income, native-born Americans who are often Black. These residents are an integral part of refugee resettlement and directly influence how and if refugees can feel at home in the United States. This fact is not adequately considered by VOLAGs and others involved in thinking about resettlement policies. For example, the Migration Policy Institute's report titled *The*

Unmet Potential of Community Consultations in U.S. Refugee Resettlement (Hinkle 2023) encourages closer collaboration and exchange of information and data among VOLAGs, U.S. government agencies involved in the USRAP, and "community stakeholders" (e.g., education and health care providers). Absent from the report's recommendations, despite its emphasis on "community," are local residents. But these local residents are crucial. This study about Liberian refugees in Staten Island and other research (Besteman 2012) have demonstrated that long-time native-born American residents—especially those marginalized due to socioeconomic status, race, or the intersection of these—can resent newcomers, especially if they perceive that refugees are getting resources that have been denied to them. This outlook, mixed with (cultural) misinformation and stereotypes, does not bode well for either group.

Thus, I recommend that VOLAGs and state refugee coordinators actively engage with the people already living in the neighborhoods where refugees are being resettled. One first step would be to facilitate an orientation designed specifically for long-term American residents, sharing information about the newly arriving refugees and their cultures and general information about the USRAP. This could also be an opportunity to clear up commonly held misconceptions and/or lack of knowledge about refugees, for example, by explaining the vetting process and the requirements that refugees pay for their own flights and attain fast economic self-sufficiency. Ideally, through an ongoing dialogue among VOLAGs, community organizations, local governments, religious institutions, refugees, and long-term residents, coalitions that seek to improve the lives of all can be formed and nurtured. Such coalitions could, for example, work toward a local food pantry and accessible and affordable health care that would benefit many lower-income residents. At times, the long-term residents could also be a valuable resource to (Black) refugees as they undergo racial naturalization (Carbado 2005), providing strategies and integrating them into established organizations that are committed to fighting racial and socioeconomic injustices. This is exactly the area where the Cultural Orientations currently fall short. Finally, sharing experiences with anti-Black racism in the workplace and housing market, in public spaces, and with the police can buttress alliances between native-born Black Americans and Black refugees.

A LOOK AHEAD: MORE REFUGEES AND A NEED FOR ADAPTIVE SOLUTIONS

This study makes clear that obtaining refugee status and finding true and lasting refuge is hard for most forcibly displaced people, in particular for Black refugees in the United States. A look into the immediate future indicates that many nation-states, especially those in the Global North, are becoming more reluctant to admit refugees and asylum seekers, above all those whom they perceive as "unassimilable" or "a threat" to their current population or mainstream culture. Attacks on and lies about refugees, asylees, asylum seekers, and immigrants are the fodder of right-wing nationalist parties. This is all happening while the number of forcibly displaced people grows at a steady rate. In fact, there have never been more forcibly displaced people than there are today. This number is only expected to rise, as these individuals will be joined by millions of climate refugees in the next decades. Thus, what is needed is an honest conversation about how to address the various refugee, asylum seeker, and IDP crises around the world. This includes reassessing the process of how individuals are selected for resettlement in a third country and how they are supported in the process. Refugees, asylum seekers, IDPs, policymakers, and human rights organizations need to envision new and improved solutions in addition to the current three durable solutions ([voluntary] repatriation, local integration in the first country of asylum, resettlement in a third country) that the UNHCR currently supports. One possible approach would be adapting what Achiume (2022) describes as an "empire-centric approach" to international displacement, implying that nation-states are responsible for granting refuge to those displaced through their actions (e.g., neocolonial ties, military interventions). In this way, the United States would have a unique obligation to Liberian refugees since it created the social dynamics and social hierarchies in Liberia that brought about the upheaval.

Whatever approach is taken to reimagine new and more just and equitable solutions and policies, it is absolutely necessary to center the voices of refugees, asylum seekers, and IDPs, as these decisions directly affect them, and they have unique lived experiences that can and must inform proposals of how to alleviate human suffering and to allow them to prosper.

The same applies to how refugee and immigration policies are made and revised in the United States. Refugee voices must be represented and given weight and not just be a pure performative act. In addition, immigration advocates and policymakers must recognize that immigration is not just a "Hispanic issue." There are countless accounts of non-Hispanic immigrants who are left out of the conversation (S. M. Kim and Yellow Horse 2018; Kolawole 2016; Lauby 2020). This also applies to "crimmigration," which has frequently been framed as a "Hispanic issue" (Armenta 2017; Arriaga 2023) that, as data and studies have shown, very much also affects Black refugees and immigrants (Ibrahim 2020; Palmer 2017) as well as others.[9] Take, for example, the introduction of H.R.5248—Southeast Asian Deportation Relief Act of 2023, which would halt the removal of certain Vietnamese, Cambodian, and Laotian nationals who had arrived in the United State as refugees. But it is not just Southeast Asian refugees who are being deported; so are refugees from Liberia, Somalia, Sudan, and so forth. Hence, what is needed are conversations and coalitions that bring to light that the proposed policies should be extended in their scope. At the same time, it is important that immigration reforms and relief are not offered to one group of immigrants or refugees at the expense of another group. For example, in 2013, the S.744—Border Security, Economic Opportunity, and Immigration Modernization Act, developed and introduced by the "Gang of Eight," proposed a pathway to 11 million undocumented immigrants (predominantly from Latin America) while eliminating the Diversity Immigrant Visa Program, which would have disproportionately affected immigrants from Africa (B. I. Logan and Thomas 2012).[10]

Finally, while it is important to overhaul and address biases of "an immigration system that does not recognize constitutional norms of equality" (McKanders 2020, 1150), the continued institutional anti-Black racism in the larger U.S. society also requires systemic changes. It appeared that some of this happened in the aftermath of the nation's reckoning of George Floyd's murder. However, as more recent developments have shown, the United States is moving once again away from much-needed policies, laws, and programs that address centuries of anti-Black racism. What we need is not the banning of diversity, equity, inclusion, and accessibility programming, books, and critical race theory but real knowledge and conversations about centuries of (racial) injustices, so we can as a society create a more just world. I hope that this book contributes to this.

APPENDIX 1

Liberian Research Participants

Liberian Research Participants

Pseudonym	Gender	Ethnicity	Entrance mode	Arrival year	Age (beginning of study)	Formal education
Annie Quide	F	Grebo	Refugee	2004	35	11th grade
Baka Wehjay	M	Bassa	Asylee	1988	46	BA
Beatrice Akoi	F	Loma	Refugee	2010	18	HS
Bernice Richards	F	Kru	Refugee	1996	30	HS
Beverly Coleman	F	Americo Liberian & Vai	Immigrant	1988	48	HS
Boakai Boakai	M	Americo Liberian & Gola	Immigrant (de facto refugee)	1992	70	AA
Comfort Johnson	F	Bassa	Refugee	2003	70	None
Cynthia Sherif	F	Americo Liberian	Refugee	1986	44	BA
Danny Gayflor	M	Loma	n/a (UNHCR employee)	n/a	35	BA
David Joe	M	Americo Liberian	U.S. citizen	1990	58	BA
Desai Kpoe Monbello	F	Bassa	Refugee	2001	67	None
Dorgbah Weemongar	M	Bassa	Refugee	1998	44	MA
Elizabeth Kamara	F	Vai	Immigrant (de facto refugee)	2002	34	HS

(continued)

Liberian Research Participants (*continued*)

Pseudonym	Gender	Ethnicity	Entrance mode	Arrival year	Age (beginning of study)	Formal education
Enid Browning	F	Americo Liberian	Immigrant	1979	50	MA
Estella Konde	F	Bassa	Refugee	2005	27	8th grade
Everliner Ethridge	F	Americo Liberian	Immigrant	1995	43	HS
Flomo Yakpazua	M	Kpelle	DV immigrant	2009	34	HS
Garmuyou Dyemene	M	Bassa	Refugee	2001	41	AA
Garpu Garbleh	M	Krahn	Asylee	1996	49	BA
Garsuah Janjay	M	Bassa	Asylee	2000	60	AA
Gloria Adams	F	Grebo	Asylee	1998	51	BA
Isaac Cheeks	M	Americo Liberian	U.S. citizen	1960	79	BA
Israel Youkonjay Ways	M	Bassa	Refugee	2001	26	HS
Jacob Jallah	M	Bassa	Refugee	2003	30	BA
James Paye	M	Gio	Asylee	2002	40	MA
Janjay Waggah	F	Bassa	Refugee	1998	56	HS
Juah Nimley	F	Kru	Immigrant (de facto refugee)	1987	40	AA
Keisha Kole	F	Bassa	Refugee	2003	18	HS
Kormassa Kollie	F	Loma	Refugee	2004	72	None
Loko Pella	F	Gio	TPS	1989	74	None
Love Juah	F	Kru	Immigrant (de facto refugee)	2007	40	BA
Maymay Bensing	F	Vai	Immigrant (de facto refugee)	2002	40	HS
Memba Wesseh	M	Bassa	Refugee	2000	57	BA
Mr. Baby	M	Loma	Refugee	2002	35	10th grade
Nowa Namo	F	Kpelle	Refugee	2003	53	None
Nyema Browne	F	Grebo	Immigrant	1986	60	HS
Oman Zumo	M	Loma	Immigrant	1986	48	MA
Osiemeo Boye	M	Bassa	Refugee	2003	47	AA
Philip Kollie	M	Loma	DV immigrant (de facto refugee)	2007	32	HS

Liberian Research Participants (*continued*)

Pseudonym	Gender	Ethnicity	Entrance mode	Arrival year	Age (beginning of study)	Formal education
Saah Kandakai	M	Kissi	Immigrant	2011	39	BA
Sam Collins	M	Americo Liberian	Immigrant (IRCA; de facto refugee)	1981	43	AA
Samuel Black	M	Mende	Refugee	2000	20	HS
Sarah Beh	F	Krahn	Asylee	1998	72	None
Sunday John	F	Bassa	Refugee	2000	30	HS
Thomas Bono	M	Gola	Asylee	2000	44	MA
Vanessa Jallah	F	Bassa	Refugee	1998	18	HS
Varney Konneh	M	Mandingo	DV immigrant (de facto refugee)	2008	53	MA
Varney Yarkpolo	M	Gbandi	Asylee	1998	54	BA
Wannie Jacobs	F	Bassa	Refugee	1997	22	BA
Winnifred Fassah	F	Kissi	Refugee	2004	50	None
Wright Talley	M	Krahn	Refugee	2003	54	BA
Yassah Flomo	F	Loma	Refugee	2006	27	HS
Younger Dugbo	F	Bassa	Refugee	2010	35	6th grade
Zaiway Paye	F	Krahn	Refugee	2005	52	HS
Zubah Kpadeh	M	Loma	Refugee	2002	28	HS

NOTE: Names in bold indicate (previous) employment with a refugee/immigrant aid organization.

APPENDIX 2

Other Research Participants

Other Research Participants

Pseudonym	Gender	Nationality (ethnicity/race)	Entrance mode	Arrival year	Age	Formal education
Asha Onyango	F	Kenya (Luo)	n/a (UNHCR employee)	n/a	35	LLM
Eva McGovern	F	American (White)	n/a	n/a	32	MA
Diasa Minong	M	Senegal (Wolof)	Immigrant	2002	37	BA
Nigel Baba	M	American (Black)	n/a	n/a	35	BA
Michael Lewis	M	American (Black)	n/a	n/a	52	HS
Mac Willi	M	American (Black)	n/a	n/a	68	HS
Ezi West	F	American (Black)	n/a	n/a	19	HS
Mr. Black	M	American (Black)	n/a	n/a	22	HS
Tracey Rogers	F	American (Black)	n/a	n/a	22	HS
Dee Love	F	American (Black)	n/a	n/a	49	HS
Lemon Angel	F	American (Black)	n/a	n/a	20	HS
Little T	M	American (Black)	n/a	n/a	38	HS
Brendan Mack	M	American (Black)	n/a	n/a	20	BA

NOTE: Names in bold indicate (previous) employment with a refugee/immigrant aid organization.

ACKNOWLEDGMENTS

I owe thanks and gratitude to many people who made this book a reality. First and foremost, I am deeply indebted to the Liberian refugees and immigrants in Staten Island who took time out of their busy schedules and welcomed me into their homes and lives and shared with me their perspectives about coming to and living in the United States. Without their generosity, insights, and hospitality, this book would not exist. So, let me once again express my sincerest thanks. I am especially grateful to Solomon Reeves, James Kollie, and Telee Brown, who introduced me to many of their family members, friends, and community members. Unbounded gratitude also to my friend Adama Fassah, a steadfast supporter of this research project from its inception, who included me in countless family and community events and invited me to serve on the board of Napela, Inc. Words will never be able to express how grateful I am for our conversations and shared laughter.

I also wish to extend my gratitude to the native-born Black American residents of Park Hill who were willing to discuss their experiences of living in this neighborhood, which included, but were not limited to, encounters with anti-Black racism in Staten Island and interactions with their Liberian and other African refugee and immigrant neighbors. I am grateful as well to Titus Leo and Tylia Ferone, who, as undergraduate students at Wagner College, conducted this subset of interviews with me.

I am also grateful for the staff members of international refugee and humanitarian organizations who shared their experiences in working and supporting Liberian refugees in West Africa and in Staten Island with me.

My thanks go to Sara Rowbottom, who created an opportunity for me to become involved with the IRC in New York and let me analyze and subsequently use the data the IRC had collected on Liberian youth and their families. Additionally, Gerald Barclay (Gee Bee Productions) generously shared photographs from the Liberian community, which are included in this book and I have used in presentations across the country. Special thanks also to Jever Mariwala for her detailed literature reviews. I am also indebted to my brother Gerold Ludwig for creating the maps.

This book project began when I was a doctoral student at The Graduate Center, The City University of New York. I am forever grateful to Nancy Foner, who has championed me and my work since our first meeting, providing extremely fast and insightful feedback and mentorship well beyond my student years. Phil Kasinitz and Holly Reed have also provided feedback in the early stages of this project. I also want to recognize the late William Helmreich, who was a supporter of this project from the first time I discussed this in his class. A special thank you to Vilna Bashi, who gave me the tools and confidence to undertake this study.

Many colleagues offered invaluable feedback and comments on earlier drafts of chapters. I am grateful to Orly Clergé, Vadricka Etienne, Laura Limonic, Koby Oppenheim, Stephen Ruszczyk, Alexis Silver, and Jessica Sperling for their time and insights. I owe particular thanks to Rachel Kravetz, Elizabeth Miller, Kaleefa Munroe-Peters, and Jen Sloan for their constructive suggestions and comments, editing, friendship, and continued encouragement. Micha Rahder's guidance was instrumental in helping me revise the initial chapters and book proposal as well as indexing. With the help of Rachel Kravetz's detailed feedback and suggestions, I was able to complete the manuscript. My gratitude also goes to Helena Zeweri and an anonymous reviewer for their thoughtful critiques and suggestions, which considerably strengthened my arguments. This book has also benefited from the feedback that audiences provided at the Annual Meetings of the American Sociological Association and the Eastern Sociological Society Conferences, and UCLA's Emerging Immigration Scholars Conference.

The research was supported by Wagner College's Faculty (Research) Aid awards, Maureen Robinson Fellowship, Zolberg Institute on Migration and Mobility Research Grant, Lang Faculty Opportunity Award Fund, National Science Foundation-funded Alliances for Graduate Education and the Professoriate (AGEP) Program in Social, Behavioral and Economic Sciences (SBES) Summer Research Award (NSF/CUNY AGEP SBES # 0753623), and The Graduate Center's Dissertation Fellowship.

Portions of the book were published in *International Migration* (2016), "'Wiping the Refugee Dust from My Feet': Advantages and Burdens of Refugee Status and the Refugee Label" 54, no. 1: 5–18 and in *African and Black Diaspora: An International Journal* (2019), "It Is Tough to Be a Liberian Refugee in Staten Island, NY: The Importance of Context for Second-Generation African Immigrant Youth" 12, no. 2: 189–210.

At Rutgers University Press, I would like to thank Peter Mickulas for his enthusiastic support of this book project and for guiding me from the beginning to the final process of getting this book into print. I am also grateful to Catherine Denning at Rutgers University Press and Helen Wheeler at Westchester Publishing Services for their work on the book production.

Vielen Dank to my sister, Gundula Ludwig, who not only offered her home as a writing retreat but whose steadfast encouragement helped move this project along.

Last but not least, my thanks go to Glen Patterson, who has been there for me since long before I started this research, steadily reminding me "to write that book."

NOTES

CHAPTER 1 THE UNITED STATES, A HOME AND A REFUGE FOR BLACK PEOPLE?

1. The descendants of Black people who left the United States. "Settlers" is the term used by these (forced) migrants then and by today's Liberians.
2. "American" throughout the book refers to things or identities related to the United States of America.
3. While some distinguish between the first (1989–1997) and the second Liberian (1999–2003) war, I refer to the entire period between 1989 and 2003 as one civil war, as fighting never totally stopped and most people remained displaced during much of that time. This also reflects how most Liberians speak about that time, by just calling it "the war."
4. The full definition of the 1951 Convention can be found in chapter 4.
5. Generally, in the U.S. context "refugees" are individuals who are outside the United States and were approved for resettlement by U.S. immigration officials based on a number of criteria and thus enter the country with this legal status. Asylees are those who meet the legal definition of "refugee" but are either already physically in the United States or are seeking admission at a U.S. border. The details and complexities of these legal categories are discussed in depth in the following chapters.
6. Therefore, this neighborhood shares at times similarities with new immigrant destinations (Massey 2010) where many refugees have been resettled (Singer and Wilson 2006).
7. This is an increase from 23 percent in 2000.
8. For example, Donald Trump has fueled the flames of White supremacy many times, including when he first demanded proof of Barack Obama's U.S. citizenship and some years later told four congresswomen, among them Somali American Ilhan Omar and native-born Black American Ayanna Pressley, to "go back . . . to their countries," insinuating that they are not Americans; and there are countless more.
9. Like with the ACS a century before, some native-born Black American leaders did support the idea to leave the United States, although they had different motives.
10. The United States has at times haphazardly come to the aid of those impacted (and displaced) by direct U.S. government and military actions, such as Vietnamese, Cambodians, Laotians, Iraqis, and Afghans. This has not happened in the cases of Liberia, Haiti, and El Salvador.
11. This approach focuses on the strength of refugees and immigrants instead of their shortcomings (deficits).
12. For example, since one of the nonprofit organizations that I worked for received grants from the ORR and management of this grant was part of my portfolio, I not only knew about the requirements around service provisions for individual refugees but also how and what kind of reporting the government asked for. Some of it left me utterly speechless, such as having to enter job skills for each individual in a large Somali or Liberian refugee family. Many of these refugees were illiterate and had been farmers before, so their job skills did not match most of the jobs available in metro Atlanta, and this data entry seemed pointless.
13. Executive Order 14161 bars entry for nationals twelve countries, seven of them in Africa, Haiti and the remaining four in the Middle East and Asia.
14. There are sixteen Indigenous ethnic groups in Liberia; those represented here are listed in alphabetical order, not by sample size.

15. I acknowledge that there are other genders, but all research participants in this study identified as either female or male.
16. These legal categories are discussed in chapter 4.
17. The Diversity Visa Program makes fifty-five thousand permanent resident visas available annually by lottery to people from countries with low immigration rates to the United States.
18. IRCA included a provision that legalized undocumented immigrants who had not been found guilty of any crime and had been continuously present in the United States since before January 1, 1982.
19. Forcibly displaced people is not a legal category but an umbrella term that captures all those individuals who were forced or felt compelled to leave their residency due to overwhelming force beyond their control and elements of coercion including those listed in the 1951 Convention, but also generalized violence, natural disasters, and so forth (Reed et al. 2016).
20. Research participants gave oral consent in lieu of signing consent forms. I opted for this approach to ensure that Liberians who are illiterate would not feel alienated.
21. I have also served as the vice chair of a grassroots organization that provides educational and cultural programming for older West African refugee and immigrant women in Staten Island's North Shore.
22. The applicant has to demonstrate that it is more likely than not that they will be tortured if they are sent back to their country of origin. Torture here is defined as inhumane and cruel treatment.
23. Deportable crimes include, but are not limited to, aggravated felony convictions (e.g., rape, human trafficking), convictions of crimes of moral turpitude (e.g., murder, burglary), domestic violence convictions, and firearm convictions.
24. The data from ORR is very incomplete as the earlier system did not capture "bio data" such as education. In addition, a lot of the columns just list "bio data not complete."
25. At the same time, it is worth noting that I am a first-generation college graduate and not a native-English speaker, and as such, I did not always have this cultural capital.

CHAPTER 2 WHEN THE WAR CAME, EVERYONE SCATTERED

1. More than a month later, the *Elizabeth* arrived in Freetown, Sierra Leone, because Liberia did not exist yet.
2. Listed here from the largest ethnic group to the smallest.
3. The "Native Plan" of 1904, presented by President Arthur Barclay, only granted Liberian citizenship to Americo Liberians and Indigenous men who were formally educated, owned land, had converted to Christianity, and adopted a "Western form of dress."
4. The Liberian Constitution of 1847, which remained in effect until 1980, was prepared by Simon Greenleaf, a native-born White American Harvard Law professor. Originally, the Liberian Constitution used the phrase "persons of color." "Persons of color" was amended to "Negroes or persons of Negro descent" in 1907 (Tannenbaum et al. 2009). This change was made because the original phrase was seen as too ambiguous. While in the United States, whose norms and laws served as a model for Liberia, "colored person"/"person of color" was synonymous for "Black," this was not the case on the African continent. This became evident when a number of North Africans of "pure Arab blood" and Jews from Morocco tried to become citizens of Liberia, arguing that they were of African descent (Huberich 2010 [1947], 1018).
5. At the same time the Liberian Constitution explicitly outlawed slavery.
6. A wraparound skirt.
7. Like earlier, among solely Indigenous groups, this led to a "flexible definition of family" (Dick 2002a, 13) among Liberians that continues until today and, as I discuss in chapter 4,

had significant implications for refugee resettlement (and reunification) of Liberian families.

8. Later, some Americo Liberian men also married Indigenous women; only on rare occasions did Americo Liberian women marry Indigenous men.

9. Rural areas.

10. Indigenous Liberians, who did not hold legal land titles, were disproportionately affected by this.

11. The U.S. government "rewarded" Doe for the coup "with a massive package of American military aid" that funded weapons that "would later be turned on the Liberian people" (Moran 2012, 56).

12. Reports suggest that more than two hundred people were killed in just three days following the coup (Lawyers Committee for Human Rights 1986).

13. The elections were most likely rigged and under no circumstance fair (Dolo 2002).

14. Mandingos belonging to Liberia has long been questioned. Most Mandingos, unlike the other ethnic groups, are predominantly Muslim and not Christian, and as such are commonly labeled "foreigners," regardless of the fact that they migrated as traders from the Mali Empire to what is Liberia today between the fourteenth and fifteenth centuries (Konneh 1996).

15. Observers estimate that around 15 percent of all combatants were child soldiers (Advocates for Human Rights 2006; Utas 2003).

16. For a more detailed description and analysis of the Liberian civil war see Berkeley (2002), J. Levitt (2005), and Advocates for Human Rights (2006).

17. It should be noted that most Liberian refugees returned in unassisted spontaneous repatriations and not in organized repatriations and thus did not receive any financial and logistical support (Ecke et al. 2016).

18. This was the case, especially after the invocation of the cessation clause on June 30, 2012, which ended official UNHCR refugee status for all but a few hundred Liberians in Ghana and other countries in West Africa (see chapter 4). The cessation clause was invoked after the Ghana Refugee Board and the Ghanaian minister for the interior in collaboration with the UNHCR determined that it was safe for Liberian refugees to move to Liberia; although many Liberian refugees disagreed with this assessment (Crawley and Fynn Bruey 2022; Omata 2012b).

19. Local integration was almost a nonissue in Côte d'Ivoire and Guinea since most Liberian refugees had left due to the outbreak of civil wars and conflicts there.

20. Trapp's (2015, 37) study also reports the wide usage of "already in America" among Liberian refugees in the Buduburam camp when they spoke about the (relative) wealth and comfortable lifestyle of some refugees.

21. See Jacobsen (2005) and Jansen (2008) for examples of these activities in refugee camps in Kenya.

22. Prostitution.

CHAPTER 3 SEARCHING FOR HOME IN STATEN ISLAND

1. Between 1989 and 1995, more than one hundred thousand refugees were resettled on an annual basis, reflecting the large influx of refugees from the former Soviet Union (FSU). Following the two years after the 9/11 attacks, fewer than thirty thousand refugees were admitted. Other events have significantly impacted the number of refugees admitted under the USRAP: the COVID-19 pandemic, as well as the Trump presidencies. During his first term, Trump lowered the number significantly and in the second term he has suspended it totally, with the exception of Afrikaners who were classified as "refugees"—while not meeting the criteria of being refugees. This follows, the more than one hundred thousand refugees from across the globe who were resettled in fiscal year (FY) 2024 under Joe Biden.

2. Liberian refugees arrived in the United States in larger numbers until the mid-2000s because their paperwork—which they had filed many years ago—took such a long time to process. A handful of Liberian refugees were resettled until 2024.
3. Priority 1, 2, and 3 cases are described in detail in chapter 4.
4. There are two reasons for the prevalence of P3 cases of Liberians in Staten Island; first, due to the high cost of living in New York City, only refugees who have familial ties in the city are being resettled here, and second, P3 has been the major avenue for African refugees to be resettled in the United States (see chapter 4 for details).
5. The U.S. government requires proof of such sponsors to ensure that these new immigrants will not become a (financial) burden to American society.
6. After one year in the United States, refugees need to file with USCIS to have their status adjusted to "permanent resident."
7. Standardized English is a variety of English that is privileged by those who have historically held power in society. Standardized instead of "standard" reflects that this language is continuously in flux and actively standardized.
8. There have been incidents of racist attacks and hate crimes in other boroughs as well, such as in Crown Heights, Howard Beach, and East Harlem, but in these cases, the entire borough was not labeled racist, whereas this is the case for Staten Island. However, the 120th Precinct, which encompasses Staten Island's North Shore, had the highest rate of reported (and confirmed) hate crimes; the majority of victimized individuals were Black (New York Police Department 2020).
9. This was a special election following the resignation of Michael Grimm.
10. Michael E. McMahon, U.S. congressman from 2008 until 2010, and Richmond County's district attorney since 2015, stated that "racism exists in our country and is way too much in Staten Island" during a virtual "Community Dialogue on Race" with the African immigrant community and the New York Police Department on June 10, 2020.
11. Although there have been some exceptions. For example, Barack Obama won in Staten Island in 2012, as well as the aforementioned election of Max Rose in 2018.
12. Not a pseudonym.
13. The 120th Precinct, which encompasses most of the North Shore, had twenty-one reported murders in 1993, seven in 2001, twelve in 2023, and one in 2024 (Police Department, City of New York 2025).
14. According to the Refugee Act of 1980, refugees can only be resettled in geographic areas with employment opportunities, affordable housing, and public and private resources. As noted, Park Hill provided some, but not all, of these requirements. According to the law, however, refugees who have a spouse, parent, sibling, son, or daughter living in an area that does not meet all the requirements can still be resettled there.
15. Brandt (2010) documents that VOLAGs in Philadelphia shared this view as well.
16. This is a conventional "Western" handshake followed by mutual pressing of fingers that produce a "snap sound."
17. According to U.S. law and American mainstream culture, this is not her daughter but her niece. However, in Liberian culture, someone is considered a daughter if she is raised by that person (see also chapter 4).
18. Ethiopian immigrants encountered similar opposition from native-born Black Americans when they tried to rename an area in Washington, D.C., "Little Ethiopia" (Habecker 2012).

CHAPTER 4 SOMEONE CALL ME A "DAMN" REFUGEE

1. Many refugees move in and out of refugee camps, either back to their native countries, somewhere else in the host country, or to another refugee camp (Agier 2011; Jansen 2016).
2. There are some exceptions to this rule that are discussed later in the chapter, but to be clear, African refugees have never benefited from these.

3. The geographical parameters of the 1951 Convention are not surprising when one keeps in mind who was in power then (and to a large extent now), as well as the fact that most of the countries in the Caribbean and Africa, and several countries in the Middle East and Asia, were under colonial rule, and thus colonial powers did not want to grant protection to people subjected to their colonial rule. Although it is worth noting that not all Europeans are White.

4. This change came about since other refugee crises outside of Europe emerged coupled with increasing efforts to end colonial rule.

5. Not all authoritarian regimes were treated equally by the U.S. government, which meant that those fleeing regimes propped up by the United States, such as in El Salvador (Stokes 2003) and Haiti (Gerlus 1995), did not receive the same kind of welcome and protection, often indeed none. For example, "between 1981 and 1990, the United States did not accept a single Haitian refugee or asylee for permanent refugee status" (DenUyl 2022, 772).

6. Between FY 1980 and FY 2023, 451,676 African refugees were resettled compared to 1,244,687 from East and Southeast Asia—not including all Amerasians; 498,700 from the Middle East and South Asia (predominantly Iraq, Syria, Iran, and Afghanistan; this number does not account for the ten thousands of Afghan and Iraqi SIVs [Special Immigrant Visas] whose recipients have also been resettled along with their families); 886,504 from Europe and the FSU, with the FSU accounting for close to two-thirds; and 121,597 from Latin America and the Caribbean (mostly Cuban; this number does not include the ten thousands of Cubans who were admitted annually under the Cuban Adjustment Act of 1966 [until 2017] and the Special Cuban Migration Lottery [until 1998]) (author's tabulation of WRAPS data).

7. The fast tracking of the resettlement of Afrikaners in 2025 is another example.

8. Not all Marielitos were Black, but they were more likely to be Black or biracial Black-White than the earlier wave of Cubans, who were almost exclusively White.

9. Despite these strategies, the resettlement of Syrian refugees and other refugees from predominantly Muslim countries was stopped by one of the first executive orders that Trump issued after taking office in January 2017.

10. This was a response to a campaign promise to cut refugee admission overall but also reflects Islamophobia and anti-Black sentiments, as well as the goal to deter Central Americans from seeking asylum at the U.S. border. The second term has been marked by even more xenophobic and anti-immigrant rhetoric and policies.

11. I chose to keep this is present tense, with the hope that the USRAP's pause is temporary.

12. Muslim African refugees are additionally stereotyped as terrorists (C. Abdi 2015a; Crosby and Brazelton 2017), something they share with other Muslim refugees (Gowayed 2019).

13. A quick *New York Times* search revealed that since 1851, over 2,046 articles mention Syrian refugees, 1,284 Afghan refugees, 1,487 Cuban refugees, and 537 Ukrainian refugees, compared to 194 Somali refugees, 250 Sudanese refugees, and 64 Liberian refugees (as of late-May 2025).

14. Liberians also had TPS due to the Ebola virus outbreak in West Africa from November 21, 2014, until May 21, 2017, although these were not the same Liberians who were originally under TPS related to the civil war in Liberia.

15. The reasons for the low enrollment are manifold and include various bureaucratic and financial hurdles (having to renew TPS and later DED, as well as work permit cards almost every year, which involves a new set of administrative fees and getting fingerprinted every time) and lack of knowledge or information about the process. Finally, there is also a substantiated fear of what the U.S. government may do with the information, as the applications include applicants' current addresses and fingerprints, leaving them vulnerable to deportation (Heeren 2015; Reilly 2016).

16. "There is no legislation permitting TPS holders to adjust their status to that of lawful permanent residents; in fact, the 1990 Immigration Act expressly prohibited the enactment of such legislation unless affirmatively approved by a three-fifths supermajority of the Senate" (Bergeron 2014, 25).

17. The Liberian Refugee Immigration Fairness Act was available to Liberian nationals who had been continuously physically present in the United States since November 20, 2014, met a set of other requirements, and applied by December 20, 2021. While an estimated ten thousand Liberians were eligible, only close to thirty-five hundred applications were received. Reasons for this low number include the immense paperwork required, a $1,125 application fee per person, the USCIS backlogs, and issues related to COVID-19 (American Immigration Lawyers Association 2021).

18. Jewish Syrian nationals also benefited from Public Law 106–378, which allowed them to adjust their status to lawful permanent residents in 2001.

19. Out of twenty-eight nations that were or are currently on the list, twelve are in Africa, and two others have predominantly Black populations (Haiti and Montserrat) (American Immigration Council 2024).

20. UNHCR refugee status does not automatically translate to having refugee status in the United States or another country.

21. This was the case until 2000, when the Ghanaian government instituted "a much stricter screening process, and assistance was limited only to 'vulnerable' populations'" (Byrne 2013, 55). Côte d'Ivoire stopped recognizing Liberian refugees on a prima facie basis in 2004 (U.S. Committee for Refugees and Immigrants 2007).

22. According to the Organisation of African Unity Convention Governing the Specific Aspects of Refugee Problems in Africa (1974, Article 1), the term refugee also applies "to every person who, owing to external aggression, occupation, foreign domination or events seriously disturbing public order in either part of or the whole of his country of origin or nationality, is compelled to leave his place of habitual residence in order to seek refuge in another place outside his country of origin or nationality." In expanding the parameters of the 1951 Convention, the OAU makes provisions for recognizing large groups of refugees whose fear of persecution does not have to be individualized but rather is due to generalized violence such as war in their country of residence.

23. Not only did Ghana host Liberian refugees the longest out of the various West African countries where Liberians sought refuge, but it also became a destination for Liberians who first fled to Guinea, Côte d'Ivoire, and Sierra Leone and had to leave because of conflicts there, as well as due to language barriers, since French is the official language in Guinea and Côte d'Ivoire. Ghana granted certain Liberian refugees an exemption from the cessation clause.

24. Again, this does not apply to Afrikaners who left directly from South Africa.

25. The same applies to expected "appropriate" performance in terms of sexual orientation for LGBTQ+ refugees (D. A. Morgan 2006).

26. The flipside of this emphasis on women's vulnerability is that it ignores gendered vulnerability that men and other genders face (for example, Janmyr 2017). In addition, these gender narratives regularly rely "on the biologically sexed body" (Llewellyn 2017, 1120).

27. Some of this fudging included at times presenting a different marital status.

28. Indeed, official U.S. government documents state that certain religious minorities from the FSU—who are processed while living in their own homes and under P2, "are considered under a reduced evidentiary standard for establishing a well-founded fear of persecution" (U.S. Department of State 2021, 14).

29. Some of these national groups (e.g., Burmese) remained a P2 for over a decade, whereas other groups were only designated for several years. For the majority of the existence of USRAP, the quota allocated to Europe, East Asia, Latin America, and to some extent, the Middle East and Southeast Asia, was almost exclusively for P2 cases, whereas for the African quota only in some years about half the cases were for P2. Other times, refugee status under P2 was generously extended: "Bhutanese refugees who had migrated for work and settled across the subcontinent and Gulf states were invited to come back to Nepal to claim resettlement" (Watson 2023, 699).

30. Under the Biden administration changes were implemented that considered common-law spouses and life partners if "evidence of an ongoing relationship with the partner for at least one year overseas prior to the submission of the affidavit of relationship and evidence that legal marriage could not be obtained due to social and/or legal prohibitions" can be provided (U.S. Department of State 2023, 29).

31. Furthermore, it often becomes virtually impossible for families to reunite when some members are resettled and others are left behind (Fee 2023).

32. For Liberians this was even more problematic, as the U.S. government had issued a "temporary suspension of Priority 3 family reunion processing of Liberians to avoid interfering with ongoing repatriation to Liberia" in FY 2006 (U.S. Department of State 2006, 19).

33. In 2006, the U.S. government, or more specifically, the USCIS, wanted to pilot a program requiring DNA tests to establish eligibility. The official explanation for "focus[ing] exclusively on Africans [was] because fraud was suspected . . . and because 95 percent of beneficiaries of the family reunification program are currently African" (Esbenshade 2011, 176). In addition, these African refugees lack legal protection and advocates in positions of power in the United States, making it the "logical place to implement a pilot" (185).

34. This is despite evidence that individuals in the FSU falsified claims that they were Jewish in order to be eligible as refugees for resettlement in the United States (Orleck 2013).

35. These numbers are based on the author's tabulations from publicly available data from the Department of Homeland Security and the Department of Justice for the time period from FY 1980 until FY 2024.

36. Important here is that they "must—with a few exceptions—apply for asylee status within one year of their arrival in the US" (Reilly 2016, 102).

37. Asylum cases can also be expensive if asylum seekers are not fortunate enough to secure a pro bono lawyer. But attorneys are crucial, as data show that having one significantly increases one's odds of obtaining asylum (Transactional Records Access Clearinghouse 2016).

38. Although my data analysis of affirmative and defensive asylum decisions pertaining to Liberians from across the country during the height of the war does not necessarily support this conclusion. However, in general there are wide discrepancies by circuits and judges that were exacerbated during the Trump presidencies. In addition, the New York asylum office has had significant lower grant rates than the Newark asylum office (Human Rights First, 2022).

39. Approval rates are listed online by jurisdiction and judge.

40. Data for other national groups represent a mixed picture. For example, Burmese consistently had low denial rates and Somali relatively high, while Eritreans had during one time period very low denial rates but higher in the others, and Cubans had higher denial rates than almost all African nationalities (Transactional Records Access Clearinghouse 2007; 2016). Although in the Cuban case it should be noted that deportation was a nonissue until the end of the "wet-foot, dry-foot" policy in 2017.

41. Between 2012 and 2017, asylum seekers from Haiti had the second-highest denial rate (87 percent) despite having the world's highest per capita kidnapping rate along with other violent political persecution; the denial rate for Mexicans during the same time was 88 percent (Herrera 2021).

42. I witnessed this firsthand when I served as a country conditions expert for Liberian asylum and deportation hearings throughout the United States. For example, an immigration judge in the Southwest steadfastly proclaimed that "there is no Liberian diaspora in the U.S." since "they went back."

43. The case contains additional information that is omitted here to protect the Liberian asylum seeker's anonymity.

44. White men in the U.S. government, society, and mainstream culture continue to be imbued by hegemonic masculinity (Connell 2005), which, in turn, situates White, heterosexual, able-bodied cis men at the top of society's hierarchy.

45. Immigrants have been barred from these through the Personal Responsibility and Work Opportunity Reconciliation Act since 1996. Legal permanent residents (with some exceptions) become eligible after they have legal permanent residency for five years or longer.
46. Here, my findings differ significantly from H. E. Brown's (2011, 146–147) observations about Liberians in California who used their "legal [refugee] status to make claims for social and political membership . . . [and] rights."
47. At the same time, I note that native-born Black Americans have also been frequently infantilized in mainstream society, while native-born Black American youth are simultaneously being adultified and criminalized (Gilmore and Bettis 2021; Ladson Billings 2011).
48. Tang (2015, 153) states that "the [Cambodian] refugee mother in the hyperghetto remained on welfare for long periods of time and exhibited high fertility[;] she was quickly exempted from welfare queen status," a derogatory racist label that has been applied to poor Black women.
49. Eritrean and Ethiopian refugees also made that connection to being equated to "beggars" (McSpadden and Moussa 1993, 210).
50. The preference for "settlers" is a nod to her Americo Liberian paternal ancestors who are known as "settlers."
51. See an earlier description of how some refugees obtained "spots" to be resettled in the United States.
52. While this group of Sudanese people were children when they initially became refugees, they were mostly young adults when resettled to the United States, and as such calling Black men "boys" is especially problematic given the racial history around this term when applied to Black people. In addition, this is an example of infantilizing African refugees, perhaps to emphasize their innocence and therefore counteract dominant racist stereotypes about Black men.

CHAPTER 5 WHITES ARE THE BOSS

1. Liberian refugees in California had similar inclinations (H. E. Brown 2011).
2. Following Lamont et al. (2016), discrimination here is also defined as denial of resources and opportunities; however, anti-Black racism also exists among other ethnoracial minority groups (for example, C. V. Morgan et al. 2017).
3. Here, this research as well other scholarship (Covington-Ward 2017a; Pierre 2004; Showers 2015a) sharply converges from Holtzman (1999, 115), who contends that "racism [experienced by Nuer refugees] should not be overemphasized . . . few and far . . . instances have occurred . . . Africans are frequently viewed with substantially less racism by whites than African Americans."
4. For example, for many years while teaching at Wagner College, which is a twenty-minute walk from Park Hill, I requested that the college van service provide a shuttle for college students volunteering with different organizations in Park Hill. While the senior administration was supportive, in the first two-and-a-half years, the van drivers and their director were more than reluctant to drive my students because "it is dangerous there," as they said. Most of the drivers are native-born White Staten Islanders who retired from government agencies, including the New York City Police Department and the New York City Department of Sanitation. One time I went in person to follow up on the van request and ensure the staff that it was safe to go. I cited my ongoing ethnographic work as evidence that nothing ever had happened to me, but I was mocked by the then-director and several drivers who were present at the time. "Let's fill you up with water and see where the bullet holes are," said one of the drivers with a sarcastic laugh. Only after years of intervention, the work of dedicated and committed students, and a change in leadership (director), Wagner College vans went to Park Hill and without incident. It should also be noted that these same van drivers were going for many years to a predominantly non-White Hispanic immigrant neighborhood in Staten Island's North Shore without voicing any objections, although both neighborhoods have comparable crime rates.

5. The *Staten Island Advance* ended the comment section, citing "the proliferation of other communication options; and an increase in personal-attack comments that required around-the-clock moderation" (*Staten Island Advance* 2020).
6. American Community Survey data for 2010–2014 (weighted values). For all groups, men have higher labor force participation rates than women (Hamilton 2019). (No other gender categories are listed.)
7. Publicly available data and most studies tend to rely on binary gender categories.
8. The comparison with native-born White and Black Americans is a bit more complex: All African men earn less than native-born White American men, but some African immigrant men earn more than native-born Black American men. Nigerian immigrant women earn more than native-born White American women, whereas all other African immigrant and refugee women earn less than native-born White American and Nigerian women in the United States (Hamilton 2019, 127).
9. Hispanic immigrants.
10. Those murdered include, but are not limited to, Ernest Sayon (born to Liberian parents, 1994), Amadou Diallo (Guinea, 1999), Jonathan Deng (Sudan, 2009), Deng Manyoun (Sudan, 2015), Alfred Olango (Uganda, 2016), Lindani Myeni (South African, 2021), and Patrick Lyoya (Democratic Republic of Congo, 2022).
11. "Seventy-six percent of Black immigrants are deported on criminal grounds, compared to 45 percent of all immigrants." In addition, Black refugees and immigrants are also overrepresented among the people facing deportation on criminal grounds (Ibrahim 2020, para. 12).
12. Official statistics from the U.S. Immigration and Customs Enforcement show that in FY 2016, 27 Liberians were deported compared to anywhere between 108 and 112 in FYs 2017–2020. The numbers were lower during the Biden administration.
13. There are important and notable exceptions: White refugees, refugees with more formal education who tend to have had the opportunity to engage in global travel and/or work with people from different national backgrounds, refugees who had previously worked with the U.S. military (e.g., during wars in Laos, Vietnam, Afghanistan, Iraq), and so forth.
14. A version of the White savior complex is central in the 2014 movie *The Good Lie*, which features Sudanese refugees.
15. Undoubtedly, refugees whose applications for resettlement were denied will have different views from those who were among the fortunate few to be given a chance to create a new home in the United States.
16. Many of the refugees who have been resettled in the United States over the past decades fled ethnic and/or religious persecution. Among them are Dinka and Nuer from (South) Sudan, Somalis, Somali Bantus, Rwandans, Tigrinya and Kunama from Ethiopia and Eritrea, religious minorities from the FSU and Iran, Bosnian Muslims, Kosovo Albanians, Meskhetian Turks, Iraqi Kurds, Sino-Vietnamese, and different ethnic groups from Myanmar, Liberia, and the Democratic Republic of Congo.
17. Remittances make up a large share of Liberia's gross domestic product (Hamilton 2019).
18. With money and prestige.
19. In contrast, Colic-Peisker (2009) found that some African refugees who were resettled in Australia expected to be discriminated against due to prevalent (global) anti-Black racism.
20. However, data show that anti-Black racism has led to significantly higher fatality rates for Black people in the United States due to excessive and deadly force in policing (Embrick 2015), lack of care and resources in health care (Yearby et al. 2022), and exposure to environmental hazards and poor living conditions (Henderson and Wells 2021), among other outcomes.
21. The knowledge about (historic) relations between White and Black people in the United States was even more important for the few Liberians who settled in the United States around the time of the Civil Rights movement, long before the outbreak of the war in Liberia. Among

them was Isaac Cheeks, another Americo Liberian, whose parents had left the Jim Crow South for Liberia as children several decades prior. In the 1960s, when Mr. Cheeks came to New York on a ship from Monrovia, a fellow passenger told him about a place that he could rent in the Bronx. At first, he was hesitant to accept this offer because he "didn't know whether they were . . . going to lynch him or not . . . because in a strange place and . . . heard about the lynching [of] Black people." Indeed, it was the lynching, abuse, and anti-Black racism that had pushed Mr. Cheeks's own ancestors to leave the United States for Liberia.

22. "No more war" for almost all Liberians does not mean the end of the armed conflict and the signing of the peace treaty but rather that there is permanent peace and economic stability and thus, it is safe to return; this did not happen until recently. (See also discussions about the subjective vs. the objective assessment of "safe return" for refugees [Chimni 2004; Ecke et al. 2016].)

CHAPTER 6 WE HAVE THE SAME SKIN COLOR

1. H.Res.1055 (115th Congress, 2nd Session)—To affirm strong United States–Liberia ties and support for democratic principles, and call for full implementation of the Truth and Reconciliation Commission recommendations, including the establishment of an Extraordinary Criminal Tribunal for Liberia.

2. Names are omitted to protect the privacy of both individuals, since some of this exchange took place in writing in a public forum.

3. Guluma (2023) reported the same among first- and second-generation Oromo immigrants from Ethiopia, which is in contrast to other ethnic groups (e.g., Amhara or Tigrayan) who tend to emphasize non-Black identities.

4. The racial category for "White" also did not allow for any distinctions in terms of ethnicity and nationality until 2020.

5. Congos is interchangeably used with "Americo Liberian."

6. After researching and teaching about Liberian refugees, I have found that most Americans, regardless of their race, are often unaware of this historical connection between Liberia and the United States (see also House 2024). Another example is when Donald Trump asked Liberian President Boakai, "And such good English. Such beautiful. Where did you learn to speak so beautifully? Where were you educated?," indicating his lack of knowledge about Liberia's origins.

7. "African American"—native-born Black Americans without recent migration history—is itself already a pan-ethnic group (Yang and Brown 2022).

8. Although very often different Asian (American) groups are also lumped together.

9. Americo Liberians, due to their ancestral ties to American slavery, did not make these comparisons.

10. Berlin (2010) describes how generations before, Africans who were born on the continent and subsequently forcibly enslaved viewed native-born Black American people as morally and culturally inferior to them.

11. A spicy bean/pea-based stew.

12. The show was released the same year Juah Nimley came to the United States.

13. Several of the native-born Black Americans in this study also remarked how they experienced anti-Black racism at the hands of Asian immigrants in Staten Island and how this was even more bewildering than having been discriminated against by native-born White Americans. For example, Mac Willi noted, "If you wanna be in this country, you should not bring your prejudice with you. We've had enough of our own. We don't need anyone else to bring their own. . . . The nerve to actually come in and . . . bring this new type of racism." This may indicate

that Black people have come to expect native-born White Americans to be racist but are startled when encountering discrimination from those who are not White.

14. One of the three activists who cofounded the Black Lives Matter movement following the acquittal of George Zimmerman, who killed Trayvon Martin, is Ayọ Tometi, a second-generation Nigerian American.

15. At the same time, it must be noted that many of today's immigrants in the United States, including myself, owe our ability to be here to the battle that native-born Black Americans fought. It was the Civil Rights movement that paved the way for the Immigration and Nationality Act of 1965, which removed national quotas that discriminated against certain national, ethnic, and racial groups.

16. Kasinitz et al. (2008, 303) concluded that first- and second-generation Black immigrants and refugees have benefited from "the institutions, political strategies, and notions of rights developed in the aftermath of the civil rights movement precisely because they have been nonwhite."

17. In order to protect the anonymity of the research participant, the pseudonym is omitted.

18. This person's race was given as "White" in other reports and news coverage about this hate crime.

19. Not a pseudonym.

20. Mr. Richards explained to me that attending an educational program about race and racism was a condition of the racist offender's guilty plea. This arrangement was made between the district attorney's office, the court-appointed lawyer, and the "bigot" as Mr. Richards said. He added that this was preferable to the offender going to jail.

21. Not a pseudonym.

22. Language was not the reason for the separate meetings, as both were facilitated in English, despite the presence of West African refugees and immigrants whose first language is not English.

23. Black immigrants and refugees make up less than 10 percent of the noncitizen population but 20 percent of immigrants facing deportation on criminal grounds (Palmer 2017, 102).

24. In one instance, a Liberian refugee was forced to watch one of his close female family members being sexually assaulted during the Liberian civil war when he was a young child. He recounted how he felt helpless as he was prevented by armed rebels from intervening. Once resettled in the United States with his fractured family, he dealt with post-traumatic stress disorder and not feeling safe. In his words, he chose to arm himself with a gun without a permit to get a sense of control and to be able to protect others, "just in case."

25. The shared celebration does not mean that events that focus on, for example, African heritage, are not happening. For example, the African Community Alliance of Staten Island has organized an African Heritage Cultural Festival in Park Hill for the last couple of years.

CHAPTER 7 THERE ARE LIBERIAN REFUGEES IN THE FUTURE

1. Recall the global outcry about injustices when media outlets, humanitarian organizations, and individuals shared the picture of Aylan Kurdî, the three-year-old refugee boy from Syria who drowned in Turkey in 2015. None of the bodies of drowned African children that washed up on European beaches in the months before received comparable attention (El-Enany 2016).

2. As noted before, the travel ban in the second Trump administration was even more anti-Black.

3. Since 2020, the Cultural Orientation Resource Exchange (CORE), a technical assistance program, has provided the support and material for this Cultural Orientation. CORE is funded by the U.S. Department of State, Bureau of Population, Refugees, and Migration and administered by the IRC. Previously, this service was delivered by the Cultural Orientation Resource Center.

4. "Switchboard's mission is to provide comprehensive support and guidance to professionals and organizations involved in refugee resettlement. . . . We aim to empower and equip service providers with the tools they need to facilitate successful and sustainable integration for newcomers in their new communities" (Switchboard, n.d.).

5. In some regards, that can be understood as similar to "the talk" that parents/caregivers have with their Black children in the United States (L. A. Anderson et al. 2022). This is not to equate Black refugees with children but rather involve them in a process about learning about a society's norms, cultures, history, and so forth.

6. There have also been reports about inaccurate translations for Haitian Creole. In 2024, the CBP One app supported five languages (English, Spanish, Russian, Portuguese, and Haitian Creole), but certain aspects of the app (e.g., registration) were available only in Spanish and English. In 2025, it appears that most of the app's functions can only be accessed in English, Spanish, and Haitian Creole.

7. Only once in all these years, I was contacted by an immigration lawyer with the request to assist in finding an interpreter who spoke Mandigo for a detained Liberian asylum seeker.

8. But revoking Executive Order 13166 "will lead to less coordinated and consistent efforts by federal agencies to provide language access in programs they directly deliver" (Hofstetter 2025, para. 3).

9. For a notable exception see Menjívar et al. (2018).

10. This bill proposed several other changes as well.

REFERENCES

Abdi, Cawo. 2011. "The Newest African-Americans?: Somali Struggles for Belonging." *Bildhaan: An International Journal of Somali Studies* 11:90–107.

———. 2015a. "Disclaimed or Reclaimed? Muslim Refugee Youth and Belonging in the Age of Hyperbolisation." *Journal of Intercultural Studies* 36 (5): 564–578. https://doi.org/10.1080/07256868.2015.1072905.

———. 2015b. *Elusive Jannah: The Somali Diaspora and a Borderless Muslim Identity*. Minneapolis: University of Minnesota Press.

Abdi, Nimo M. 2020. "Immigrant Hierarchies and White Supremacy: Race and Representation among East African Immigrant Muslims." *International Journal of Qualitative Studies in Education* 33 (2): 274–284. https://doi.org/10.1080/09518398.2019.1681542.

Abrego, Leisy J. 2019. "Relational Legal Consciousness of U.S. Citizenship: Privilege, Responsibility, Guilt, and Love in Latino Mixed-Status Families." *Law & Society Review* 53 (3): 641–670.

Abu-Sada, Caroline, ed. 2012. *In the Eyes of Others. How People in Crises Perceive Humanitarian Aid*. New York: Doctors Without Borders. https://www.msf.org/sites/default/files/msf-in-the-eyes-of-others.pdf.

Achebe, Chinua, and Robert Lyons, eds. 1998. *Another Africa*. London: Lund Humphries.

Achiume, E. Tendayi. 2021. "Race, Refugees, and International Law." In *The Oxford Handbook of International Refugee Law*, edited by Cathryn Costello, Michelle Foster, and Jane McAdam. Oxford: Oxford University Press.

———. 2022. "Empire, Borders, and Refugee Responsibility Sharing." *California Law Review* 110:1011–1039. https://doi.org/10.15779/Z38HH6C669.

Adjepong, Anima. 2018. "Afropolitan Projects: African Immigrant Identities and Solidarities in the United States." *Ethnic and Racial Studies* 41 (2): 248–266. https://doi.org/10.1080/01419870.2017.1281985.

Adombila, Maxwell Akalaare. 2024. "Liberia's Civil War Refugees Left Destitute After Decades-Old Ghana Camp Demolished." *Reuters*, March 5, sec. Africa. https://www.reuters.com/world/africa/liberias-civil-war-refugees-left-destitute-after-decades-old-ghana-camp-2024-03-05/.

Advocates for Human Rights, The. 2006. "A House with Two Rooms: Final Report of the Truth and Reconciliation Commission of Liberia Diaspora Project." Dispute Resolution Institute Press. https://www.theadvocatesforhumanrights.org/uploads/a_house_with_two_rooms.pdf.

Agadjanian, Victor, Cecilia Menjívar, and Natalya Zotova. 2017. "Legality, Racialization, and Immigrants' Experience of Ethnoracial Harassment in Russia." *Social Problems* 64 (4): 558–576. https://doi.org/10.1093/socpro/spw042.

Agblorti, Samuel K. M., and Miriam R. Grant. 2019. "Conceptualising Obstacles to Local Integration of Refugees in Ghana." *Refugee Survey Quarterly* 38 (2): 195–213. https://doi.org/10.1093/rsq/hdz005.

Agier, Michel. 2011. *Managing the Undesirables: Refugee Camps and Humanitarian Government*. Cambridge: Polity Press.

Ahmad, Muneer I. 2002. "The Ethics of Narrative." *Journal of Gender, Social Policy & the Law* 11 (1): 117–127.

Aizenobie, Aituaje. 2019. "Interpreting Global Statistics on Resettlement of Refugees Through the Lens of Critical Race Theory: A Consideration of Canada." LLM thesis, University of Windsor. https://scholar.uwindsor.ca/etd/7775.

Ajrouch, Kristine J., and Amaney Jamal. 2007. "Assimilating to a White Identity: The Case of Arab Americans." *International Migration Review* 41 (4): 860–879.

Alao, Temi. 2023. "Diasporic Consciousness in African Immigrants' Support for #BlackLivesMatter." *Journal of Race, Ethnicity, and Politics* 8 (2): 141–163. https://doi.org/10.1017/rep.2023.10.

Alba, Richard D., and Victor Nee. 2003. *Remaking the American Mainstream: Assimilation and Contemporary Immigration*. Cambridge, MA: Harvard University Press.

Albert, Matthew. 2010. "Prima Facie Determination of Refugee Status: An Overview and Its Legal Foundation." Working Paper Series 55. University of Oxford. https://www.rsc.ox.ac.uk/publications/prima-facie-determination-of-refugee-legal-status-an-overview-of-its-legal-foundation.

Alboim, Naomi. 2016. "Lessons Learned from the Indochinese and Syrian Refugee Movements." Montréal, Canada: Institute for Research on Public Policy. https://policyoptions.irpp.org/magazines/may-2016/lessons-learned-from-the-indochinese-and-syrian-refugee-movements/.

Aleinikoff, T. Alexander. 1996. "United States Refugee Law and Policy: Past, Present and Future." *International Migration Review* 30 (1): 245–257. https://doi.org/10.1177/019791839603001S15.

———. 2015. "Ending the Second Exile." *UNHCR Tracks* (blog). June 20. http://tracks.unhcr.org/2015/06/ending-the-second-exile/.

Aleinikoff, T. Alexander, and Rubén G. Rumbaut. 1998. "Terms of Belonging: Are Models of Membership Self-Fulfilling Prophecies?" *Georgetown Immigration Law Journal* 13 (1): 1–24.

Alexander, Michelle. 2010. *The New Jim Crow: Mass Incarceration in the Age of Colorblindness*. New York: New Press.

Alves, Giavanni. 2021. "NYC Subsidized Housing Crisis: A Look Inside the Park Hill Apartments; 'This Is Not the Way We're Supposed to Live.'" *Staten Island Advance*, November 24, sec. News. https://www.silive.com/news/2021/11/nyc-public-housing-crisis-a-look-inside-the-park-hill-apartments-this-is-not-the-way-were-supposed-to-live.html.

American Immigration Council. 2024. "Temporary Protected Status: An Overview." Fact Sheet. Washington, D.C. https://www.americanimmigrationcouncil.org/sites/default/files/research/temporary_protected_status_an_overview_2024.pdf.

American Immigration Lawyers Association. 2021. "Eliminate or Extend the Deadline of the Liberian Refugee Immigration Fairness Program," December 17. https://www.aila.org/File/DownloadEmbeddedFile/91125.

Anderson, Elijah. 2011. *The Cosmopolitan Canopy: Race and Civility in Everyday Life*. New York: W. W. Norton & Company.

Anderson, Leslie A., Margaret O'Brien Caughy, and Margaret T. Owen. 2022. "'The Talk' and Parenting While Black in America: Centering Race, Resistance, and Refuge." *Journal of Black Psychology* 48 (3–4): 475–506. https://doi.org/10.1177/00957984211034294.

Appiah, Kwame Anthony. 1992. *In My Father's House: Africa in the Philosophy of Culture*. New York: Oxford University Press.

Apraku, Kofi Konadu. 1996. *Outside Looking In: An African Perspective on American Pluralistic Society*. Westport, CT: Praeger.

Aptekar, Sofya. 2015. *The Road to Citizenship: What Naturalization Means for Immigrants and the United States*. New Brunswick, NJ: Rutgers University Press.

Armenta, Amada. 2017. "Racializing Crimmigration: Structural Racism, Colorblindness, and the Institutional Production of Immigrant Criminality." *Sociology of Race and Ethnicity* 3 (1): 82–95. https://doi.org/10.1177/2332649216648714.

Arriaga, Felicia. 2023. *Behind Crimmigration: ICE, Law Enforcement, and Resistance in America*. Chapel Hill: University of North Carolina Press.

Arthur, John A. 2000. *Invisible Sojourners: African Immigrant Diaspora in the United States*. Westport, CT: Praeger.

———. 2009. *African Women Immigrants in the United States: Crossing Transnational Borders.* New York: Palgrave Macmillan.

Asante, Godfried Agyeman, Sachi Sekimoto, and Christopher Brown. 2016. "Becoming 'Black': Exploring the Racialized Experiences of African Immigrants in the United States." *Howard Journal of Communications* 27 (4): 367–384. https://doi.org/10.1080/10646175.2016.1206047.

Auer, Doug. 2008. "As Staten Islanders Rally Against Gun Violence, North Shore Records Another Shooting." *Staten Island Advance,* December 31. http://www.silive.com/news/index.ssf/2008/12/a_staten_island_rally_against.html.

Awokoya, Janet. 2012. "Identity Constructions and Negotiations Among 1.5- and Second-Generation Nigerians: The Impact of Family, School, and Peer Contexts." *Harvard Educational Review* 82 (2): 255–281. https://doi.org/10.17763/haer.82.2.9v77p329367116vj.

Baldassar, Loretta. 2015. "Guilty Feelings and the Guilt Trip: Emotions and Motivation in Migration and Transnational Caregiving." *Emotion, Space and Society* 16 (August): 81–89. https://doi.org/10.1016/j.emospa.2014.09.003.

Baranik De Alarcón, Sarah, David Secor, and Norma Fuentes-Mayorga. 2020. "'We Are Asking Why You Treat Us This Way. Is It Because We Are Negroes?' A Reparations-Based Approach to Remedying the Trump Administration's Cancellation of TPS Protections for Haitians." *Michigan Journal of Race & Law* 26 (1): 1–47. https://doi.org/10.36643/mjrl.26.1.we.

Barth, Fredrik, ed. 1998. *Ethnic Groups and Boundaries: The Social Organization of Culture Difference.* Long Grove, IL: Waveland Press.

Bashi, Vilna. 1998. "Racial Categories Matter Because Racial Hierarchies Matter: A Commentary." *Ethnic & Racial Studies* 21 (5): 959–968.

———. 2004. "Globalized Anti-Blackness: Transnationalizing Western Immigration Law, Policy, and Practice." *Ethnic and Racial Studies* 27 (4): 584–606. https://doi.org/10.1080/01491987042000216726.

———. 2007. *Survival of the Knitted: Immigrant Social Networks in a Stratified World.* Stanford, CA: Stanford University Press.

Beaman, Jean, and Orly Clergé. 2024. "Ain't I a Migrant?: Global Blackness and the Future of Migration Studies." *International Migration Review* 58 (4): 1727–1756. https://doi.org/10.1177/01979183241271685.

Bell, Katherine M. 2013. "Raising Africa?: Celebrity and the Rhetoric of the White Saviour." *Journal of Multidisciplinary International Studies* 10 (1): 1–24.

Berger, Iris. 2015. "Between Advocacy and Deception." In *African Asylum at a Crossroads: Activism, Expert Testimony, and Refugee Rights,* edited by Iris Berger, Tricia Redeker Hepner, Benjamin N. Lawrance, Joanna T. Tague, and Meredith Terretta. Athens: Ohio University Press.

Berger, Joseph, and Ian Urbina. 2003. "Along with Population and Diversity, Stress Rises on Staten Island." *New York Times,* September 25. http://www.nytimes.com/2003/09/25/nyregion/along-with-population-and-diversity-stress-rises-on-staten-i.html?pagewanted=all&src=pm.

Bergeron, Claire. 2014. "Temporary Protected Status after 25 Years: Addressing the Challenge of Long-Term 'Temporary' Residents and Strengthening a Centerpiece of US Humanitarian Protection." *Journal on Migration and Human Security* 2 (1): 23–43. https://doi.org/10.14240/jmhs.v2i1.23.

Berkeley, Bill. 2002. *The Graves Are Not Yet Full: Race, Tribe, and Power in the Heart of Africa.* New York: Basic Books.

Berlin, Ira. 2010. *The Making of African America: The Four Great Migrations.* New York: Viking Adult.

Bernstein, Richard. 1994. "One Neighborhood, Two Lives—A Special Report. A Death on Staten Island: 2 Paths Cross on Familiar Ground." *New York Times,* May 15, sec. 1.

Besbris, Max, Jacob William Faber, Peter Rich, and Patrick Sharkey. 2015. "Effect of Neighborhood Stigma on Economic Transactions." *Proceedings of the National Academy of Sciences* 112 (16): 4994–4998.

Besteman, Catherine. 2012. "Somali Bantus in a State of Refuge." *Bildhaan: An International Journal of Somali Studies* 12 (8): 11–33.

———. 2016. *Making Refuge: Somali Bantu Refugees and Lewiston, Maine*. Durham, NC: Duke University Press.

Binder, Susanne, and Jelena Tošić. 2005. "Refugees as a Particular Form of Transnational Migrations and Social Transformations: Socioanthropological and Gender Aspects." *Current Sociology* 53 (4): 607–624.

Black, Richard. 2001. "Fifty Years of Refugee Studies: From Theory to Policy." *International Migration Review* 35 (1): 57–78.

Blyden, Edward Wilmot. 1856. *A Voice from Bleeding Africa on Behalf of Her Exiled Children*. Monrovia, Liberia: G. Killian Printer.

Boas, Heidi H. 2006. "The New Face of America's Refugees: African Refugee Resettlement to the United States." *Georgetown Immigration Law Journal* 21 (3): 431–468.

Boaz, Danielle N. 2011. "Dividing Stereotyping and Religion: The Legal Implications of the Ambiguous References to Voodoo in U.S. Court Proceedings." *Scholar: St. Mary's Law Review on Race and Social Justice* 14 (2): 251–299.

Bolter, Jessica, and Muzaffar Chishti. 2022. "Welcoming Afghans and Ukrainians to the United States: A Case in Similarities and Contrasts." Washington, D.C.: Migration Policy Institute. https://www.migrationpolicy.org/article/afghan-ukrainian-us-arrivals-parole.

Bonilla-Silva, Eduardo. 1996. "Rethinking Racism: Toward a Structural Interpretation." *American Sociological Review* 62 (3): 465–480.

Bonilla-Silva, Eduardo, and Sarah Mayorga. 2011. "On (Not) Belonging. Why Citizenship Does Not Remedy Racial Inequality." In *State of White Supremacy: Racism, Governance, and the United States*, edited by Moon-Kie Jung, João H. Costa Vargas, and Eduardo Bonilla-Silva. Stanford, CA: Stanford University Press.

Bonsu, Samuel K. 2009. "Colonial Images in Global Times: Consumer Interpretations of Africa and Africans in Advertising." *Consumption Markets & Culture* 12 (1): 1–25.

Bradburn, Douglas. 2009. *The Citizenship Revolution: Politics and the Creation of the American Union, 1774–1804*. Charlottesville: University of Virginia Press.

Brandt, Karin Leah. 2010. "Making Immigrant Integration Work: A Case Study of Refugee Resettlement in Philadelphia, PA." Master's thesis, Massachusetts Institute of Technology. https://dspace.mit.edu/handle/1721.1/59716.

Brondolo, Elizabeth, Nisha Brady Ver Halen, Melissa Pencille, Danielle Beatty, and Richard J. Contrada. 2009. "Coping with Racism: A Selective Review of the Literature and a Theoretical and Methodological Critique." *Journal of Behavioral Medicine* 32 (1): 64–88.

Brown, Chip. 1994. "Escape from New York." *New York Times*, January 30.

Brown, Hana E. 2011. "Refugees, Rights, and Race: How Legal Status Shapes Liberian Immigrants' Relationship with the State." *Social Problems* 58 (1): 144–163. https://doi.org/10.1525/sp.2011.58.1.144.

———. 2013. "Race, Legality, and the Social Policy Consequences of Anti-Immigration Mobilization." *American Sociological Review* 78 (2): 290–314. https://doi.org/10.1177/0003122413476712.

Brown, Tamara Mose. 2011. *Raising Brooklyn: Nannies, Childcare, and Caribbeans Creating Community*. New York: New York University Press.

Bryce-Laporte, Roy Simon. 1972. "Black Immigrants: The Experience of Invisibility and Inequality." *Journal of Black Studies* 3 (1): 29–56.

Bunyasi, Tehama Lopez, and Candis Watts Smith. 2019. "Do All Black Lives Matter Equally to Black People? Respectability Politics and the Limitations of Linked Fate." *Journal of Race, Ethnicity, and Politics* 4 (1): 180–215. https://doi.org/10.1017/rep.2018.33.

Buscher, Dale. 2017. "Formidable Intersections: Forced Migration, Gender and Livelihoods." In *Gender, Violence, Refugees*, edited by Susanne Buckley-Zistel and Ulrike Krause. New York: Berghahn Books.

Byrne, Jennifer. 2013. "Should I Stay or Should I Go? National Identity and Attitudes Towards Local Integration Among Liberian Refugees in Ghana." *Refugee Survey Quarterly* 32 (1): 50–73. https://doi.org/10.1093/rsq/hds020.

Campbell, Elizabeth H., Jean D'Arc Kakusu, and Iddi Musyemi. 2006. "Congolese Refugee Livelihoods in Nairobi and the Prospects of Legal, Local Integration." *Refugee Survey Quarterly* 25 (2): 93–108. https://doi.org/10.1093/rsq/hdi0128.

Capps, Randy, and Michael Fix. 2015. "Ten Facts about U.S. Refugee Resettlement." Migration Policy Institute. https://www.migrationpolicy.org/research/ten-facts-about-us-refugee-resettlement.

Capps, Randy, Kathleen Newland, Susan Fratzke, Susannah Groves, Greg Auclair, Michael Fix, and Margie McHugh. 2015. "Integrating Refugees in the United States: The Successes and Challenges of Resettlement in a Global Context." *Journal of the International Association for Official Statistics* 31:341–367. https://doi.org/10.3233/SJI-150918.

Carbado, Devon W. 2005. "Racial Naturalization." *American Quarterly* 57 (3): 633–658. https://doi.org/10.1353/aq.2005.0042.

Casavantes Bradford, Anita. 2019. "'Another Foothold in Our Fight Against Communism': Race, Religion, and Public Relations in the Hungarian and Cuban Refugee Programs, 1956–1961." *U.S. Catholic Historian* 37 (3): 43–76. https://doi.org/10.1353/cht.2019.0017.

Castles, Stephen. 2003. "Towards a Sociology of Forced Migration and Social Transformation." *Sociology* 37 (1): 13–34. https://doi.org/10.1177/0038038503037001384.

Chacko, Elizabeth. 2003. "Identity and Assimilation Among Young Ethiopian Immigrants in Metropolitan Washington." *Geographical Review* 93 (4): 491–506.

Chandler, Mittie Olion. 1992. "Public Housing Desegregation: What Are the Options?" *Housing Policy Debate* 3 (2): 509–534. https://doi.org/10.1080/10511482.1992.9521102.

Charles, Carolle. 2006. "Political Refugees or Economic Immigrants? A New 'Old Debate' Within the Haitian Immigrant Communities but with Contestations and Division." *Journal of American Ethnic History* 25 (2/3): 190–208.

Chimni, Bhupinder S. 1998. "The Geopolitics of Refugee Studies: A View from the South." *Journal of Refugee Studies* 11 (4): 350–374. https://doi.org/10.1093/jrs/11.4.350-a.

———. 2004. "From Resettlement to Involuntary Repatriation: Towards a Critical History of Durable Solutions to Refugee Problems." *Refugee Survey Quarterly* 23 (3): 55–73. https://doi.org/10.1093/rsq/23.3.55.

Chisholm, Shirley. 1982. "U.S. Policy and Black Refugees." *Issue: A Journal of Opinion* 12 (1/2): 22–24. https://doi.org/10.2307/1166533.

Chommie, John C. 1963. "The University of Miami Program for Cuban Lawyers: A Report." *Inter-American Law Review* 5:177.

Church World Service. 2015. "Faith Leaders Join Together, Ask U.S. to Increase Support for Syrian Refugees—United States of America." Reliefweb. https://reliefweb.int/report/united-states-america/faith-leaders-join-together-ask-us-increase-support-syrian-refugees.

Ciment, James. 2013. *Another America. The Story of Liberia and the Former Slaves Who Ruled It.* New York: Hill & Wang.

Clark, Msia Kibona. 2008. "Identity Among First and Second Generation African Immigrants in the United States." *African Identities* 6 (2): 169–181. https://doi.org/10.1080/14725840801933999.

Clarke, Leah K., and L. DiAnne Borders. 2014. "'You Got to Apply Seriousness': A Phenomenological Inquiry of Liberian Refugees' Coping." *Journal of Counseling & Development* 92 (3): 294–303. https://doi.org/10.1002/j.1556-6676.2014.00157.x.

Clergé, Orly. 2019. *The New Noir: Race, Identity, and Diaspora in Black Suburbia.* Oakland: University of California Press.

Cohen, Michael. 2009. "Staten Island's Race Problem." *Interactive Journalism 2010* (blog). October 4. http://interactive2010.journalism.cuny.edu/2009/10/04/staten-islands-race-problem/.

Colic-Peisker, Val. 2005. "'At Least You're the Right Colour': Identity and Social Inclusion of Bosnian Refugees in Australia." *Journal of Ethnic and Migration Studies* 31 (4): 615–638. https://doi.org/10.1080/13691830500109720.

———. 2009. "Visibility, Settlement Success and Life Satisfaction in Three Refugee Communities in Australia." *Ethnicities* 9 (2): 175–199. https://doi.org/10.1177/1468796809103459.

Congressional Research Service. 2011. "U.S. Refugee Resettlement Assistance." R41570. https://crsreports.congress.gov/product/pdf/R/R41570.

Connell, R. W. 2005. *Masculinities*. 2nd ed. Berkeley: University of California Press.

CORE. 2019. "Cultural Orientation Objectives and Indicators." CORE. https://coresourceexchange.org/cultural-orientation-objectives-and-indicators/.

———. 2020a. "Addressing Social Unrest, U.S. Laws, Diversity and Tolerance in Cultural Orientation Delivery." CORE. June 10. https://coresourceexchange.org/2020/06/10/addressing-social-unrest-u-s-laws-diversity-and-tolerance-in-cultural-orientation-delivery/.

———. 2020b. "Supplemental Lesson Plan Public Safety and Police Interactions." CORE. August 2020. https://coresourceexchange.org/cultural-orientation-objectives-and-indicators/.

Corrie, Bruce P., and Sarah Radosevic. 2013. "The Economic Contributions of Immigrants in Minnesota." St. Paul: Minnesota Chamber of Commerce. http://cdn2.hubspot.net/hub/172912/file-371412567-pdf/Economic_Contributions_of_Immigrants_in_Minnesota_2013.pdf.

Covington-Ward, Yolanda. 2017a. "African Immigrants in Low-Wage Direct Health Care: Motivations, Job Satisfaction, and Occupational Mobility." *Journal of Immigrant and Minority Health* 19 (3): 709–715. https://doi.org/10.1007/s10903-016-0400-8.

Covington-Ward, Yolanda. 2017b. "'Back Home, People Say America Is Heaven': Pre-Migration Expectations and Post-Migration Adjustment for Liberians in Pittsburgh." *Journal of International Migration and Integration* 18 (4): 1013–1032. https://doi.org/10.1007/s12134-017-0511-7.

Cox, Kiana, and Christine Tamir. 2022. "Race Is Central to Identity for Black Americans and Affects How They Connect with Each Other." Washington, D.C.: Research Center. https://www.pewresearch.org/race-ethnicity/2022/04/14/race-is-central-to-identity-for-black-americans-and-affects-how-they-connect-with-each-other/.

Crawley, Heaven, and Veronica Fynn Bruey. 2022. "'Hanging in the Air': The Experiences of Liberian Refugees in Ghana." In *Migration in West Africa: IMISCOE Regional Reader*, edited by Joseph Kofi Teye. Cham, Switzerland: Springer International Publishing.

Creese, Gillian. 2011. *The New African Diaspora in Vancouver: Migration, Exclusion and Belonging*. Toronto: University of Toronto Press.

Crenshaw, Kimberle W. 2011. "From Private Violence to Mass Incarceration: Thinking Intersectionally About Women, Race, and Social Control." *UCLA Law Review* 59:1418–1473.

Crosby, Dorian B., and Shenita R. Brazelton. 2017. "The Disadvantages of African American and Somali Men in the US Criminal Justice System." *Spectrum: A Journal on Black Men* 6 (1): 99–120. https://doi.org/10.2979/spectrum.6.1.05.

Current, Brewer Cheris. 2008. "Normalizing Cuban Refugees: Representations of Whiteness and Anti-Communism in the USA During the Cold War." *Ethnicities* 8 (1): 42–66. https://doi.org/10.1177/1468796807087019.

Dabney, Dean A., Brent Teasdale, Glen A. Ishoy, Taylor Gann, and Bonnie Berry. 2017. "Policing in a Largely Minority Jurisdiction: The Influence of Appearance Characteristics Associated with Contemporary Hip-Hop Culture on Police Decision-Making." *Justice Quarterly* 34 (7): 1310–1338. https://doi.org/10.1080/07418825.2017.1382557.

D'Alisera, JoAnn. 2004. *An Imagined Geography: Sierra Leonean Muslims in America*. Philadelphia: University of Pennsylvania Press.

Dallaire, Roméo. 2009. *Shake Hands with the Devil: The Failure of Humanity in Rwanda*. Toronto: Random House of Canada.

Dalmage, Heather M. 2000. *Tripping on the Color Line: Black-White Multiracial Families in a Racially Divided World*. New Brunswick, NJ: Rutgers University Press.

David, John Seh. 2014. *The American Colonization Society: And the Founding of the First African Republic*. Bloomington, IN: iUniverse LLC.

Davis, Darren W. 1997. "The Direction of Race of Interviewer Effects Among African-Americans: Donning the Black Mask." *American Journal of Political Science* 41 (1): 309–322. https://doi.org/10.2307/2111718.

Dawsey, Josh. 2018. "Trump Derides Protections for Immigrants from 'Shithole' Countries." *Washington Post*, January 12, sec. Politics. https://www.washingtonpost.com/politics/trump-attacks-protections-for-immigrants-from-shithole-countries-in-oval-office-meeting/2018/01/11/bfc0725c-f711-11e7-91af-31ac729add94_story.html.

Dawson, Michael C. 1994. *Behind the Mule: Race and Class in African-American Politics*. Princeton, NJ: Princeton University Press.

DenUyl, Sophia. 2022. "The Particular Harms of the 'Good Immigrant' Versus 'Bad Immigrant' Construction on Black Immigrants in the United States." *Georgetown Immigration Law Journal* 36:775–774.

Department of International Protection (DIP). 2005. "Self-Study Module 2: Refugee Status Determination. Identifying Who Is a Refugee." UNHCR. http://www.refworld.org/docid/43141f5d4.html.

Desbarats, Jacqueline. 1985. "Indochinese Resettlement in the United States." *Annals of the Association of American Geographers* 75 (4): 522–538.

Devroy, Ann, and Molly Moore. 1990. "61 Americans Evacuated from Liberia." *Washington Post*, August 6.

Dick, Shelly. 2002a. "Liberians in Ghana: Living Without Humanitarian Assistance." Working Paper 57. New Issues in Refugee Research. Geneva, Switzerland: UNHCR. http://www.unhcr.org/3c8398f24.html.

———. 2002b. "Responding to Protracted Refugee Situations: A Case Study of Liberian Refugees in Ghana." Evaluation and Policy Analysis. Geneva, Switzerland: UNHCR. http://www.unhcr.org/3d40059b4.html.

Dobbs, Leo, and Adrian Edwards. 2012. "Protracted Refugee Situations in Liberia and Angola to Finally End." Geneva, Switzerland: UNHCR. http://www.unhcr.org/news/latest/2012/6/4fed81049/protracted-refugee-situations-liberia-angola-finally-end.html.

Dolo, Emmanuel. 2002. *Democracy Versus Dictatorship: The Quest for Freedom and Justice in Africa's Oldest Republic—Liberia*. Lanham, MD: University Press of America.

———. 2007. *Ethnic Tensions in Liberia's National Identity Crisis: Problems and Possibilities*. Cherry Hill, NJ: Africana Homestead Legacy Publishers.

Donnelly, Frank. 2012. "Staten Island Cop Who Falsely Arrested Black Man Insists He's Not Racist." *Staten Island Advance*, June 18. http://www.silive.com/news/index.ssf/2012/06/staten_island_cop_who_falsely.html.

———. 2021. "He Admits Hate Crime for Racist Graffiti on S.I. Campaign Posters. Must Undergo Racial-Insensitivity Treatment." *Staten Island Advance*, December 1, sec. Crime & Safety. https://www.silive.com/crime-safety/2021/12/he-admits-hate-crime-for-racist-graffiti-on-si-campaign-posters-must-undergo-racial-insensitivity-treatment.html.

Dove, Edward S. 2013. "Back to Blood: The Sociopolitics and Law of Compulsory DNA Testing of Refugees." *University of Massachusetts Law Review* 8 (2): 466–531.

Du Bois, W.E.B. 1994. *The Souls of Black Folk*. New York: Dover Publications.

Dutt, Anjali, Farrah Jacquez, Autumn Kirkendall, Bryan Wright, and Riham Alwan. 2022. "Refugee Experiences in Cincinnati, Ohio: A Local Case Study in the Context of Global Crisis." *Journal of Social Issues* 78 (1): 126–145. https://doi.org/10.1111/josi.12471.

Dwyer, Tatiana. 2010. "Refugee Integration in the United States: Challenges & Opportunities." White Paper. New York: Church World Service. http://www.churchworldservice.org/site/DocServer/Refugee_Integration_in_the_United_States.pdf?docID=3923.

Eager, Page Whaley. 2011. "The Voice of the Congressional Black Caucus in American Foreign Policy." In *The Expanding Boundaries of Black Politics*, edited by Georgia A. Persons. The National Political Science Review. New Brunswick, NJ: Transaction Publishers.

Eberhardt, Jennifer L., Paul G. Davies, Valerie J. Purdie-Vaughns, and Sheri Lynn Johnson. 2006. "Looking Deathworthy: Perceived Stereotypicality of Black Defendants Predicts Capital-Sentencing Outcomes." *Psychological Science* 17 (5): 383–386. https://doi.org/10.1111/j.1467-9280.2006.01716.x.

Ecke, Jonas, Geetor Saydee, Joseph W. Nyan, Kalilu Donzo, Mackie K. Dolo, and Richard Russ. 2016. "The Subjective and Economic Well-Being of Repatriated Liberian Refugees from Ghana." *Refugee Survey Quarterly* 35 (3): 119–143. https://doi.org/10.1093/rsq/hdw011.

Eckstein, Susan. 2022. *Cuban Privilege*. Cambridge: Cambridge University Press.

Ekeh, Peter. 2001. "Kinship and State in African and African American Histories." In *The African Diaspora: African Origins and New World Identities*, edited by Isidore Okpewho, Carole Boyce Davies, and Ali Al'Amin Mazrui. Bloomington: Indiana University Press.

El-Enany, Nadine. 2016. "Aylan Kurdi: The Human Refugee." *Law and Critique* 27 (1): 13–15. https://doi.org/10.1007/s10978-015-9175-7.

Ellis, B. Heidi, Alisa K. Lincoln, Saida M. Abdi, Elizabeth A. Nimmons, Osob Issa, and Scott H. Decker. 2020. "'We All Have Stories': Black Muslim Immigrants' Experience with the Police." *Race and Justice* 10 (3): 341–362. https://doi.org/10.1177/2153368718754638.

Ellis, Stephen. 1999. *The Mask of Anarchy: The Destruction of Liberia and the Religious Dimension of an African Civil War*. New York: New York University Press.

Elo, Irma T., Elizabeth Frankenberg, Romeo Gansey, and Duncan Thomas. 2015. "Africans in the American Labor Market." *Demography* 52 (5): 1513–1542. https://doi.org/10.1007/s13524-015-0417-y.

Embrick, David G. 2015. "Two Nations, Revisited: The Lynching of Black and Brown Bodies, Police Brutality, and Racial Control in 'Post-Racial' Amerikkka." *Critical Sociology* 41 (6): 835–843. https://doi.org/10.1177/0896920515591950.

Enos, Olivia. 2022. "Why the U.S. Should Extend 'Priority 2' Refugee Status to Uyghurs and Hong Kong Citizens." The Heritage Foundation. https://www.heritage.org/asia/report/why-the-us-should-extend-priority-2-refugee-status-uyghurs-and-hong-kong-citizens.

Enriquez, Laura E. 2015. "Multigenerational Punishment: Shared Experiences of Undocumented Immigration Status Within Mixed-Status Families." *Journal of Marriage and Family* 77 (4): 939–953.

Ernyes, Klara, and Ellen Pulleyblank Coffey. 2006. "Pushing Against the Stream: Building Community with Bosnian Refugees in Oakland, California." In *Immigrant Families and Immigration: Therapeutic Work*, edited by Gonzalo Bacigalupe and Janine Roberts. Vol. 2. Monograph Series. Washington, DC: American Family Therapy Academy.

Esbenshade, Jill. 2010. *An Assessment of DNA Testing for African Refugees*. Special Reports on Immigration. Washington, D.C.: American Immigration Council. https://www.americanimmigrationcouncil.org/research/assessment-dna-testing-african-refugees.

———. 2011. "Discrimination, DNA Testing, and Dispossession: Consequences of U.S. Policy for African Refugees." *Souls* 13 (2): 175–196. https://doi.org/10.1080/10999949.2011.574571.

Essed, Philomena. 1991. *Understanding Everyday Racism: An Interdisciplinary Theory*. Vol. 2. Sage Series on Race and Ethnic Relations. Newbury Park, CA: Sage Publications.

Essuman-Johnson, Abeeku. 2011. "When Refugees Don't Go Home: The Situation of Liberian Refugees in Ghana." *Journal of Immigrant & Refugee Studies* 9 (2): 105–126. https://doi.org/10.1080/15562948.2011.567139.

Etienne, Vadricka Y. 2020. "Rather Be Known as Haitian: Identity Construction of the Ethnically-Identified Second Generation." *Ethnic and Racial Studies* 43 (12): 2158–2175. https://doi.org/10.1080/01419870.2019.1677927.

Fábos, Anita. 2012. "Resisting Blackness, Embracing Rightness: How Muslim Arab Sudanese Women Negotiate Their Identity in the Diaspora." *Ethnic and Racial Studies* 35 (2): 218–237. https://doi.org/10.1080/01419870.2011.592594.

Fair, Jo Ellen, and Lisa Parks. 2001. "Africa on Camera: Television News Coverage and Aerial Imaging of Rwandan Refugees." *Africa Today* 48 (2): 35–57.

Feagin, Joe R. 1991. "The Continuing Significance of Race: Antiblack Discrimination in Public Places." *American Sociological Review* 56 (1): 101–116.

———. 2009a. "Global Impacts of White Racism: Americo-Liberians." *Racism Review* (blog), January 4. http://www.racismreview.com/blog/2009/01/04/global-impacts-of-white-racism-americo-liberians/.

———. 2009b. *The White Racial Frame: Centuries of Racial Framing and Counter-Framing.* New York: Routledge.

Fee, Molly. 2023. "Humanitarian Protection and the Reconstitution of Refugee Families." Paper presented at American Sociological Association Annual Meeting. Philadelphia.

Ferber, Abby L. 2007. "The Construction of Black Masculinity: White Supremacy Now and Then." *Journal of Sport and Social Issues* 31 (1): 11–24. https://doi.org/10.1177/0193723506296829.

Ferris, Elizabeth. 2014. "Ten Years after Humanitarian Reform: How Have IDPs Fared?" Washington, D.C.: Brookings Institution. https://www.africaportal.org/publications/ten-years-after-humanitarian-reform-how-have-idps-fared/.

Fiddian-Qasmiyeh, Elena. 2010. "'Ideal' Refugee Women and Gender Equality Mainstreaming in the Sahrawi Refugee Camps: 'Good Practice' for Whom?" *Refugee Survey Quarterly* 29 (2): 64–84. https://doi.org/10.1093/rsq/hdq023.

FitzGerald, David Scott, and Rawan Arar. 2018. "The Sociology of Refugee Migration." *Annual Review of Sociology* 44 (1): 387–406. https://doi.org/10.1146/annurev-soc-073117-041204.

Fitzgerald, Michael W. 1997. "'We Have Found a Moses': Theodore Bilbo, Black Nationalism, and the Greater Liberia Bill of 1939." *Journal of Southern History* 63 (2): 293–320. https://doi.org/10.2307/2211284.

Foner, Nancy. 2005. *In a New Land: A Comparative View of Immigration.* New York: New York University Press.

———. 2018. "Race in an Era of Mass Migration: Black Migrants in Europe and the United States." *Ethnic and Racial Studies* 41 (6): 1113–1130. https://doi.org/10.1080/01419870.2018.1411600.

Forrest, Anika, and Haddy Gassama. 2023. "What Is 'Freedom' to Black Migrants?" *AFRO American Newspapers*, September 12. http://afro.com/what-is-freedom-to-black-migrants/.

Fox, Cybelle, and Thomas A. Guglielmo. 2012. "Defining America's Racial Boundaries: Blacks, Mexicans, and European Immigrants, 1890–1945." *American Journal of Sociology* 118 (2): 327–379. https://doi.org/10.1086/666383.

Franz, Barbara. 2005. *Uprooted and Unwanted: Bosnian Refugees in Austria and the United States.* College Station: Texas A&M University Press.

Frelick, Bill, and Barbara Kohnen. 1995. "Filling the Gap: Temporary Protected Status." *Journal of Refugee Studies* 8 (4): 339–363. https://doi.org/10.1093/jrs/8.4.339.

Gale, Peter. 2004. "The Refugee Crisis and Fear: Populist Politics and Media Discourse." *Journal of Sociology* 40 (4): 321–340. https://doi.org/10.1177/1440783304048378.

García, María Cristina. 1997. *Havana USA: Cuban Exiles and Cuban Americans in South Florida, 1959–1994.* Berkeley: University of California Press.

Gbowee, Leymah, and Carol Lynn Mithers. 2011. *Mighty Be Our Powers: How Sisterhood, Prayer, and Sex Changed a Nation at War.* New York: Beast Books.

Gerlus, Jean-Claude. 1995. "The Effects of the Cold War on U.S.-Haiti's Relations." *Journal of Haitian Studies* 1 (1): 34–56.

Gershoni, Yekutiel. 1985. *Black Colonialism: The Americo-Liberian Struggle for the Hinterland.* Boulder, CO: Westview Press.

Gilmore, Amir A., and Pamela J. Bettis. 2021. "Antiblackness and the Adultification of Black Children in a U.S. Prison Nation." In *Oxford Research Encyclopedia of Education.* Oxford: Oxford University Press.

Gmelch, George. 1992. *Double Passage: The Lives of Caribbean Migrants Abroad and Back Home.* Ann Arbor: University of Michigan Press.

Golash-Boza, Tanya. 2006. "Dropping the Hyphen? Becoming Latino(a)-American Through Racialized Assimilation." *Social Forces* 85 (1): 27–55. https://doi.org/10.1353/sof.2006.0124.

Gold, Steven J. 1992. *Refugee Communities: A Comparative Field Study.* Newbury Park, CA: Sage Publications.

Goodkind, Jessica R., and Zermarie Deacon. 2004. "Methodological Issues in Conducting Research with Refugee Women: Principles for Recognizing and Re-Centering the Multiply Marginalized." *Journal of Community Psychology* 32 (6): 721–739. https://doi.org/10.1002/jcop.20029.

Gosin, Monika. 2019. *The Racial Politics of Division: Interethnic Struggles for Legitimacy in Multicultural Miami.* Ithaca, NY: Cornell University Press. https://doi.org/10.7591/cornell/9781501738234.003.0003.

Gowayed, Heba. 2019. "Resettled and Unsettled: Syrian Refugees and the Intersection of Race and Legal Status in the United States." *Ethnic and Racial Studies* 43 (2): 275–293. https://doi.org/10.1080/01419870.2019.1583350.

Gray, Harriet, and Anja K Franck. 2019. "Refugees as/at Risk: The Gendered and Racialized Underpinnings of Securitization in British Media Narratives." *Security Dialogue* 50 (3): 275–291. https://doi.org/10.1177/0967010619830590.

Greer, Christina M. 2013. *Black Ethnics: Race, Immigration, and the Pursuit of the American Dream.* New York: Oxford University Press.

———. 2018. "Hart-Celler and the Effects on African American and Immigrant Incorporation." *National Political Science Review* 19 (1): 18–28.

Gualtieri, Sarah. 2001. "Becoming 'White': Race, Religion and the Foundations of Syrian/Lebanese Ethnicity in the United States." *Journal of American Ethnic History* 20 (4): 29–58.

Guarnizo, Luis Eduardo, Alejandro Portes, and William Haller. 2003. "Assimilation and Transnationalism: Determinants of Transnational Political Action Among Contemporary Migrants." *American Journal of Sociology* 108 (6): 1211–1248.

Guenther, Katja M., Sadie Pendaz, and Fortunata Songora Makene. 2011. "The Impact of Intersecting Dimensions of Inequality and Identity on the Racial Status of Eastern African Immigrants." *Sociological Forum* 26 (1): 98–120. https://doi.org/10.1111/j.1573-7861.2010.01226.x.

Guluma, Beka. 2023. "I'm Not Habesha, I'm Oromo: Immigration, Ethnic Identity, and the Transnationality of Blackness." *Sociology of Race and Ethnicity* 9 (4): 486–501.

Gupte, Jaideep, and Lyla Mehta. 2007. "Disjunctures in Labelling Refugees and Oustees." In *The Power of Labelling: How People Are Categorized and Why It Matters,* edited by Joy Moncrieffe and Rosalind Eyben. London: Routledge.

Gurung, Shobha Hamal. 2015. *Nepali Migrant Women: Resistance and Survival in America.* Syracuse, New York: Syracuse University Press.

Gutsche, Robert E, Xinhe Cong, Feihong Pan, Yiyi Sun, and LaTasha DeLoach. 2022. "#DiminishingDiscrimination: The Symbolic Annihilation of Race and Racism in News Hashtags of 'Calling 911 on Black People.'" *Journalism* 23 (1): 259–277. https://doi.org/10.1177/1464884920919279.

Habecker, Shelly. 2012. "Not Black, but Habasha: Ethiopian and Eritrean Immigrants in American Society." *Ethnic and Racial Studies* 35 (7): 1200–1219. https://doi.org/10.1080/01419870.2011.598232.

Haddow, Gary Laurence. 2015. "(Trans)Formation of Liberian Immigrant Identities in the United States." Master's thesis, University of California, Santa Barbara. https://escholarship.org/uc/item/9j54c62t.

Hadley, Craig, and Crystal Patil. 2009. "Perceived Discrimination Among Three Groups of Refugees Resettled in the USA: Associations with Language, Time in the USA, and Continent of Origin." *Journal of Immigrant and Minority Health* 11 (6): 505–512. https://doi.org/10.1007/s10903-009-9227-x.

Haffejee, Badiah, and Jean F. East. 2015. "African Women Refugee Resettlement: A Womanist Analysis." *Affilia* 31 (2): 232–242. https://doi.org/10.1177/0886109915595840.

Haines, David W. 2007. "Ethnicity's Shadows: Race, Religion, and Nationality as Alternative Identities Among Recent United States Arrivals." *Identities* 14 (3): 285–312. https://doi.org/10.1080/10702890601162773.

———. 2010. *Safe Haven? A History of Refugees in America*. Sterling, VA: Kumarian Press.

Haines, David W., and Karen E. Rosenblum. 2010. "Perfectly American: Constructing the Refugee Experience." *Journal of Ethnic & Migration Studies* 36 (3): 391–406. https://doi.org/10.1080/13691830903358445.

Hall, Brian J., Melissa R. Garabiles, and Carl A. Latkin. 2019. "Work Life, Relationship, and Policy Determinants of Health and Well-Being Among Filipino Domestic Workers in China: A Qualitative Study." *BMC Public Health* 19 (1): 1–14. https://doi.org/10.1186/s12889-019-6552-4.

Hall, Stuart. 1996. "Race, Articulation, and Societies Structured in Dominance." In *Black British Cultural Studies: A Reader*, edited by Houston A. Baker Jr., Manthia Diawara, and Ruth H. Lindeborg. Chicago: University of Chicago Press.

Hamilton, Tod G. 2019. *Immigration and the Remaking of Black America*. New York: Russell Sage Foundation.

Hampshire, Kate, Gina Porter, Kate Kilpatrick, Peter Kyei, Michael Adjaloo, and George Oppong. 2008. "Liminal Spaces: Changing Inter-Generational Relations Among Long-Term Liberian Refugees in Ghana." *Human Organization* 67 (1): 25–36.

Hanson-Easey, Scott, and Martha Augoustinos. 2010. "Out of Africa: Accounting for Refugee Policy and the Language of Causal Attribution." *Discourse & Society* 21 (3): 295–323. https://doi.org/10.1177/0957926509360744.

Harrell-Bond, Barbara. 2002. "Can Humanitarian Work with Refugees Be Humane?" *Human Rights Quarterly* 24 (1): 51–85.

Hauser, Christine. 2009. "After a Hate Crime Spree, an Intense Effort to Make Arrests." *New York Times*, January 12, sec. New York Region.

Hawkins, Virgil. 2008. *Stealth Conflicts: How the World's Worst Violence Is Ignored*. Burlington, VT: Ashgate Publishing Company.

Heeren, Geoffrey. 2015. "The Status of Nonstatus." *American University Law Review* 64: 1115–1182.

Henderson, Sheree, and Rebecca Wells. 2021. "Environmental Racism and the Contamination of Black Lives: A Literature Review." *Journal of African American Studies* 25 (1): 134–151. https://doi.org/10.1007/s12111-020-09511-5.

Herrera, Jack. 2021. "Black Immigrants Matter." *Nation*, March 24. https://www.thenation.com/article/society/black-immigrants-asylum-deportation/.

Hess, Julia Meredith, Brian L. Isakson, Suha Amer, Eric Ndaheba, Brandon Baca, and Jessica R. Goodkind. 2019. "Refugee Mental Health and Healing: Understanding the Impact of Policies of Rapid Economic Self-Sufficiency and the Importance of Meaningful Work." *Journal of International Migration and Integration* 20 (3): 769–786. https://doi.org/10.1007/s12134-018-0628-3.

Hilario, Carla T., John L. Oliffe, Josephine P. Wong, Annette J. Browne, and Joy L. Johnson. 2019. "'I Tend to Forget Bad Things': Immigrant and Refugee Young Men's Narratives of Distress." *Health* 23 (6): 587–601. https://doi.org/10.1177/1363459318763865.

Hing, Bill Ong. 2002. "Vigilante Racism: The De-Americanization of Immigrant America." *Michigan Journal of Race and Law* 7 (2): 441–456.

Hing, Bill Ong. 2022. "Addressing the Intersection of Racial Justice and Immigrant Rights." *Belmont Law Review* 9 (March): 357–405.

Hinkle, Lillie. 2023. *The Unmet Potential of Community Consultations in U.S. Refugee Resettlement*. Washington, D.C.: Migration Policy Institute. https://www.migrationpolicy.org/sites/default/files/publications/mpi-us-resettlement-consultations_final.pdf.

Hirsch, Shirin. 2019. "Racism, 'Second Generation' Refugees and the Asylum System." *Identities* 26 (1): 88–106. https://doi.org/10.1080/1070289X.2017.1361263.

Hofstetter, Jacob. 2025. "Shifting Priorities: How the Official English Executive Order Could Affect Language Access Efforts." Washington, D.C.: Migration Policy Institute. https://www.migrationpolicy.org/news/official-english-order-language-access.

Holland, Emily. 2011. "Moving the Virtual Border to the Cellular Level: Mandatory DNA Testing and the U.S. Refugee Family Reunification Program." *California Law Review* 99 (6): 1635–1682.

Holtzman, Jon D. 1999. *Nuer Journeys, Nuer Lives: Sudanese Refugees in Minnesota*. Boston: Allyn & Bacon.

Holzer, Elizabeth. 2015. *The Concerned Women of Buduburam: Refugee Activists and Humanitarian Dilemmas*. Ithaca, NY: Cornell University Press.

Horowitz, Juliana Menasce, Anna Brown, and Kiana Cox. 2019. "Race in America 2019." Washington, D.C.: Pew Research Center. https://www.pewresearch.org/social-trends/wp-content/uploads/sites/3/2019/04/Race-report_updated-4.29.19.pdf.

Horst, Cindy. 2007. *Transnational Nomads. How Somalis Cope with Refugee Life in the Dadaab Camps of Kenya*. Oxford: Berghahn Books.

House, Roger. 2024. "Why Black Americans Should Commemorate the History of Liberia." *Hill*, February 11, sec. Opinion—Civil Rights. https://thehill.com/opinion/civil-rights/4460990-why-black-americans-should-commemorate-the-history-of-liberia/.

Huberich, Charles Henry. 2010. *The Political and Legislative History of Liberia*. Clark, NJ: Lawbook Exchange Ltd.

Human Rights First. 2022. USCIS Records Reveal Systemic Disparities in Asylum Decisions. https://humanrightsfirst.org/wp-content/uploads/2022/09/AsylumOfficeFOIASystemicDisparities.pdf.

Humphries, Jill M. 2009. "Resisting 'Race': Organizing African Transnational Identities in the United States." In *The New African Diaspora*, edited by Isidore Okpewho and Nkiru Nzegwu. Bloomington: Indiana University Press.

Hylton, Annie. 2019. "How the U.S. Became a Haven for War Criminals." *New Republic*, April 29. https://newrepublic.com/article/153416/us-became-haven-war-criminals.

Hyndman, Jennifer. 2000. *Managing Displacement: Refugees and the Politics of Humanitarianism*. Minneapolis: University of Minnesota Press.

———. 2019. "Unsettling Feminist Geopolitics: Forging Feminist Political Geographies of Violence and Displacement." *Gender, Place & Culture* 26 (1): 3–29. https://doi.org/10.1080/0966369X.2018.1561427.

Hyndman, Jennifer, and Wenona Giles. 2011. "Waiting for What? The Feminization of Asylum in Protracted Situations." *Gender, Place & Culture* 18 (3): 361–379. https://doi.org/10.1080/0966369X.2011.566347.

Ibe, Peniel. 2021. "Immigration Is a Black Issue." Philadelphia: American Friends Service Committee. https://afsc.org/news/immigration-black-issue.

Ibrahim, Shamira. 2020. "The NYPD's Long History of Targeting Black Immigrants." *Documented*, July 1. https://documentedny.com/2020/07/01/the-nypds-long-history-of-targeting-black-immigrants/.

Iceland, John. 2009. *Where We Live Now: Immigration and Race in the United States*. Berkeley: University of California Press.

Imoagene, Onoso. 2015. "Broken Bridges: An Exchange of Slurs Between African Americans and Second Generation Nigerians and the Impact on Identity Formation Among the Second Generation." *Language Sciences* 52:176–186. https://doi.org/10.1016/j.langsci.2015.03.010.

———. 2017. *Beyond Expectations: Second-Generation Nigerians in the United States and Britain*. Oakland: University of California Press.

———. 2019. "Gauging Panethnicity: Affirmative Action, African Americans, and Children of Black Immigrants." *African and Black Diaspora: An International Journal* 12 (2): 156–170. https://doi.org/10.1080/17528631.2018.1559790.

Internal Displacement Monitoring Center. 2023. *Global Report on Internal Displacement 2022*. https://api.internal-displacement.org/sites/default/files/publications/documents/IDMC_GRID_2022_LR.pdf.

Iversen, Ivar A. 2007. "Evangelicals and US Policy on Sudan." In *Foreign Policy in God's Name*. Oslo, Norway: Norwegian Institute for Defence Studies. https://core.ac.uk/download/pdf/225932968.pdf.

Jackson, Jennifer, and Mary E. Cothran. 2003. "Black Versus Black: The Relationships Among African, African American, and African Caribbean Persons." *Journal of Black Studies* 33 (5): 576–604.

Jackson, Regine O. 2010. "Black Immigrants and the Rhetoric of Social Distancing." *Sociology Compass* 4 (3): 193–206. https://doi.org/10.1111/j.1751-9020.2009.00266.x.

Jacobsen, Karen. 2005. *The Economic Life of Refugees*. Sterling, VA: Kumarian Press.

Jacobsen, Karen, and Loren B. Landau. 2003. "The Dual Imperative in Refugee Research: Some Methodological and Ethical Considerations in Social Science Research on Forced Migration." *Disasters* 27 (3): 185–206. https://doi.org/10.1111/1467-7717.00228.

Jang, Yuri, Ahyoung A. Lee, Michelle Zadrozny, Sung-Heui Bae, Miyong T. Kim, and Nathan C. Marti. 2017. "Determinants of Job Satisfaction and Turnover Intent in Home Health Workers: The Role of Job Demands and Resources." *Journal of Applied Gerontology* 36 (1): 56–70. https://doi.org/10.1177/0733464815586059.

Janmyr, Maja. 2017. "Military Recruitment of Sudanese Refugee Men in Uganda: A Tale of National Patronage and International Failure." In *Gender, Violence, Refugees*, edited by Susanne Buckley-Zistel and Ulrike Krause. New York: Berghahn Books.

———. 2021. "Sudanese Refugees and the 'Syrian Refugee Response' in Lebanon: Racialised Hierarchies, Processes of Invisibilisation, and Resistance." *Refugee Survey Quarterly* 41 (September): 131–156. https://doi.org/10.1093/rsq/hdab012.

Jansen, Bram J. 2008. "Between Vulnerability and Assertiveness: Negotiating Resettlement in Kakuma Refugee Camp, Kenya." *African Affairs* 107 (429): 569–587. https://doi.org/10.1093/afraf/adn044.

———. 2016. "'Digging Aid': The Camp as an Option in East and the Horn of Africa." *Journal of Refugee Studies* 29 (2): 149–165. https://doi.org/10.1093/jrs/fev018.

Johnson, Kevin R. 2007. *Opening the Floodgates: Why America Needs to Rethink Its Borders and Immigration Laws*. New York: New York University Press.

Johnson, Violet Showers. 2016. "When Blackness Stings: African and Afro-Caribbean Immigrants, Race, and Racism in Late Twentieth-Century America." *Journal of American Ethnic History* 36 (1): 31–62. https://doi.org/10.5406/jamerethnhist.36.1.0031.

Jones-Correa, Michael. 1998. "Different Paths: Gender, Immigration and Political Participation." *International Migration Review* 32 (2): 326–349. https://doi.org/10.2307/2547186.

Jubany, Olga. 2011. "Constructing Truths in a Culture of Disbelief: Understanding Asylum Screening from Within." *International Sociology* 26 (1): 74–94. https://doi.org/10.1177/0268580910380978.

Kaj, Nisreen. 2012. "Why a Non-Black Identity—the Lebanese—as Part of Nigeria's National Polity Has Been Problematic." CERS Working Paper. University of Leeds. cers.leeds.ac.uk/files/2013/05/Lebanese_and_Nigeria_Nisreen_Kaj.pdf.

Kälin, Walter. 2000. *Guiding Principles on Internal Displacement: Annotations*. Vol. 38. Studies in Transnational Legal Policy. Washington, DC: The American Society of International Law. http://www.asil.org/pdfs/stlp.pdf.

Kamara, Alpha. 2020. "Simmering Tensions Between Africans and African Americans in Staten Island Ease—Pavement Pieces." *Pavement Pieces* (blog), June 17. https://pavementpieces.com/tensions-between-africans-and-african-americans-in-staten-island-ease/, https://pavementpieces.com/tensions-between-africans-and-african-americans-in-staten-island-ease/.

Kamara-Umunna, Agnes Fallah, and Lauren Feeney. 2011. "From Liberia to Staten Island: A Former Child Soldier Shares His Story." *Women, War, & Peace*. A Five-Part Special Series on PBS. http://www.pbs.org/wnet/women-war-and-peace/features/from-liberia-to-staten-island-a-former-child-soldier-shares-his-story/.

Kasinitz, Philip. 1992. *Caribbean New York: Black Immigrants and the Politics of Race*. Ithaca, NY: Cornell University Press.

———. 2008. "Becoming American, Becoming Minority, Getting Ahead: The Role of Racial and Ethnic Status in the Upward Mobility of the Children of Immigrants." *ANNALS of the American Academy of Political and Social Science* 620 (1): 253–269. https://doi.org/10.1177/0002716208322880.

Kasinitz, Philip, John H. Mollenkopf, Mary C. Waters, and Jennifer Holdaway. 2008. *Inheriting the City: The Children of Immigrants Come of Age*. Cambridge, MA: Harvard University Press.

Kawahara, Yumeka, Lucy Mastellar, Sarah Rose Morehouse, Charlie Williams, and Karen Jacobsen. 2022. "Assessing Refugees' Understanding of and Responses to U.S. Race Relations: An Analysis of Findings." Henry J. Leir Institute for Migration and Human Security, The Fletcher School, Tufts University. https://sites.tufts.edu/ihs/files/2023/02/LeirInstitute_RITReport_v4_FINAL.pdf.

Kebede, Kassahun. 2017. "Twice-Hyphenated: Transnational Identity among Second-Generation Ethiopian-American Professionals in the Washington, DC, Metropolitan Area." *African and Black Diaspora: An International Journal* 10 (3): 252–268. https://doi.org/10.1080/17528631.2017.1319146.

Kelling, George L., and James Q. Wilson. 1982. "Broken Windows." *Atlantic Monthly* 249 (3): 29–38.

Kelly, Melissa, and Lina Hedman. 2016. "Between Opportunity and Constraint: Understanding the Onward Migration of Highly Educated Iranian Refugees from Sweden." *Journal of International Migration and Integration* 17 (3): 649–667. https://doi.org/10.1007/s12134-015-0422-4.

Kibreab, Gaim. 2004. "Pulling the Wool over the Eyes of the Strangers: Refugee Deceit and Trickery in Institutionalized Settings." *Journal of Refugee Studies* 17 (1): 1–26. https://doi.org/10.1093/jrs/17.1.1.

Kim, Anna Joo, and Ashley Bozarth. 2021. "Refuge City: Creating Places of Welcome in the Suburban U.S. South." *Journal of Urban Affairs* 43 (6): 851–871. https://doi.org/10.1080/07352166.2020.1718506.

Kim, Soo Mee, and Aggie J. Yellow Horse. 2018. "Undocumented Asians, Left in the Shadows." *Contexts* 17 (4): 70–71. https://doi.org/10.1177/1536504218812875.

King, Candace S., and Emmanuel Adero. 2020. "Crafting the Racial Frame: Blackness and the Myth of the Monolith." In *Black in America: The Paradox of the Color Line*, edited by Enobong Hannah Branch and Christina Jackson. Medford, MA: Polity Press.

Kolawole, Bolatito. 2016. "African Immigrants, Intersectionality, and the Increasing Need for Visibility in the Current Immigration Debate." *Columbia Journal of Race and Law* 7:373–409.

Konneh, Augustine. 1996. "Citizenship at the Margins: Status, Ambiguity, and the Mandingo of Liberia." *African Studies Review* 39 (2): 141–154. https://doi.org/10.2307/525439.

Koyama, Jill. 2015. "Constructing Gender: Refugee Women Working in the United States." *Journal of Refugee Studies* 28 (2): 258–275.

Krogstad, Jens Manuel, and Jynnah Radford. 2017. "Key Facts about Refugees to the U.S." Washington, D.C.: Pew Research Center. http://www.pewresearch.org/fact-tank/2017/01/30/key-facts-about-refugees-to-the-u-s/.

Lacroix, Marie. 2004. "Canadian Refugee Policy and the Social Construction of the Refugee Claimant Subjectivity: Understanding Refugeeness." *Journal of Refugee Studies* 17 (2): 147–166. https://doi.org/10.1093/jrs/17.2.147.

Ladson Billings, Gloria. 2011. "Boyz to Men? Teaching to Restore Black Boys' Childhood." *Race Ethnicity and Education* 14 (1): 7–15. https://doi.org/10.1080/13613324.2011.531977.

Lamont, Michèle, Ann Morning, and Margarita Mooney. 2002. "Particular Universalisms: North African Immigrants Respond to French Racism." *Ethnic and Racial Studies* 25 (3): 390–414. https://doi.org/10.1080/01419870020036701e.

Lamont, Michèle, Graziella Moraes Silva, Jessica Welburn, Joshua Guetzkow, Nissim Mizrachi, Hanna Herzog, and Elisa Reis. 2016. *Getting Respect: Responding to Stigma and Discrimination in the United States, Brazil, and Israel.* Princeton, NJ: Princeton University Press.

Landes, Scott D., and Suzie S. Weng. 2020. "Racial–Ethnic Differences in Turnover Intent Among Home Health Aides." *Journal of Applied Gerontology* 39 (5): 490–501. https://doi.org/10.1177/0733464819827806.

Landry, Ava. 2018. "Black Is Black Is Black?: African Immigrant Acculturation in Chimamanda Ngozi Adichie's *Americanah* and Yaa Gyasi's *Homegoing*." *MELUS: Multi-Ethnic Literature of the U.S.* 43 (4): 127–147. https://doi.org/10.1093/melus/mly044.

Larson, Eric D. 2016. "Black Lives Matter and Bridge Building: Labor Education for a 'New Jim Crow' Era." *Labor Studies Journal* 41 (1): 36–66. https://doi.org/10.1177/0160449X16638800.

Lauby, Fanny. 2020. "Diversity, Leadership, and Authenticity in the Undocumented Youth Movement." *Journal of Race, Ethnicity and Politics* 5 (1): 37–61. https://doi.org/10.1017/rep.2019.28.

Lawrence, Charles R. 1987. "The Id, the Ego, and Equal Protection: Reckoning with Unconscious Racism." *Stanford Law Review* 39 (2): 317–388. https://doi.org/10.2307/1228797.

Lawyers Committee for Human Rights. 1986. *Liberia: A Promise Betrayed:* New York: Lawyers Committee for Human Rights.

Layne, Asha. 2021. "It's Not Just Black and White: How Black Immigrants Continue to Influence the Fight Against Police Violence." *Journal of Liberal Arts and Humanities* 2 (6): 1–7.

Lazin, Fred. 2009. "The Role of Ethnic Politics in U.S. Immigration and Refugee Policy: The Case of Soviet Jewry." Working Paper 175. The Center for Comparative Immigration Studies, University of California, San Diego.

Lee, Cynthia. 2004. "But I Thought He Had a Gun—Race and Police Use of a Deadly Force." *Hastings Race and Poverty Law Journal* 2:1–52.

Lee, Wonhyung, and Lindsey Disney. 2024. "Resettled Refugees and African Americans in the Same Neighborhoods: Insights for Intergroup Dynamics and Multicultural Community Building." *Urban Affairs Review* 60 (3): 864–891. https://doi.org/10.1177/10780874231209971.

Lenette, Caroline, and Sienna Cleland. 2016. "Visual Representations of Asylum Seekers in Times of Crisis." *Creative Approaches in Research* 9 (1): 68–83.

Lennox, Malissia. 1993. "Refugees, Racism, and Reparations: A Critique of the United States' Haitian Immigration Policy." *Stanford Law Review* 45 (3): 687–724.

Levitt, Jeremy. 2005. *The Evolution of Deadly Conflict in Liberia: From "Paternaltarianism" to State Collapse*. Durham, NC: Carolina Academic Press.

Levitt, Peggy. 2001. *The Transnational Villagers*. Berkeley: University of California Press.

Liebenow, J. Gus. 1969. *Liberia: The Evolution of Privilege*. Ithaca, NY: Cornell University Press.

Liotta, Paul. 2019. "'Like We're Living in a Third World Country': Park Hill Tenants Fed Up, Say Conditions Are Worst Ever." *Silive*, July 31, sec. News. https://www.silive.com/news/2019/07/like-were-living-in-a-third-world-country-park-hill-tenants-fed-up-say-conditions-are-worst-ever.html.

Lipsitz, George. 1998. *Possessive Investment in Whiteness*. Philadelphia: Temple University Press.

Llewellyn, Cheryl. 2017. "Sex Logics: Biological Essentialism and Gender-Based Asylum Cases." *American Behavioral Scientist* 61 (10): 1119–1133. https://doi.org/10.1177/0002764217734261.

Logan, B. Ikubolajeh, and Kevin J. A. Thomas. 2012. "The U.S. Diversity Visa Programme and the Transfer of Skills from Africa." *International Migration* 50 (2): 1–19. https://doi.org/10.1111/j.1468-2435.2011.00711.x.

Logan, John R. 2013. "The Persistence of Segregation in the 21st Century Metropolis." *City & Community* 12 (2): 160–168. https://doi.org/10.1111/cico.12021.

Long, Katy. 2013. "When Refugees Stopped Being Migrants: Movement, Labour and Humanitarian Protection." *Migration Studies* 1 (1): 4–26. https://doi.org/10.1093/migration/mns001.

Loury, Glenn C. 2002. *The Anatomy of Racial Inequality*. Cambridge, MA: Harvard University Press.

Lubkemann, Stephen C. 2017. "The Lack of Liberty Drove Us There. Spatialized Instantiations of Hope and Contested Diasporan Identity in the Liberian-American Transnational Field (1810–2010)." In *Hope and Uncertainty in Contemporary African Migration*, edited by Nauja Kleist and Dorte Thorsen. New York: Routledge. https://library.oapen.org/bitstream/id/52cf13f7-c2b9-4396-9ace-a1150dc644bb/9781317335481.pdf.

Ludwig, Bernadette. 2016a. "A Black Republic: Citizenship and Naturalisation Requirements in Liberia." *Migration Letters* 13 (1): 84–99.

———. 2016b. "From 'Oh My Gosh I'm Going to Get Mugged' to 'See[ing] Them as People Who Are Just Like Me.'" In *Handbook of Research on Effective Communication in Culturally Diverse Classrooms*, edited by Katia Gonzalez and Rhoda Frumkin. Hershey, PA: IGI Global.

———. 2016c. "Thrust into the Spotlight: Liberian Refugees Dealing with Ebola and Other Stigmas." In *The Psychosocial Aspects of a Deadly Epidemic: What Ebola Has Taught Us about Holistic Healing*, edited by Judy Kuriansky. Westport, CT: Praeger.

———. 2017. "Looking for Refuge in the Other New York City: Liberian Refugees in Staten Island." In *Maintaining Refuge: Anthropological Reflections in Uncertain Times*, edited by David W. Haines, Jayne Howell, and Fethi Keles. Washington, DC: American Anthropological Association.

Ludwig, Bernadette, and Holly Reed. 2016. "'When You Are Here You Have High Blood Pressure': Liberian Refugees' Health and Access to Healthcare in Staten Island, NY." *International Journal of Migration, Health and Social Care* 12 (1): 26–37.

Lumley-Sapanski, Audrey. 2021. "The Survival Job Trap: Explaining Refugee Employment Outcomes in Chicago and the Contributing Factors." *Journal of Refugee Studies* 34 (2): 2093–2123. https://doi.org/10.1093/jrs/fez092.

Magan, Ifrah Mahamud. 2020. "On Being Black, Muslim, and a Refugee: Stories of Somalis in Chicago." *Journal of Immigrant & Refugee Studies* 18 (2): 172–188. https://doi.org/10.1080/15562948.2019.1617451.

Majavu, Mandisi. 2017. *Uncommodified Blackness: The African Male Experience in Australia and New Zealand*. New York: Palgrave Macmillan.

Malkki, Liisa H. 1995. "Refugees and Exile: From 'Refugee Studies' to the National Order of Things." *Annual Review of Anthropology* 24 (1): 495–523. https://doi.org/10.1146/annurev.an.24.100195.002431.

———. 1996. "Speechless Emissaries: Refugees, Humanitarianism, and Dehistoricization." *Cultural Anthropology* 11 (3): 377–404.

Marie, Erika. 2021. "Lucia Roberts, 16: Detective Alleges Police Were Responsible for 1982 Murder." Our Black Girls. July 8. https://ourblackgirls.com/2021/07/08/lucia-roberts-16-detective-alleges-police-were-responsible-for-1982-murder/.

Marrow, Helen. 2011. *New Destination Dreaming: Immigration, Race, and Legal Status in the Rural American South.* Stanford, CA: Stanford University Press.

Martin, Ben L. 1991. "From Negro to Black to African American: The Power of Names and Naming." *Political Science Quarterly* 106 (1): 83–107. https://doi.org/10.2307/2152175.

Marwell, Nicole P. 2009. *Bargaining for Brooklyn: Community Organizations in the Entrepreneurial City.* Chicago: University of Chicago Press.

Mascini, Peter, and Marjolein van Bochove. 2009. "Gender Stereotyping in the Dutch Asylum Procedure: 'Independent' Men Versus 'Dependent' Women." *International Migration Review* 43 (1): 112–133. https://doi.org/10.1111/j.0197-9183.2008.01149.x.

Masquelier, Adeline. 2006. "Why Katrina's Victims Aren't Refugees: Musings on a 'Dirty' Word." *American Anthropologist* 108 (4): 735–743. https://doi.org/10.1525/aa.2006.108.4.735.

Massey, Douglas S. 2010. *New Faces in New Places: The Changing Geography of American Immigration.* New York: Russell Sage Foundation.

Massey, Douglas S., and Garvey Lundy. 2001. "Use of Black English and Racial Discrimination in Urban Housing Markets: New Methods and Findings." *Urban Affairs Review* 36 (4): 452–469. https://doi.org/10.1177/10780870122184957.

Maxwell, Joseph A. 2004. *Qualitative Research Design: An Interactive Approach.* 2nd ed. Applied Social Research Methods Series. Thousand Oaks, CA: Sage Publications.

May, Jeff. 2015. "Racial Vibrations, Masculine Performances: Experiences of Homelessness Among Young Men of Colour in the Greater Toronto Area." *Gender, Place & Culture* 22 (3): 405–421. https://doi.org/10.1080/0966369X.2013.817970.

McKanders, Karla M. 2019. "Immigration and Blackness." *Human Rights* 44 (1): 20–23.

———. 2020. "Immigration and Racial Justice: Enforcing the Borders of Blackness." *Georgia State University Law Review* 37 (4): 1139–1176.

McKinnon, Sara L. 2008. "Unsettling Resettlement: Problematizing 'Lost Boys of Sudan' Resettlement and Identity." *Western Journal of Communication* 72 (4): 397–414. https://doi.org/10.1080/10570310802446056.

———. 2009. "Citizenship and the Performance of Credibility: Audiencing Gender-Based Asylum Seekers in U.S. Immigration Courts." *Text and Performance Quarterly* 29 (3): 205–221. https://doi.org/10.1080/10462930903017182.

McMichael, Celia, Caitlin Nunn, Sandra M. Gifford, and Ignacio Correa-Velez. 2015. "Studying Refugee Settlement Through Longitudinal Research: Methodological and Ethical Insights from the Good Starts Study." *Journal of Refugee Studies* 28 (2): 238–257. https://doi.org/10.1093/jrs/feu017.

McNamarah, Chan Tov. 2018. "White Caller Crime: Racialized Police Communication and Existing While Black." *Michigan Journal of Race & Law* 24 (2): 335–416.

McSpadden, Lucia Ann, and Helene Moussa. 1993. "I Have a Name: The Gender Dynamics in Asylum and in Resettlement of Ethiopian and Eritrean Refugees in North America." *Journal of Refugee Studies* 6 (3): 203–225.

Menjívar, Cecilia. 2006. "Liminal Legality: Salvadoran and Guatemalan Immigrants' Lives in the United States." *American Journal of Sociology* 111 (4): 999–1037.

Menjívar, Cecilia, and Leisy Abrego. 2009. "Parents and Children Across Borders: Legal Instability and Intergenerational Relations in Guatemalan and Salvadoran Families." In *Across*

Generations: Immigrant Families in America, edited by Nancy Foner. New York: New York University Press.

Menjívar, Cecilia, Andrea Gómez Cervantes, and Daniel Alvord. 2018. "The Expansion of 'Crimmigration,' Mass Detention, and Deportation." *Sociology Compass* 12 (4): e12573. https://doi.org/10.1111/soc4.12573.

Mfum-Mensah, Obed. 2020. *We Come as Members of the Superior Race: Distortions and Education Policy Discourse in Sub-Saharan Africa*. New York: Berghahn Books.

Mills, Jesse. 2012. "Somali Social Justice Struggle in the U.S.: A Historical Context." *Race, Gender & Class* 19 (3/4): 52–74.

Minor, Olive Melissa, and Michelle Cameo. 2018. "A Comparison of Wages by Gender and Region of Origin for Newly Arrived Refugees in the USA." *Journal of International Migration and Integration* 19 (3): 813–828. https://doi.org/10.1007/s12134-018-0581-1.

Mittelberg, David, and Mary C. Waters. 1992. "The Process of Ethnogenesis Among Haitian and Israeli Immigrants in the United States." *Ethnic and Racial Studies* 15 (3): 412–435. https://doi.org/10.1080/01419870.1992.9993755.

Moncarz, Raul. 1970. "Professional Adaptation of the Cuban Teachers in the United States, 1959–1969." *International Migration* 8 (3): 110–116.

Moore, Tina, and Daniel Cassady. 2020. "Cops Investigating Hate Crime Against Staten Island City Council Candidate." *New York Post*, March 16, sec. Metro. https://nypost.com/2020/03/16/cops-probe-potential-hate-crime-against-city-council-candidate/.

Moran, Mary H. 2012. "Uneasy Images. Contested Representations of Gender, Modernity and Nationalism in Pre-War Liberia." In *Gender Ironies of Nationalism: Sexing the Nation*, edited by Tamar Mayer. New York: Routledge.

Morgan, Charlie V., Rubén G. Rumbaut, and Lisa Anh Nguyen. 2017. "Crossing Lines and Imagining the Future: Transitions to Adulthood and Mixed Couples in California and New York." In *Crossings to Adulthood: How Diverse Young Americans Understand and Navigate Their Lives*, edited by Teresa Toguchi Swartz, Douglas Hartmann, and Rubén G. Rumbaut. Boston: Brill.

Morgan, Deborah A. 2006. "Not Gay Enough for the Government: Racial and Sexual Stereotypes in Sexual Orientation Asylum Cases." *Law & Sexuality: A Review of Lesbian, Gay, Bisexual, and Transgender Legal Issues* 15:135–161.

Morgan-Trostle, Juliana, Kexin Zheng, and Carl Lipscombe. 2020. "The State of Black Immigrants." New York: Black Alliance for Just Immigration. https://baji.org/wp-content/uploads/2021/01/The-Impact-of-Anti-Black-Racism-on-African-Migrants-at-Mexico.pdf.

Motomura, Hiroshi. 2019. "The New Migration Law: Migrants, Refugees, and Citizens in an Anxious Age." *Cornell Law Review* 105 (2): 457–548.

Mott, Tamar E. 2009. *African Refugee Resettlement in the United States*. El Paso, TX: LFB Scholarly Publishing LLC.

Mullen, Mike. 2009. "Liberia: The Untold Stories." *Minnesota Daily* (blog), November 9. https://mndaily.com/252106/uncategorized/liberia-untold-stories/.

Nagel, Joane. 1994. "Constructing Ethnicity: Creating and Recreating Ethnic Identity and Culture Special Issue on Immigration, Race, and Ethnicity in America." *Social Problems* 41 (1): 152–176.

Nakano Glenn, Evelyn. 2002. *Unequal Freedom: How Race and Gender Shaped American Citizenship and Labor*. Cambridge, MA: Harvard University Press.

Nawyn, Stephanie J. 2010. "Institutional Structures of Opportunity in Refugee Resettlement: Gender, Race/Ethnicity, and Refugee NGOs." *Journal of Sociology & Social Welfare* 37 (1): 149–167.

———. 2011. "'I Have so Many Successful Stories': Framing Social Citizenship for Refugees." *Citizenship Studies* 15 (6–7): 679–693.

Nawyn, Stephanie J., and Linda Gjokaj. 2014. "The Magnifying Effect of Privilege: Earnings Inequalities at the Intersection of Gender, Race, and Nativity." *Feminist Formations* 26 (2): 85–106. https://doi.org/10.1353/ff.2014.0015.

Neal, Joan F. 2020. "Being Black and Immigrant in America." New York: Center for Migration Studies. https://cmsny.org/being-black-and-immigrant-in-america/.

Neckerman, Kathryn M., and Joleen Kirschenman. 1991. "Hiring Strategies, Racial Bias, and Inner-City Workers." *Social Problems* 38 (4): 433–447. https://doi.org/10.2307/800563.

New York Civil Liberties Union. 2019. "Stop-and-Frisk in the de Blasio Era." New York Civil Liberties Union. https://www.nyclu.org/sites/default/files/field_documents/20190314_nyclu_stopfrisk_singles.pdf.

———. 2022. "Stop-and-Frisk Data." New York Civil Liberties Union. https://www.nyclu.org/en/stop-and-frisk-data.

New York Police Department. 2020. "Hate Crimes Dashport." https://app.powerbigov.us/view?r=eyJrIjoiYjg1NWI3YjgtYzkzOSooNzcoLTkwMDAtNTgzM2I2M2JmYWE1IiwidCI6IjJiOWY1N2ViLTc4ZDEtNDZmYi1iZTgzLWEyYWZkZDdjNjAoMyJ9.

Ngai, Mae M. 2014. *Impossible Subjects: Illegal Aliens and the Making of Modern America*. Princeton, NJ: Princeton University Press.

Ngom, Fallou. 2015. "Afterword." In *African Asylum at a Crossroads: Activism, Expert Testimony, and Refugee Rights*, edited by Iris Berger, Tricia Redeker Hepner, Benjamin N. Lawrance, Joanna T. Tague, and Meredith Terretta. Athens: Ohio University Press.

Nopper, Tamara K. 2008. "Why Black Immigrants Matter: Re-Focusing the Discussion on Racism and Immigration Enforcement." In *Keeping Out the Other: A Critical Introduction to Immigration Enforcement Today*, edited by David Brotherton and Philip Kretsedemas. New York: Columbia University Press.

Nsangou, Ashly, and Lauren Dundes. 2018. "Parsing the Gulf Between Africans and African Americans." *Social Sciences* 7 (2): 1–26. https://doi.org/10.3390/socsci7020024.

Nunnally, Shayla C. 2010. "Linking Blackness or Ethnic Othering? African Americans' Diasporic Linked Fate with West Indian and African Peoples in the United States." *Du Bois Review: Social Science Research on Race* 7 (2): 335–355. https://doi.org/10.1017/S1742058X10000305.

Nyamwange, Monica. 2014. "Analysis of Modes of Entry and Legal Statuses of African Immigrants in the United States." *International Journal for Innovation Education and Research* 2 (3): 84–91.

Ogbu, John U. 1994. "From Cultural Differences to Differences in Cultural Frame of Reference." In *Cross-Cultural Roots of Minority Child Development*, edited by Patricia M. Greenfield and Rodney R. Cocking. New York: Psychology Press.

Okamoto, Dina, and G. Cristina Mora. 2014. "Panethnicity." *Annual Review of Sociology* 40:219–239.

Okonofua, Benjamin Aigbe. 2013. "'I Am Blacker Than You': Theorizing Conflict Between African Immigrants and African Americans in the United States." *SAGE Open* 3 (3): 1–14. https://doi.org/10.1177/2158244013499162.

Olayiwola, J. Nwando. 2016. "Racism in Medicine: Shifting the Power." *Annals of Family Medicine* 14 (3): 267–269. https://doi.org/10.1370/afm.1932.

Omata, Naohiko. 2012a. "Repatriation and Integration of Liberian Refugees from Ghana: The Importance of Personal Networks in the Country of Origin." *Journal of Refugee Studies* 26 (2): 265–282. https://doi.org/10.1093/jrs/fes023.

———. 2012b. "Struggling to Find Solutions: Liberian Refugees in Ghana." Research Paper 234. New Issues in Refugee Research. Geneva, Switzerland: UNHCR.

Omi, Michael, and Howard Winant. 1994. *Racial Formation in the United States: From the 1960s to the 1990s*. 2nd ed. New York: Routledge.

Ong, Aihwa. 2003. *Buddha Is Hiding: Refugees, Citizenship, the New America*. Berkeley: University of California Press.

Orleck, Annelise. 1999. *The Soviet Jewish Americans*. Westport, CT: Greenwood Press.

———. 2001. "Soviet Jews: The City's Newest Immigrants Transform New York Jewish Life." In *New Immigrants in New York*, edited by Nancy Foner. New York: Columbia University Press.

———. 2013. "Soviet Jews: The Continuing Russification of Jewish New York." In *One out of Three: Immigrant New York in the 21st Century*, edited by Nancy Foner. New York: Columbia University Press.

Osirim, Mary Johnson. 2010. "The New African Diaspora: Transnationalism and Transformation in Philadelphia." In *Global Philadelphia: Immigrant Communities Old and New*, edited by Ayumi Takenaka and Mary Johnson Osirim. Philadelphia: Temple University Press.

Oxford, Connie G. 2005. "Protectors and Victims in the Gender Regime of Asylum." *National Women's Studies Association (NWSA) Journal* 17 (3): 18–38.

Pager, Devah. 2007. *Marked: Race, Crime, and Finding Work in an Era of Mass Incarceration*. Chicago: University of Chicago Press.

Pailey, Robtel Neajai. 2012. "The Negro Clause in Liberia's Constitution Is Not Racist; It Is Protectionary." *New Narratives. Africans Reporting Africa* (blog), October 21. http://www.newnarratives.org/stories/robtel-pailey/the-negro-clause-in-liberias-constitution-is-not-racist-it-is-protectionary/.

———. 2016. "Birthplace, Bloodline and Beyond: How 'Liberian Citizenship' Is Currently Constructed in Liberia and Abroad." *Citizenship Studies* 20 (6–7): 811–829. https://doi.org/10.1080/13621025.2016.1204269.

Palmer, Breanne J. 2017. "The Crossroads: Being Black, Immigrant, and Undocumented in the Era of #BlackLivesMatter." *Georgetown Journal of Law & Modern Critical Race Perspectives* 9:99–121.

Patel, Leigh. 2017. "The Ink of Citizenship." *Curriculum Inquiry* 47 (1): 62–68. https://doi.org/10.1080/03626784.2016.1254503.

Patterson, Roza E. 2019. "Black Bodies Drowning in the Mediterranean Sea: Why Does the World Not Care?" *UCLA Journal of International Law and Foreign Affairs* 23 (1): 183–219.

Pear, Robert. 1992. "Bias Is Admitted by New York City in Public Housing." *New York Times*, July 1, sec. A.

Perreault, Gregogry, and Newly Paul. 2018. "An Image of Refugees Through the Social Media Lens: A Narrative Framing Analysis of the Humans of New York Series 'Syrian Americans.'" *Journal of Applied Journalism & Media Studies* 7 (1): 79–102.

Pierre, Jemima. 2004. "Black Immigrants in the United States and the 'Cultural Narratives' of Ethnicity." *Identities: Global Studies in Power and Culture* 11 (2): 141–170.

Pierre, Jemima. 2013. "Race in Africa Today: A Commentary." *Cultural Anthropology* 28 (3): 547–551. https://doi.org/10.1111/cuan.12023.

Police Department, City of New York. 2025. "CompStat 120th Precinct. Report Covering the Week 5/12/2025 Through 5/18/2025" 32 (20). https://www.nyc.gov/assets/nypd/downloads/pdf/crime_statistics/cs-en-us-120pct.pdf.

Porter, Gina, Kate Hampshire, Peter Kyei, Michael Adjaloo, George Rapoo, and Kate Kilpatrick. 2008. "Linkages Between Livelihood Opportunities and Refugee–Host Relations: Learning from the Experiences of Liberian Camp-Based Refugees in Ghana." *Journal of Refugee Studies* 21 (2): 230–252. https://doi.org/10.1093/jrs/fen015.Portes, Alejandro, and Rubén G. Rumbaut. 1996. *Immigrant America: A Portrait*. 2nd ed. Berkeley: University of California Press.

Portes, Alejandro, Rubén G. Rumbaut. 2001. *Legacies: The Story of the Immigrant Second Generation*. Berkeley: University of California Press.

Potocky-Tripodi, Miriam. 2002. *Best Practices for Social Work with Refugees and Immigrants*. New York: Columbia University Press.

Puar, Jashir K. 1996. "Nicaraguan Women, Resistance, and the Politics of Aid." In *Women and Politics in the Third World*, edited by Haleh Afshar. New York: Routledge.

Quart, Alissa. 2007. "The Child Soldiers of Staten Island. While Hollywood Swoons over Teen Guerrillas, the Real Lost Boys Are Hidden in Plain Sight." *Mother Jones*, June 29. http://www.motherjones.com/politics/2007/06/child-soldiers-staten-island.

Rajasingham-Senanayake, Darini. 2004. "Between Victim and Agent: Women's Ambivalent Empowerment in Displacement." In *Refugees and the Transformation of Societies: Agency, Policies, Ethics and Politics*, edited by Philomena Essed, Georg Frerks, and Joke Schrijvers. New York: Berghahn Books.

Ramji-Nogales, Jaya, Andrew I. Schoenholtz, and Philip G. Schrag. 2009. *Refugee Roulette: Disparities in Asylum Adjudication and Proposals for Reform*. New York: New York University Press.

Ray, Rashawn. 2022. "The Russian Invasion of Ukraine Shows Racism Has No Boundaries." Brookings Institution. https://www.brookings.edu/blog/how-we-rise/2022/03/03/the-russian-invasion-of-ukraine-shows-racism-has-no-boundaries/.

Reed, Holly, Bernadette Ludwig, and Laura Braslow. 2016. "Forced Migration." In *Handbook of Migration and Population Distribution*, edited by Michael White and Josh DeWind. New York: Springer.

Reilly, Janet E. 2014. "Becoming Transnational Citizens: The Liberian Diaspora's Civic Engagement in the United States and in Homeland Peacebuilding." PhD diss., The Graduate Center, The City University of New York.

———. 2016. "Temporary Refugees: The Impact of US Policy on Civic Participation and Political Belonging Among Liberians in the United States." *Refugee Survey Quarterly* 35 (3): 94–118. https://doi.org/10.1093/rsq/hdw009.

Reno, William. 1995. "Reinvention of an African Patrimonial State: Charles Taylor's Liberia." *Third World Quarterly* 16 (1): 109–120. https://doi.org/10.1080/01436599550036266.

Rhodes, P. J. 1994. "Race-of-Interviewer Effects: A Brief Comment." *Sociology* 28 (2): 547–558. https://doi.org/10.1177/0038038594028002011.

Riak Akuei, Stephanie. 2005. "Remittances as Unforeseen Burdens: The Livelihoods and Social Obligations of Sudanese Refugees." *Global Migration Perspectives* 18. Geneva, Switzerland: Global Commission on International Migration. https://www.refworld.org/docid/42ce4d354.html.

Roberts, Sam. 2005. "More Africans Enter U.S. Than in Days of Slavery." *New York Times*, February 21. http://www.nytimes.com/2005/02/21/nyregion/more-africans-enter-us-than-in-days-of-slavery.html.

Robertson, Cheryl Lee, Linda Halcon, Kay Savik, David Johnson, Marline Spring, James Butcher, Joseph Westermeyer, and James Jaranson. 2006. "Somali and Oromo Refugee Women: Trauma and Associated Factors." *Journal of Advanced Nursing* 56 (6): 577–587. https://doi.org/10.1111/j.1365-2648.2006.04057.x.

Rodriguez, Clara E., and Hector Cordero-Guzman. 1992. "Placing Race in Context." *Ethnic and Racial Studies* 15 (4): 523–542. https://doi.org/10.1080/01419870.1992.9993762.

Roediger, David R. 2005. *Working Toward Whiteness: How America's Immigrants Became White*. New York: Basic Books.

Rogers, Reuel R. 2001. "'Black Like Who?' Afro-Caribbean Immigrants, African Americans and the Politics of Group Identity." In *Islands in the City: West Indian Migration to New York*, edited by Nancy Foner. Berkeley: University of California Press.

———. 2004. "Race-Based Coalitions Among Minority Groups: Afro-Caribbean Immigrants and African-Americans in New York City." *Urban Affairs Review* 39 (3): 283–317. https://doi.org/10.1177/1078087403258960.

Rogers, Reuel R., and Jae Yeon Kim. 2023. "Rewiring Linked Fate: Bringing Back History, Agency, and Power." *Perspectives on Politics* 21 (1): 288–301. https://doi.org/10.1017/S1537592721003261.

Roscigno, Vincent J., Diana L. Karafin, and Griff Tester. 2009. "The Complexities and Processes of Racial Housing Discrimination." *Social Problems* 56 (1): 49–69. https://doi.org/10.1525/sp.2009.56.1.49.

Roubeni, Sonia, Lucia De Haene, Eva Keatley, Nira Shah, and Andrew Rasmussen. 2015. "'If We Can't Do It, Our Children Will Do It One Day': A Qualitative Study of West African Immigrant Parents' Losses and Educational Aspirations for Their Children." *American Educational Research Journal* 52 (2): 275–305. https://doi.org/10.3102/0002831215574576.

Russell, Felecia S., and Alonso R. Reyna Rivarola. 2023. "What Does It Mean to Be UndocuBlack? Exploring the Double Invisibility of Black Undocumented Immigrant Students in U.S. Colleges and Universities." *New Directions for Higher Education* 2023 (203): 61–76. https://doi.org/10.1002/he.20480.

Ryo, Emily, and Reed Humphrey. 2022. "The Importance of Race, Gender, and Religion in Naturalization Adjudication in the United States." *Proceedings of the National Academy of Sciences* 119 (9). https://doi.org/10.1073/pnas.2114430119.

Sackett, Blair, and Annette Lareau. 2023. *We Thought It Would Be Heaven: Refugees in an Unequal America*. Oakland: University of California Press.

Sáenz, Rogelio, and Karen Manges Douglas. 2015. "A Call for the Racialization of Immigration Studies: On the Transition of Ethnic Immigrants to Racialized Immigrants." *Sociology of Race and Ethnicity* 1 (1): 166–180. https://doi.org/10.1177/2332649214559287.

Sall, Dialika. 2019. "Convergent Identifications, Divergent Meanings: The Racial and Ethnic Identities of Second-Generation West African Youth." *African and Black Diaspora: An International Journal* 12 (2): 137–155. https://doi.org/10.1080/17528631.2018.1559785.

———. 2022. "Love Thy Neighbour? Religion and Ethnoracial Boundaries Among Second-Generation West African Youth." *Ethnic and Racial Studies* 45 (12): 2223–2245. https://doi.org/10.1080/01419870.2021.2001026.

Sampson, Robert J. 2008. "Rethinking Immigration and Crime." *Contexts* 7 (Winter): 28–33.

Sampson, Robert J., and Stephen W. Raudenbush. 2004. "Seeing Disorder: Neighborhood Stigma and the Social Construction of 'Broken Windows.'" *Social Psychology Quarterly* 67 (4): 319–342. https://doi.org/10.1177/019027250406700401.

Sanneh, Lamin. 2001. *Abolitionists Abroad: American Blacks and the Making of Modern West Africa*. Cambridge, MA: Harvard University Press.

Selee, Andrew. 2023. "Regional Processing Centers: Can This Key Component of the Post-Title 42 U.S. Strategy Work?" Washington, D.C.: Migration Policy Institute. https://www.migrationpolicy.org/news/regional-processing-centers-post-title-42-strategy.

Sengupta, Somini. 2003. "Enraged Liberians Call for U.S. Help as Rebels Attack." *New York Times*, July 21, sec. World. https://www.nytimes.com/2003/07/21/international/africa/enraged-liberians-call-for-us-help-as-rebels-attack.html.

Shahi, Priya. 2025. "Park Hill Apartments Face Nearly 400 Violations in 2025, Records Show." *Staten Island Advance*, April 17. https://www.silive.com/news/2025/04/park-hill-apartments-face-nearly-400-violations-in-2025-records-show.html.

Shammas, Brittany. 2022. "For Patrick Lyoya, the American Dream Became the American Nightmare." *Washington Post*, May 2, sec. National. https://www.washingtonpost.com/nation/2022/05/02/patrick-lyoya-grand-rapids/.

Shaw-Taylor, Yoku, and Steven A. Tuch, eds. 2007. *The Other African Americans: Contemporary African and Caribbean Immigrants in the United States*. Lanham, MD: Rowman & Littlefield.

Showers, Fumilayo. 2015a. "Being Black, Foreign and Woman: African Immigrant Identities in the United States." *Ethnic and Racial Studies* 38 (10): 1815–1830. https://doi.org/10.1080/01419870.2015.1036763.

———. 2015b. “Professional Identities, Boundary Work and Meaning Making Among West African Nurses.” In *Caring on the Clock: The Complexities and Contradictions of Paid Care Work*, edited by Mignon Duffy, Amy Armenia, and Clare L. Stacey. New Brunswick, NJ: Rutgers University Press.

———. 2023. *Migrants Who Care: West Africans Working and Building Lives in U.S. Health Care*. New Brunswick, NJ: Rutgers University Press.

Sienkiewicz, Holly C., Kelly G. Mauceri, Emma Catherine Howell, and Daniel L. Bibeau. 2013. “Untapped Resources: Refugee Employment Experiences in Central North Carolina.” *Work: A Journal of Prevention, Assessment and Rehabilitation* 45 (1): 17–24. https://doi.org/10.3233/WOR-131599.

Sigona, Nando. 2014. “The Politics of Refugee Voices: Representations, Narratives, and Memories.” In *The Oxford Handbook of Refugee and Forced Migration Studies*, edited by Elena Fiddian-Qasmiyeh, Gil Loescher, Katy Long, and Nando Sigona. London: Oxford University Press.

Simmelink, Jennifer. 2011. “Temporary Citizens: U.S. Immigration Law and Liberian Refugees.” *Journal of Immigrant & Refugee Studies* 9 (4): 327–344. https://doi.org/10.1080/15562948.2011.616793.

Singer, Audrey, and Jill H. Wilson. 2006. “From ‘There’ to ‘Here’: Refugee Resettlement in Metropolitan America.” Washington, D.C.: The Brookings Institution. https://www.brookings.edu/articles/from-there-to-here-refugee-resettlement-in-metropolitan-america/.

Singler, John Victor. 2015. “African American English over Yonder.” *The Oxford Handbook of African American Language*, edited by Jennifer Bloomquist, Lisa J. Green, and Sonja L. Lanehart. Oxford: Oxford University Press. https://doi.org/10.1093/oxfordhb/9780199795390.013.9.

Sjursen, Danny. 2017. “Disturbing, Deep-Rooted Patterns in Staten Island’s Racial Geography.” *Staten Island Advance*, May 22. https://www.silive.com/news/2017/05/disturbing_deep-rooted_pattern.html.

Smalls, Krystal A. 2018. “Fighting Words: Antiblackness and Discursive Violence in an American High School.” *Journal of Linguistic Anthropology* 28 (3): 356–383. https://doi.org/10.1111/jola.12197.

Smith, Candis Watts. 2014. *Black Mosaic: The Politics of Black Pan-Ethnic Diversity*. New York: New York University Press.

Smith, Christen A. 2015. “Blackness, Citizenship, and the Transnational Vertigo of Violence in the Americas.” *American Anthropologist* 117 (2): 384–387. https://doi.org/10.1111/aman.12242.

Smith, R. Scott. 2008. “The Case of a City Where 1 in 6 Residents Is a Refugee: Ecological Factors and Host Community Adaptation in Successful Resettlement.” *American Journal of Community Psychology* 42 (3–4): 328–342. https://doi.org/10.1007/s10464-008-9208-6.

Sobolik, Chelsea. 2021. “Why the U.S. Should Provide Priority 2 Refugee Status for Afghans Fleeing Persecution.” Washington, D.C.: Ethics & Religious Liberty Commission of the Southern Baptist Convention. https://erlc.com/resource-library/articles/why-the-u-s-should-provide-priority-2-refugee-status-for-afghans-fleeing-persecution/.

Sommers, Samuel R., Evan P. Apfelbaum, Kristin N. Dukes, Negin Toosi, and Elsie J. Wang. 2006. “Race and Media Coverage of Hurricane Katrina: Analysis, Implications, and Future Research Questions.” *Analyses of Social Issues and Public Policy* 6 (1): 1–17.

Sood, Aradhya, William Speagle, and Kevin Ehrman-Solberg. 2019. “Long Shadow of Racial Discrimination: Evidence from Housing Covenants of Minneapolis.” Available at SSRN: https://doi.org/10.2139/ssrn.3468520.

Sorrell, Katherine, Simranjit Khalsa, Elaine Howard Ecklund, and Michael O. Emerson. 2019. “Immigrant Identities and the Shaping of a Racialized American Self:” *Socius* 5 (June): 1–12. https://doi.org/10.1177/2378023119852788.

Sowa, Graham R. 2009. "Experiencing Refugee Resettlement in America: Exploring the Impact of Generalized Policies and Services." *Journal of Pan African Studies* 3 (2): 102–118.

Spijkerboer, Thomas. 2000. *Gender and Refugee Status*. Burlington, VT: Ashgate Publishing Company.

Spivak, Chakravorty. 2010. "Can the Subaltern Speak?" In *Can the Subaltern Speak? Reflections on the History of an Idea*, edited by Rosalind C Morris. New York: Columbia University Press.

Springer, Simon. 2012. "Neoliberalising Violence: Of the Exceptional and the Exemplary in Coalescing Moments." *Area* 44 (2): 136–143. https://doi.org/10.1111/j.1475-4762.2012.01084.x.

Staten Island Advance. 2020. "SILive to End Commenting on Website Beginning Thursday," February 17, sec. News. https://www.silive.com/news/2020/02/silive-to-end-commenting-on-website-beginning-thursday.html.

Stepakoff, Shanee. 2007. "The Healing Power of Symbolization in the Aftermath of Massive War Atrocities: Examples from Liberian and Sierra Leonean Survivors." *Journal of Humanistic Psychology* 47 (3): 400–412. https://doi.org/10.1177/0022167807301787.

Stepakoff, Shanee, Jon Hubbard, Maki Katoh, Erika Falk, Jean-Baptiste Mikulu, Potiphar Nkhoma, and Yuvenalis Omagwa. 2006. "Trauma Healing in Refugee Camps in Guinea: A Psychosocial Program for Liberian and Sierra Leonean Survivors of Torture and War." *American Psychologist* 61 (8): 921–932. https://doi.org/10.1037/0003-066X.61.8.921.

Stepick, Alex. 1992. "The Refugees Nobody Wants: Haitians in Miami." In *Miami Now: Immigration, Ethnicity, and Social Change*, edited by Guillermo J. Grenier and Alex Stepick. Gainesville: University Press of Florida.

Stier, Ken. 2009. "Stretching a Contract." *Time*, August 3. http://www.time.com/time/magazine/article/0,9171,1912403-2,00.html.

St. Louis, Brett. 2005. "The Difference Sameness Makes: Racial Recognition and the 'Narcissism of Minor Differences.'" *Ethnicities* 5 (3): 343–364. https://doi.org/10.1177/1468796805054960.

Stokes, Doug. 2003. "Countering the Soviet Threat? An Analysis of the Justifications for US Military Assistance to El Salvador, 1979–92." *Cold War History* 3 (3): 79–102. https://doi.org/10.1080/14682740312331391628.

Suárez-Orozco, Carola, and Marcelo M. Suárez-Orozco. 1994. "The Cultural Psychology of Hispanic Immigrants." In *Handbook of Hispanic Cultures in the United States: Anthropology*, edited by Nicolás Kanellos. Houston: Arte Publico Press.

Sukarieh, Mayssoun, and Stuart Tannock. 2013. "On the Problem of Over-Researched Communities: The Case of the Shatila Palestinian Refugee Camp in Lebanon." *Sociology* 47 (3): 494–508. https://doi.org/10.1177/0038038512448567.

Swanson, Kate, and Rebecca Maria Torres. 2016. "Child Migration and Transnationalized Violence in Central and North America." *Journal of Latin American Geography* 15 (3): 23–48.

Switchboard. 2020. "Talking About Race and Racism: Tips for Participating in Introductory Conversations." *Switchboard* (blog), October 9. https://www.switchboardta.org/blog/talking-about-race-and-racism-tips-for-participating-in-introductory-conversations/.

———. n.d. "Mission." Switchboard. Accessed June 19, 2024. https://www.switchboardta.org/mission/.

Taibbi, Matt. 2017. *I Can't Breathe: A Killing on Bay Street*. New York: Spiegel & Grau.

Tamir, Christine. 2022. "Key Findings About Black Immigrants in the U.S." Washington, D.C.: Pew Research Center. https://www.pewresearch.org/short-reads/2022/01/27/key-findings-about-black-immigrants-in-the-u-s/.

Tang, Eric. 2015. *Unsettled: Cambodian Refugees in the New York City Hyperghetto*. Philadelphia: Temple University Press.

Tannenbaum, Jessie, Anthony Valcke, Andrew McPherson, Leah Mueller, and Simon Conté. 2009. "Analysis of the Aliens and Nationality Law of the Republic of Liberia." Available at SSRN: http://papers.ssrn.com/abstract=1795122.

Tesfai, Rebbeca. 2019. "Double Minority Status and Neighborhoods: Examining the Primacy of Race in Black Immigrants' Racial and Socioeconomic Segregation." *City & Community* 18 (2): 509–528. https://doi.org/10.1111/cico.12384.

Tezcan, Tolga. 2019. "Return Home? Determinants of Return Migration Intention Amongst Turkish Immigrants in Germany." *Geoforum* 98 (January): 189–201. https://doi.org/10.1016/j.geoforum.2018.11.013.

Tholen, Minjon, and Church World Services. 2020. "Welcoming Refugees: Anti-Racism and Refugee Resettlement." Community Sponsorship Webinars, Church World Services, October 19. https://cwsglobal.org/lunch-and-learns/welcoming-refugees-anti-racism-and-refugee-resettlement/.

Thomas, Kevin J. A., Aggie J. Yellow Horse, and Edward D. Vargas. 2024. "Black Immigrants, Exposure to Police Violence, and Support for Black Lives Matter: Insights from the 2016 US Collaborative Multiracial Post-Election Survey." *Journal of International Migration and Integration* 25 (1): 391–420. https://doi.org/10.1007/s12134-023-01089-7.

Tracy, Thomas. 2022. "Two Shot, One Killed Outside Notorious Staten Island Apartment Building." *New York Daily News*, July 16. https://www.nydailynews.com/2022/07/16/two-shot-one-killed-outside-notorious-staten-island-apartment-building/.

Transactional Records Access Clearinghouse. 2007. "Asylum Disparities Persist, Regardless of Court Location and Nationality." September 24. https://trac.syr.edu/immigration/reports/183/.

———. 2016. "Continued Rise in Asylum Denial Rates: Impact of Representation and Nationality." December 13. https://trac.syr.edu/immigration/reports/448/.

Traoré, Rosemary. 2004. "Colonialism Continued: African Students in an Urban High School in America." *Journal of Black Studies* 34 (3): 348–369.

Trapp, Micah M. 2015. "Already in America: Transnational Homemaking Among Liberian Refugees." *Refuge* 31 (1): 31–41.

Treitler, Vilna Bashi. 2013. *The Ethnic Project: Transforming Racial Fiction into Ethnic Factions.* Stanford, CA: Stanford University Press.

———. 2015. "Social Agency and White Supremacy in Immigration Studies." *Sociology of Race and Ethnicity* 1 (1): 153–165. https://doi.org/10.1177/2332649214560796.

Trudeau, Michael, Kim Stafieri, and Matt Zeller. 2023. "Quarterly Report." Association of Wartime Allies. https://www.wartimeallies.co/_files/ugd/5887eb_fe671af8c617489b8ae94262c8671152.pdf.

Turner, Lewis. 2020. "'#Refugees Can Be Entrepreneurs Too!' Humanitarianism, Race, and the Marketing of Syrian Refugees." *Review of International Studies* 46 (1): 137–155. https://doi.org/10.1017/S0260210519000342.

Turner, Simon. 2017. "Victims of Chaos and Subaltern Sexualities? Some Reflections on Common Assumptions About Displacement and Prevalence of Sexual and Gender-Based Violence." In *Gender, Violence, Refugees*, edited by Susanne Buckley-Zistel and Ulrike Krause. New York: Berghahn Books.

Turton, David. 1996. "Migrants and Refugees: A Mursi Case Study." In *In Search of Cool Ground: War, Flight, and Homecoming in Northeast Africa*, edited by Tim Allen. London: Africa Word Press.

Tyler-McGraw, Marie. 2007. *An African Republic: Black and White Virginians in the Making of Liberia.* Chapel Hill: University of North Carolina Press.

Tyson, Tahl. 1990. "The Refugee Act of 1980: Suggested Reforms in the Overseas Refugee Program to Safeguard Humanitarian Concerns from Competing Interests Comment." *Washington Law Review* 65 (4): 921–938.

UNHCR. 2006. "UNHCR Statistical Yearbook 2005." Geneva, Switzerland: UNHCR. http://www.unhcr.org/statistics/STATISTICS/4641be64d.pdf.

———. 2013. "Note on the Mandate of the High Commissioner for Refugees and His Office." UNHCR. http://www.refworld.org/docid/5268c9474.html.

———. 2020. "Protracted Refugee Situations Explained." USA for UNHCR. The UN Refugee Agency. January 28. https://www.unrefugees.org/news/protracted-refugee-situations-explained/.

———. 2021. "UNHCR Projected Global Resettlement Needs 2022." UNHCR. https://www.unhcr.org/protection/resettlement/60d320a64/projected-global-resettlement-needs-2022-pdf.html.

U.S. Attorney's Office, Eastern District of New York. 2009. "Three Indicted for Federal Hate Crime Conspiracy. Defendants Charged with Conspiring to Assault African-Americans in Staten Island in Retaliation for President-Elect Barack Obama's Election Victory." Federal Bureau of Investigation, January 7. https://www.fbi.gov/newyork/press-releases/2009/nyfo010709.htm.

———. 2011. "Press Release: Nine Alleged Members of a Staten Island Crack Cocaine Distribution Organization Arrested." U.S. Department of Justice. https://www.justice.gov/archive/usao/nye/pr/2011/2011jun08.html.

U.S. Committee for Refugees and Immigrants. 2007. "U.S. Committee for Refugees and Immigrants World Refugee Survey 2007—Côte d'Ivoire." UNHCR. https://www.refworld.org/docid/4696387f2.html.

U.S. Department of State. 2006. *Report to Congress on Proposed Refugee Admissions for Fiscal Year 2007*. Washington, D.C. https://www.wrapsnet.org/documents/Report+to+Congress+for+FY+2007+USRAP.pdf.

———. 2021. *Report to Congress on Proposed Refugee Admissions for Fiscal Year 2022*. https://www.state.gov/report-to-congress-on-proposed-refugee-admissions-for-fiscal-year-2022/.

———. 2023. *Report to Congress on Proposed Refugee Admissions for Fiscal Year 2024*. Washington, D.C. https://www.state.gov/report-to-congress-on-proposed-refugee-admissions-for-fiscal-year-2022/.

Utas, Mats. 2003. "Sweet Battlefields: Youth and the Liberian Civil War." PhD diss., Uppsala University. http://uu.diva-portal.org/smash/get/diva2:163000/FULLTEXT01.

Valtonen, Kathleen. 1999. "The Societal Participation of Vietnamese Refugees: Case Studies in Finland and Canada." *Journal of Ethnic & Migration Studies* 25 (3): 469–491. https://doi.org/Article.

Vásquez, Tina. 2021. "Q&A: The Biden Administration Has Spent Black History Month Deporting Black Immigrants. Why Aren't People in the Streets?" *Prism*, February 11. https://prismreports.org/2021/02/11/qa-the-biden-administration-has-spent-black-history-month-deporting-black-immigrants/.

Vickerman, Milton. 1999. *Crosscurrents: West Indian Immigrants and Race*. New York: Oxford University Press.

———. 2007. "Recent Immigration and Race: Continuity and Change." *Du Bois Review: Social Science Research on Race* 4 (1): 141–165. https://doi.org/10.1017/S1742058X07070087.

Villacres, Daniela. 2013. "Beyond Remittances: Reframing Diaspora-Driven Development in El Salvador." Washington, D.C.: Migration Policy Institute. http://www.migrationpolicy.org/article/beyond-remittances-reframing-diaspora-driven-development-el-salvador.

Viteritti, Joseph. 1992. "Should Staten Island Leave the City?" *City Journal* 2 (Autumn). http://www.city-journal.org/article02.php?aid=1519.

Wacquant, Loïc. 2008. *Urban Outcasts: A Comparative Sociology of Advanced Marginality*. Malden, MA: Polity Press.

Waldinger, Roger. 1996. *Still the Promised City?: African-Americans and New Immigrants in Postindustrial New York*. Cambridge, MA: Harvard University Press.

Waldinger, Roger, and Michael I. Lichter. 2003. *How the Other Half Works: Immigration and the Social Organization of Labor*. Berkeley: University of California Press.

Wallace, Derron. 2018. "Safe Routes to School? Black Caribbean Youth Negotiating Police Surveillance in London and New York City." *Harvard Educational Review* 88 (3): 261–286. https://doi.org/10.17763/1943-5045-88.3.261.

Warriner, Doris S. 2007. "Language Learning and the Politics of Belonging: Sudanese Women Refugees Becoming and Being 'American.'" *Anthropology & Education Quarterly* 38 (4): 343–359.

Wasem, Ruth Ellen. 2011. "Asylum and 'Credible Fear' Issues in U.S. Immigration Policy." Congressional Research Service Report for Congress R41753. Washington, D.C.: Congressional Research Service. https://crsreports.congress.gov/product/details?prodcode=R41753.

Waslin, Michele. 2010. "Underrepresented African Refugees and Potential Problems with DNA Testing." *American Immigration Council: Immigration Impact* (blog), October 21. http://immigrationimpact.com/2010/10/21/underrepresented-african-refugees-and-potential-problems-with-dna-testing/.

Waters, Mary C. 1999. *Black Identities: West Indian Immigrant Dreams and American Realities.* Cambridge, MA: Harvard University Press.

Waters, Mary C., Philip Kasinitz, and Asad L. Asad. 2014. "Immigrants and African Americans." *Annual Review of Sociology* 40 (1): 369–390. https://doi.org/10.1146/annurev-soc-071811-145449.

Watson, Jake. 2023. "Standardizing Refuge: Pipelines and Pathways in the U.S. Refugee Resettlement Program." *American Sociological Review* 88 (4): 681–708. https://doi.org/10.1177/00031224231180891.

———. 2024. "Rescaling Resettlement: Local Welcoming Policies and the Shaping of Refugee Belonging." *Social Problems* 71 (3): 858–874. https://doi.org/10.1093/socpro/spac041.

Weine, Stevan, Merrill, Yael Hoffman, Norma Ware, Toni Tugenberg, Leonce Hakizimana, Gonwo Dahnweigh, Madeleine Currie, and Maureen Wagner. 2011. "Secondary Migration and Relocation Among African Refugee Families in the United States." *Family Process* 50 (1): 27–46. https://doi.org/10.1111/j.1545-5300.2010.01344.x.

Wilson, William Julius. 2012. *The Truly Disadvantaged.* 2nd ed. Chicago: University of Chicago Press.

Yang, Philip Q., and Monicka Brown. 2022. "Black Panethnicity: Origins and Evolution." *Studies in Social Science & Humanities* 1 (5): 89–103.

Yearby, Ruqaiijah, Brietta Clark, and José F. Figueroa. 2022. "Structural Racism in Historical and Modern US Health Care Policy." *Health Affairs* 41 (2): 187–194. https://doi.org/10.1377/hlthaff.2021.01466.

Yuval-Davis, Nira. 2007. "Intersectionality, Citizenship and Contemporary Politics of Belonging." *Critical Review of International Social and Political Philosophy* 10 (4): 561–574. https://doi.org/10.1080/13698230701660220.

Zetter, Roger. 2007. "More Labels, Fewer Refugees: Remaking the Refugee Label in an Era of Globalization." *Journal of Refugee Studies* 20 (2): 172–192. https://doi.org/10.1093/jrs/fem011.

———. 2011. "Unlocking the Protracted Displacement of Refugees and Internally Displaced Persons: An Overview." *Refugee Survey Quarterly* 30 (4): 1–13. https://doi.org/10.1093/rsq/hdr015.

Zolberg, Aristide R. 2005. *A Nation by Design: Immigration Policy in the Fashioning of America.* New York: Russell Sage Foundation.

Zolberg, Aristide R., Astri Suhrke, and Sergio Aguayo. 1989. *Escape from Violence: Conflict and the Refugee Crisis in the Developing World.* New York: Oxford University Press.

INDEX

Note: Page numbers followed by f *and* m *indicate figures and maps, respectively.*

ABOUT THE AUTHOR

BERNADETTE LUDWIG is a sociologist and the assistant dean of the Macricostas School of Arts and Sciences at Western Connecticut State University. She is also a part-time assistant professor at The New School and an affiliated faculty at The New School's Zolberg Institute on Migration and Mobility. Prior to entering academia, she worked with refugee and immigrant communities in Atlanta for several years. Her other research focuses on community engaged learning. Her publications include articles in journals such as *International Migration, International Journal of Migration, Health and Social Care,* and *Michigan Journal of Community Service Learning.*